Pragmatism

Pragmatism
An Introduction

Michael Bacon

Polity

First published in 2012 by Polity Press

Polity Press
65 Bridge Street
Cambridge CB2 1UR, UK

Polity Press
350 Main Street
Malden, MA 02148, USA

ISBN-13: 978-0-7456-4664-0
ISBN-13: 978-0-7456-4665-7(pb)

A catalogue record for this book is available from the British Library.

Typeset in 10.5 on 12 pt Sabon
by Toppan Best-set Premedia Limited
Printed and bound in Great Britain by MPG Books Group Limited

The publisher has used its best endeavours to ensure that the URLs for external websites referred to in this book are correct and active at the time of going to press. However, the publisher has no responsibility for the websites and can make no guarantee that a site will remain live or that the content is or will remain appropriate.

Every effort has been made to trace all copyright holders, but if any have been inadvertently overlooked the publisher will be pleased to include any necessary credits in any subsequent reprint or edition.

For further information on Polity, visit our website: www.politybooks.com

Contents

Preface   vii

INTRODUCTION   1

1   THE BIRTH OF PRAGMATISM: CHARLES SANDERS
    PEIRCE AND WILLIAM JAMES   15

2   JOHN DEWEY ON PHILOSOPHY AND DEMOCRACY   44

3   PRAGMATISM AND ANALYTIC PHILOSOPHY:
    W. V. O. QUINE, WILFRID SELLARS AND
    DONALD DAVIDSON   63

4   NEO-PRAGMATISM: RICHARD RORTY AND HILARY
    PUTNAM   92

5   BETWEEN EUROPE AND AMERICA: JÜRGEN
    HABERMAS AND RICHARD J. BERNSTEIN   122

6   THE RETURN OF PEIRCE: SUSAN HAACK AND
    CHERYL MISAK   147

7   RATIONALIST PRAGMATISM AND PRAGMATIC
    NATURALISM: ROBERT B. BRANDOM AND HUW PRICE   171

CONCLUSION   199

Works Cited   202
Index   208

Preface

Pragmatism is North America's most significant contribution to Western philosophy. This book aims to introduce readers to the ideas and arguments of some of its principal figures. These extend from its founder, Charles Sanders Peirce, writing towards the end of the nineteenth century, through to important contemporary pragmatists.

In this book, the centre of pragmatism's contribution to philosophy is shown to lie in the resources it finds in and develops from our social practices. Pragmatism challenges the often implicit assumption that our practices are necessarily inadequate and require backup from some standard or principle which lies beyond them. It does so while avoiding the kind of relativism or conservatism which holds that those practices are beyond reform and improvement. For pragmatists, suggestions for improvements are themselves worked up from elements contained within those practices. In other words, pragmatism takes our lives, in all their richness as well as their deficiencies, seriously, and theorizes from that basis.

Pragmatism is, however, a deeply contested tradition. In a famous comment, Ralph Barton Perry wrote that pragmatism originated with William James' misreading of Peirce (Perry, 1935: 410). This formulation simplifies matters somewhat; James recognized that his work extends Peirce's 'pragmatic maxim' in ways of which Peirce himself would (and did) not approve. From its beginnings through to the present day, there is no programme around which all pragmatists unite. At the same time, pragmatism constitutes a recognizable tradition of thought, one in which specific themes recur. In her introduction to a recent collection of essays entitled *New Pragmatists*

(2007a), Cheryl Misak identifies three commitments that pragmatists tend to share: (i) that standards of objectivity are historically situated but their contingency does nothing to detract from their objectivity; (ii) that knowledge has and requires no foundation; and (iii) the importance of connecting philosophical concepts to the practices of everyday life. Misak's is a helpful summary of the commitments of many pragmatists. Yet, as we shall see, the ways in which they are interpreted and connected together differ significantly between pragmatists.

The approach taken here is to offer an account of the work of some of the philosophers who have either identified with pragmatism, or recognizably developed ideas found within the pragmatist tradition.[1] This second point is important. In this book, the issue of whether a philosopher actually identifies him- or herself as a pragmatist is largely set aside.[2] The reason for this connects to an interpretive issue. The dominant interpretation of pragmatism and its history has been aptly labelled by Robert Talisse as 'the eclipse narrative' (Talisse, 2007, ch. 7). According to this narrative, pragmatism receded from view sometime after the Second World War, only to be revived with the publication of Richard Rorty's *Philosophy and the Mirror of Nature* in 1979. It will be seen that the eclipse narrative misinterprets the enduring nature of pragmatism. Pragmatist themes were in fact central to philosophy throughout the twentieth century, and remain so today.

This book examines the roots of pragmatism in the work of the classical pragmatists, considering how their ideas have been taken forward, in different ways, by more recent philosophers. In so doing, it will show that pragmatism is a living tradition, one which can properly lay claim to the attention of philosophy more generally. Owing to the nature of the large and ongoing pragmatist tradition, some major figures are not discussed. The aim is not to be exhaustive but rather to consider the writings of some of the thinkers who can be seen to have contributed to the pragmatist tradition in the hope of providing an introduction and orientation for further investigation.

I would like to express my gratitude to the Leverhulme Trust for an award which supported the project. In addition, my thanks go to Emma Hutchinson, my helpful and supportive editor at Polity. Thanks also to Leigh Mueller for carefully copy-editing the typescript. Two anonymous readers provided helpful comments for which I am very grateful. I am equally grateful to the following friends and colleagues who commented on drafts of chapters: Zara Bain, Andrew Bowie, Paul Dawson, Neil Gascoigne, Sara Wallace Goodman, Jim Hall, Eva-

Marie Nag, Jonathan Seglow, Ramida Vijitphan, Mei-Chuan Wei and Nathan Widder. Additional thanks go to Jonathan Seglow and Nathan Widder and other colleagues who help to ensure that working at Royal Holloway is an especially happy and rewarding experience.

Notes

1 That is to say, the approach focuses upon thinkers rather than themes. For an excellent thematic introduction to pragmatism, see Talisse and Aikin (2008).
2 In this I follow Misak. In her introduction to *New Pragmatists*, Misak remarks of the inclusion of philosophers who have not themselves identified with pragmatism: 'It is not of much concern in this volume whether these philosophers have in fact been influenced by the classical pragmatists or whether they see themselves as part of the pragmatist tradition. What matters is that the best of Peirce, James, and Dewey has resurfaced in deep, interesting, and fruitful ways' (Misak, 2007a: 1–2).

Introduction

In the everyday sense of the term, 'pragmatism' is associated with a matter-of-fact approach to problem-solving. The related word 'pragmatist' is sometimes used as a compliment, describing the person who 'gets results'. It is also employed pejoratively; in the case especially of politicians, the pragmatist does not stand on principle but will do whatever it takes to succeed. These connotations carry over, though often in misleading ways, into pragmatist philosophy.

The idea of pragmatism as a philosophy immediately raises a question. For if pragmatism is tied to practical success, how does it relate to philosophy, characterized as it is by the attempt to rise above everyday concerns? Pragmatists address philosophical questions, such as the nature of truth, how knowledge is possible, and the demands of moral and political life. But they do so by arguing that these questions should be addressed by drawing upon the resources offered by our practices, and with reference to the consequences they have for our lives.

The term 'pragmatism' was introduced into philosophy in a lecture given in August 1898 by William James. In his lecture, given at the University of California in Berkeley, James says that he 'will seek to define with you merely what seems to be the most likely direction in which to start upon the trail of truth' (James, 1977: 347). That direction is pragmatism, the invention of which he does not claim for himself but credits to his friend Charles Sanders Peirce. In his essay 'How to Make Our Ideas Clear' (1878), Peirce proposes that philosophy would profit by examining thought and ideas in terms of the difference they make to human behaviour. He writes there that 'we come down to what is tangible and practical, as the root of every real distinction of thought, no matter how subtile it may be; and there is no distinction of meaning so fine as to consist in anything but a possible difference of practice' (Peirce, 1992: 131).

In his lecture at Berkeley, James points out that pragmatism did not simply spring into existence in North America in the latter half of the nineteenth century; pragmatist ideas are to be found in the work of philosophers as diverse as Socrates, Aristotle, Locke and Hume. The term 'pragmatism' is, rather – in the subtitle of James' book *Pragmatism* (1907) – 'A New Name for Old Ways of Thinking'. The reason he thinks the invention of pragmatism should be attributed to Peirce is that he was the first to focus wholeheartedly on what pragmatism means and entails: 'these forerunners of pragmatism used it in fragments: they were preluders only' (James, 1977: 379). James claims that it is only with Peirce that pragmatist ideas came to be placed at the heart of philosophy.

The focus on the importance of taking seriously 'what is tangible and practical' unites pragmatists. However, what doing so means differs from pragmatist to pragmatist. Mindful of these differences, John Dewey, the third of those who have come to be referred to as the classical pragmatists, wrote in 1908 that 'the pragmatic movement is still so loose and variable that I judge one has a right to fix his own meaning, provided he serves notice and adheres to it' (Dewey, 1969–90, *Middle Works* – hereafter in text references, *MW* – 4: 128n1). In our own time, Richard Bernstein has suggested that 'the history of pragmatism has always – from its "origins" right up to the present – been a conflict of narratives. Despite family resemblances among those who are labeled pragmatists, there have always been sharp – sometimes irreconcilable – differences within this tradition. There are (as a pragmatist might expect) a *plurality* of conflicting narratives' (Bernstein, 1995: 55 – unless otherwise stated, emphasis in quotations is as in the original). For this reason, pragmatism is best viewed not as a set of doctrines but rather as a tradition of thought. As we will see in this book, various themes reappear throughout its history, but do so in different ways and with different degrees of emphasis.

The classical pragmatists

James first heard Peirce outline the position which he was to call pragmatism in meetings of the Metaphysical Club, an informal discussion group held in Cambridge, Massachusetts, in the early 1870s. In his book *The Metaphysical Club: A Story of Ideas in America*, a study of the lives of prominent members of the Club, Louis Menand presents pragmatism as resulting from the conjunction of a particular series of events (Menand, 2001). These include the widening of the franchise, the professionalization of philosophy in America, and the experience of the American Civil War. For Menand, this last is especially important. The Civil War ended in 1865 with the cost of some 600,000 lives. The rigid certainties and inflexibility that led to the War reflected a particular mindset, one attached to certainties and unwillingness to compromise. Menand suggests that the horrifying events of that tragedy gave rise in the minds of men like Peirce and James to a distrust of absolutes. In its place, they argued for an approach to philosophy which was suspicious of certainty and open to the alternatives suggested by encounters with new interests and ideas. Menand writes: 'The belief that ideas should never become ideologies – either justifying the status quo, or dictating some transcendent imperative for renouncing it – was the essence of what they taught' (Menand, 2001: xii).

In papers presented to the Metaphysical Club, Peirce presents pragmatism as a reaction to what he calls 'the spirit of Cartesianism' (Peirce, 1992: 28). Descartes is today regarded as the founder of modern philosophy. One of his innovations was to describe the mind in epistemic terms. For him the mind is a private sphere separate from the external world, to which we have privileged access. Knowledge is understood in terms of mental representations which purport accurately to 'mirror' that world. This description of the mind immediately raises a radical form of scepticism. For if we can only have immediate awareness of the contents of our own minds, how are we able to lay claim to knowledge about the world beyond us? Descartes viewed the task of philosophy as being to provide foundations for knowledge in the form of 'basic' beliefs. Other beliefs may be inferred from these basic beliefs, but to be secure they must rest firmly upon them. As we will see, pragmatists reject the very idea of immediate foundations for knowledge.

For Peirce, the centrepiece of pragmatism is one apparently very simple idea. This has become known as the 'pragmatic maxim', according to which the meaning of a concept is a matter of the practical effects of acting in accordance with it. 'Consider what effects, which might conceivably have practical bearings, we conceive the object of our concept to have. Then, our conception of these effects is the whole of our conception of the object' (Peirce, 1992: 132). To say of an object such as a diamond that it is hard means that it is difficult to scratch; if we say that something is heavy, we mean that without opposing force it will fall downwards. That is, meaning is tied to experiment, such that, in performing an action, particular consequences will follow.

These rather humdrum examples of the uses to which the pragmatic maxim might be put are a deliberate choice by Peirce. For they illustrate what for him is the important point that adherence to the pragmatic maxim brings philosophical questions into the realm of experience. In so doing, he hopes that pragmatism will clear away some of the problems with which philosophers have concerned themselves but which he takes to have come to hinder inquiry. Rather than accept at face value the textbook questions of philosophy and seek to answer them, the pragmatic maxim is presented by Peirce as a means to identify which of those questions are worth answering in the first place, by establishing whether or not they are meaningful. If a question cannot be answered in such a way that leads to some tangible difference in behaviour, then pragmatists think it unworthy of our attention.

The classical pragmatists are united in seeing the empirical approach to the world best exemplified by the natural sciences. Dewey's earliest writings were deeply influenced by Hegel, but he gradually came to focus more and more on the importance of the natural sciences for philosophy. For him, this meant in particular taking Darwin seriously. Dewey took philosophy to be mired within a pre-Darwinian worldview, one which divided sharply between humanity and nature. In its place, Dewey emphasizes the continuities between them. Darwin's importance lies in calling into question our self-image as spectators disinterestedly looking upon the world, by suggesting that we ought rather to see ourselves as agents operating within it. In place of the attempt to identify a fixed framework for inquiry, the pragmatists see inquiry as open-ended, seeking to provide tools which will enable us, as participants, to cope with the world. Dewey holds that the 'conclusions of prior knowledge are *instruments* of new inquiries, not the norm which determines their validity' (Dewey, 1969–90, *Late Works* – hereafter in text references, *LW* – 4: 149).

As we will explore, pragmatists are naturalists, thinking that philosophy must take the full measure of humans as natural creatures and that its conclusions must be consistent with our best science. And yet they do not see human activity as reducible to animal behaviour. They argue that we must attend to the normative dimension in human life by seeing humans not only as *natural* but also as *cultural* beings. Inquirers treat claims as addressed to them in their capacity as members of a social practice governed by shared norms, and must seek to justify their own claims to their peers in discussion. Writing specifically of inquiry in the natural sciences, Dewey remarks: 'No scientific inquirer can keep what he finds to himself or turn it to merely private account without losing his scientific standing. Everything discovered belongs to the community of workers. Every new idea and theory has to be submitted to this community for confirmation and test' (Dewey, *LW* 5: 115). Scientific *culture* (or practice) confers scientific *validity*, rather than the other way around.

An objection levelled at pragmatism from a variety of directions is that it allows for nothing over and above that which serves particular interests and answers particular problems. Pragmatists focus on the contingencies of human practice, denying the availability of a transcendental standpoint from which we might judge the worth of those practices. The British idealist F. H. Bradley writes that, for pragmatists, 'Our sense of value, and in the end for every man his own sense of value, is ultimate and final. And, since there is no court of appeal, it is idle even to inquire if this sense is fallible' (Bradley, 1914: 132). In his review of James' *Pragmatism*, Bertrand Russell claims that pragmatism is a philosophy suited for those unable to set their eyes beyond the here and now. 'Pragmatism', he writes, 'appeals to the temper of mind which finds on the surface of this planet the whole of its imaginative material', something which he thinks inadequate (Russell, 1910: 110). For pragmatists, however, the assumption that our practices are insufficient for the task of enabling us to understand and cope with the world is unwarranted.

In his essay 'Does Reality Possess Practical Character?' (1908), Dewey takes up themes from critics such as Bradley and Russell and offers some suggestions as to why these criticisms continue to be levelled despite his best efforts to refute them:

> In current philosophy, everything of a practical nature is regarded as 'merely' personal, and the 'merely' has the force of denying legitimate standing in the court of cosmic jurisdiction. This conception seems to me the great and the ignored assumption in contemporary philosophy; many who might shrink from the doctrine if expressly formulated hang desperately to its implications. Yet as an underlying assumption, it is sheer prejudice, a culture-survival. (Dewey, *MW* 4: 126)

In this passage Dewey calls attention to the assumption – in the 'merely' – that the standards and norms that structure our lives and inquiries are by themselves inadequate and require support from something more substantial ('in the court of cosmic jurisdiction'). He also anticipates the response that no philosopher seriously thinks this by saying that, although few may profess it, many nevertheless implicitly remain committed to it. Pragmatism, in contrast, explicitly rejects the assumption that our practices are not up to the task of enabling us to address the problems that we confront. To be sure, those practices are mutable and revisable, but they are regarded by pragmatists as sufficient for the tasks required of them until need to revise them is forthcoming. Hilary Putnam has identified this point as lying at the heart of the pragmatist tradition. He writes: 'That one can be both fallibilistic *and* antisceptical is perhaps *the* basic insight of American Pragmatism' (Putnam, 1995: 21).

The combination of fallibilism and anti-scepticism is central to the pragmatist tradition. Beyond this, however, there are significant differences between pragmatists. From its beginnings in the Metaphysical Club, pragmatism has been the product of a sharing of ideas among thinkers of very different interests and temperaments. Peirce presents pragmatism as a method of establishing the meaning of concepts in terms of the experiential consequences of applying them. A problem with this approach, however, is that it seems to deny the reality of things, such as moral values and religious and aesthetic experiences, which do not feature in our tangible experience and so cannot be brought to the test of the pragmatic maxim. In contrast to Peirce, James thinks it precisely an advantage of pragmatism that it allows for the reality of such things. He broadens the areas of life to which pragmatism might be applied, with his writings motivated in large part to show how natural science might be reconciled with religious belief. He writes: 'The whole function of philosophy ought to be to find out what definite difference it would make to you and me, at definite instants of our life, if this world-formula or that world-formula be the true one' (James, 1977: 379). Peirce was in turn sceptical of the applications which others made of pragmatism: 'Professor James remodelled the matter, and transmogrified it into a doctrine of philosophy, some parts of which I highly approved, while other and more prominent parts I regarded, and still regard, as opposed to sound logic' (Peirce, 1998: 448).

A recurring theme in the pragmatist tradition concerns the relationship between pragmatism as an epistemological and semantic theory and its role in moral and political life. Here a further difference between pragmatists emerges. Peirce strongly resists the idea of any relationship between pragmatism and workaday practical concerns but, from James and Dewey onwards, pragmatists have been inclined to see one. Peirce, trained as a laboratory scientist, is primarily interested in the implications the experimental method of inquiry might have for philosophy, distinguishing sharply between the interests which motivate scientific inquiry and the concerns of everyday life. He holds that the method of science has no relevance to political questions, and insists on the importance of distinguishing the pursuit of truth from the pursuit of the good for society. Dewey, in contrast, commends the application of the method of science to all areas of human life. In his review of James' *Pragmatism* entitled 'What Pragmatism Means by Practical', he writes that 'it lies in the nature of pragmatism that it should be applied as widely as possible; and to things as diverse as controversies, beliefs, truths, ideas, and objects' (Dewey, *MW* 4: 101). With Dewey, pragmatism is transformed into a philosophy which speaks to questions of epistemology, metaphysics, moral and political theory, and to social problems more generally.

The pragmatic century

Peirce, James and Dewey are known collectively as the classical pragmatists. Peirce wrote his anti-Cartesian essays in the 1870s but, despite the best efforts of James to bring his work to popular attention, he remained relatively unknown during his lifetime. James himself was a famous Harvard professor but, with his death in 1910, the fortunes of pragmatism came to be tied most closely to Dewey.

Dewey was active throughout his lifetime as both philosopher and participant in American public life. According to many accounts of pragmatism, however, around the time of his death in 1952, it disappeared from view, only to be revived in 1979 with the publication of Richard Rorty's book *Philosophy and the Mirror of Nature*. Robert Talisse has dubbed this account the 'eclipse narrative', with some version or another appearing in many works on pragmatism (Talisse, 2007: ch. 7). One reason for the supposed eclipse of pragmatism is suggested by Menand, who proposes that the attitude of tolerance and compromise that marked the classical pragmatists was ill-suited to the circumstances of the mid twentieth century: 'The notion that the values of the free society for which the Cold War was waged were contingent, relative, fallible constructions, good for some purposes and not so good for others, was not a notion compatible with the moral imperatives of the age' (Menand, 2001: 441). Other explanations have been offered. Within philosophy, proponents of the eclipse narrative tend to focus on the role played by the development of the tradition of thought that has become known as analytic philosophy, which grew out of the work of European philosophers, a number of whom had emigrated to America to escape Nazi persecution.

The specific movement within analytic philosophy which is some-times taken to have led to the eclipse of pragmatism is logical positiv-ism. Rather than thinking that philosophy has its own subject matter, logical positivists such as Rudolf Carnap and Hans Reichenbach argued that it is a methodology, one to be put into the service of the natural sciences. The task of natural science is empirical investigation into the world, and the role of philosophy is to analyse the meaning of the terms used in that investigation. Many of the concerns that animated James and Dewey, most especially those of moral and politi-cal life, were on this account without meaning and so of no interest to the philosopher.

By presenting analytic philosophy as having superseded pragma-tism, the eclipse narrative ignores the way in which important ana-lytic philosophers worked out themes that had animated the classical pragmatists. According to proponents of this narrative, the publica-tion of *Philosophy and the Mirror of Nature* revived pragmatism, but a reading of that book shows that Rorty himself thinks that pragma-tist ideas flourished in the years after Dewey's death, and did so among those often described as analytic philosophers. Richard Ber-nstein argues along similar lines. In his work, Bernstein demonstrates how various analytic philosophers worked out themes, such as the possibility of knowledge without foundations in immediate knowl-edge, that had occupied the classical pragmatists half a century earlier. Bernstein and Rorty show that many significant analytic philosophers can therefore be understood as contributing to an ongoing pragmatist tradition. Bernstein goes as far as to suggest that the last 100 years can properly be thought of as 'the Pragmatic Century' (Bernstein, 2006a).

If we turn to the details of the eclipse narrative, one conspicuous problem with it is that pragmatism did not disappear from the philo-sophical scene with Dewey. A second and related objection is that some of the most notable pragmatists in the generation following him can themselves be identified with analytic philosophy. As such, they call into question the assumption that pragmatism and ana-lytic philosophy are two distinct traditions of thought. In his work, C. I. Lewis addresses the relationship between the particular under-standings we bring to bear upon the world and the fact that the world exists independently of those understandings. Lewis claims that knowledge is the result of our applying a conceptual scheme (a way of organizing and understanding the world) to the 'given' (mind-independent data). The resulting understanding only counts *as* knowledge because it is constrained by the given which exists inde-pendently of and is not affected by such schemes. Lewis criticizes the classical pragmatists for missing this dimension of thought: 'The pragmatists generally have neglected to make the separation of concept and immediacy, with the result that they seem to put all truth at once at the mercy of experience and within the power of human decision or in a relation of dependence upon the human mind' (Lewis, 1929: 266). His position remains a form of pragmatism, however. For him, our choice of conceptual scheme is a practical one, keyed to the desire to achieve some particular result. And, given the plurality of human interests, this means that there might be a plurality of conceptual schemes: 'There may be alternative conceptual systems, giving rise to alternative descriptions of experience, which are equally objective and equally valid, if there be not some purely logical defect in these categorial conceptions. When this is so, choice will be determined, consciously or unconsciously, on pragmatic grounds' (Lewis, 1929: 271).

Lewis' work indicates a close relation between pragmatism and some analytic philosophers, but that relationship is even more noticeable in the generation of thinkers following him. These include Willard Van Orman Quine, Wilfrid Sellars and Donald Davidson. In his paper 'Two Dogmas of Empiricism' (1951), Quine argues that the logical positivists' distinction between conceptual (philosophical) and empirical (scientific) matters cannot be drawn, because all statements are in fact answerable to experience. Natural science requires, *contra* Descartes, no foundation but is justified in terms of its practical success in helping us cope with the world. The context of Quine's paper is not the work of Peirce, James and Dewey, but that of Lewis and Carnap, and yet the conclusion reached is presented as a form of pragmatism. A little later, in his essay 'Empiricism and the Philosophy of Mind' (1956), Sellars takes up Peirce's dismissal of the idea of immediate knowledge (the given) and presents an understanding of inquiry in which it is seen as a self-correcting enterprise, rather than one requiring philosophical foundations. And Davidson extends Quine's objections to logical positivism by arguing that natural science and empirical knowledge more generally require no foundation at all.

The new pragmatism

Pragmatism has endured and indeed grown as a field of study on both sides of the Atlantic during the twentieth century. However, this increased interest has not seen a diminution of the differences between pragmatists. Pragmatists focus on the importance of taking seriously the particularities of human practices, but there remain significant

differences about what doing so means. Among contemporary pragmatists these differences focus around the issue of how far attending
to our practices entails that we should recognize a relationship of
responsibility to the external world. This issue is central to differences
between pragmatists such as Richard Rorty, Hilary Putnam, Jürgen
Habermas, Susan Haack, Cheryl Misak, Robert B. Brandom and
Huw Price.

Some pragmatists emphasize pragmatism's radicalism, arguing that
its importance lies precisely in its freeing us from obligation to anything beyond our responsibilities to each other. This argument finds
its most thoroughgoing expression in Rorty's work. Rorty presents
pragmatism as following up on the Enlightenment suggestion that
norms be thought of not as divine commands but as the result of
agreement reached in a social contract, arguing that we have no
responsibilities to anything other than our fellow human beings. One
of his most striking claims is that objectivity should be thought a
matter of securing solidarity among communities of inquirers. This
idea is captured in his preferred definition of pragmatism, 'the doctrine that there are no constraints on inquiry save conversational
ones – no wholesale constraints derived from the nature of the
objects, or of the mind, or of language, but only those retail constraints provided by the remarks of our fellow-inquirers' (Rorty,
1982: 165).

For Rorty, seeing humanity as responsible only to itself means that
we should not erect what he calls a God-surrogate to take the place
of revealed religion. Today, philosophers seeking such a surrogate are
likely to turn to natural science as the place where we are granted
our most accurate access to reality. Rorty has written that pragmatism has itself evidenced an ambiguous relationship to science: 'pragmatism has, in the course of a hundred years, swung back and forth
between an attempt to rise the rest of culture to the epistemological
level of the natural sciences and an attempt to level down the natural
sciences to an epistemological par with art, religion, and politics'
(Rorty, 1991: 63). Admiration for the natural sciences led both Peirce
and Dewey to associate pragmatism with the methods of the natural
sciences, but Rorty takes a different view. He argues that science, just
as much as art, is a literary concern in the sense that it is a matter of
offering interesting possibilities for the future. His understanding of
pragmatism 'views science as one genre of literature – or, put the
other way round, literature and the arts as inquiries, on the same
footing as scientific inquiries' (Rorty, 1982: xliii).

Rorty is widely credited with having renewed interest in the writings of the classical pragmatists, yet very few are happy with his

position. For many, his exclusive focus on the responsibilities owed to our fellow human beings mistakenly discards the importance of our answerability to something beyond any particular human community. In reaction to Rorty's undeniable importance for contemporary pragmatism, some recent studies have set out by defining themselves in part in opposition to him. For example, in her introduction to an important collection of essays entitled *New Pragmatists*, Cheryl Misak takes Rorty's centrality to recent debates about pragmatism as a starting point, distinguishing his 'neo-pragmatism' from what she calls the 'new pragmatism' (Misak, 2007a). In his chapter in *New Pragmatists* entitled 'On Our Interest in Getting Things Right', Jeffrey Stout draws out the difference. He argues that Rorty's hope of substituting solidarity for objectivity stems from an overreaction to the attempt – one he shares with pragmatists such as Peirce and Quine – to move beyond traditional forms of metaphysics. According to Stout, Rorty mistakenly renounces any sense in which inquirers try to get things right: 'Even though inquiry is best conceived as an essentially social activity, whether what we say is correct in this objective sense is not to be understood as conforming to social consensus, for all of us could be wrong about the topic being discussed' (Stout, 2007: 7–8). 'New pragmatists' depart from Rorty in arguing that inquiry is objective in that it seeks to understand the way things are, independently of us.

One of the most eminent philosophers writing today to identify with pragmatism is Jürgen Habermas. Although his intellectual background is that of the German Frankfurt School, Habermas has long been interested in pragmatism. But, although sympathetic, he resists what he regards as the insouciant attitude which some pragmatists (he has in mind Rorty) display towards important questions, in particular how political and moral discourse can be distorted by powerful interests. In his work he offers a response to this concern in the form of what he calls 'transcendental pragmatism'. He claims that it is important to acknowledge the role played by the world in exerting influence over us, thinking this is the only way in which we can understand our practices of justification and inquiry. As he remarks, the 'supposition of an objective world that is independent of our descriptions fulfills a functional requirement of our processes of cooperation and communication. Without this supposition, everyday practices, which rest on the (in a certain sense) Platonic distinction between believing and knowing unreservedly, would come apart at the seams' (Habermas, 2000: 41).

Typically, however, pragmatists do not turn towards transcendentalism. The attempt to steer a path between transcendental philosophy and the aim of merely securing agreement with one's peers is a key objective of many pragmatists. Hilary Putnam claims that pragmatism seeks to 'do justice to our sense that knowledge claims are responsible to reality without recoiling into metaphysical fantasy' (Putnam, 1999: 4). He argues that the attempt to uncover what he calls 'the God's-eye view' – the view of the world as it is in itself, independent of any particular perspective – cannot be made sense of and should be given up. Yet this does not mean that humans are not responsible to the world at all, and he insists that our responsibilities are not exhausted by reaching agreement with our fellows. Putnam emphasizes that, contrary to what Rorty says, 'Whether a statement is warranted or not is independent of whether the majority of one's cultural peers would *say* it is warranted or unwarranted' (Putnam, 1990: 21).

Returning to the eclipse narrative, a further reason for challenging it is that it treats pragmatism as if it were a single doctrine. And indeed, in the early part of the twentieth century, pragmatism was most closely associated with Dewey. But interest in the work of other pragmatists, notably Peirce, has continued. Often this has been implicit; Bernstein suggests, for example, that Sellars' essay 'Empiricism and the Philosophy of Mind' can be read as a series of comments on Peirce's early papers, even though Peirce himself is not mentioned (Bernstein, 2006a: 4–5). But for other philosophers the interest in Peirce is explicit. Susan Haack agrees with Peirce about the importance of inquiry answering to standards beyond those of our conversational partners. She shares Peirce's 'insistence that philosophy should become scientific', in the sense that the task of philosophy should be to seek to understand reality which is entirely independent of our beliefs about it (Haack, 1998: 49). In consequence, she is critical of Rorty's position, and does not try to hide her scorn concerning his claim that science be thought of as a form of imaginative literature: 'The idea of chemistry or astrophysics as genres of literature is nothing short of laughable' (Haack, 1998: 63).

Mindful of the differences between pragmatists, some commentators have suggested not only that pragmatists do not unite around a single doctrine, but that pragmatism can no longer be said to constitute a single tradition at all. Nicholas Rescher has proposed that there are two distinct pragmatist traditions, one stemming from Peirce and the other from Jame's. According to Rescher, pragmatists can be classified by how far they retain allegiance to truth and objectivity, or whether they embrace what he calls 'subjectivist post-modernist relativism'. He distinguishes what he calls the 'pragmatism of the right', among whom he includes Peirce, Putnam and Haack, from a 'pragmatism of the left' which begins with James and leads to Rorty: 'The one views the aim of the enterprise as a matter of loosening things up, of overcoming delimiting restraints; the other as a matter of tightening things up, of providing for and implementing rationally acceptable standards of impersonal cogency and appropriateness' (Rescher, 2000: 64–5).

As we will explore in this book, such distinctions are overdrawn. For Rorty, Rescher's principal target, the idea that we could be free of the causal restraints imposed on us by the world is a deep mistake, one which reflects the continued influence of Descartes on our thinking: 'The very idea of "being out of touch with reality" presupposes the un-Darwinian, Cartesian picture of a mind which somehow swings free of the causal forces exerted on the body' (Rorty, 1999: xxiii). On Rorty's Darwinian view, we are always in touch with and constrained by reality, although how we cope with it depends on our particular purposes.

Pragmatism and its consequences for human answerability to the world are developed most fully in Robert Brandom's work. Brandom argues that the constraints we confront must be seen as *internal* to social practices; as members of such practices, we are committed to playing what he calls 'the game of giving and asking for reasons' and are constrained by the norms of that game. To this extent he is a part of what Rescher calls the pragmatism of the right. But Brandom also makes arguments which make him count as a pragmatic leftist. Rescher contrasts restraint and freedom, but Brandom sees the one as a necessary condition of the other. As he writes, 'One acquires the freedom to believe, desire, and intend the existence of novel states of affairs only insofar as one speaks some language or other, is constrained by some complex social norms. Expressive freedom is made possible only by constraint by norms, and is not some way of evading or minimising that constraint' (Brandom, 1979: 194).

The relationship between freedom and constraint naturally leads to politics, and throughout its history pragmatists have addressed political questions. Pragmatists such as Rorty and Brandom examine the relationship between the individual and society by focusing on the way in which communities provide the resources for human freedom. Others, notably Putnam and Bernstein, consider how this relationship can be a problematic one. Putnam and Bernstein both follow Dewey in calling into question the easy relationship that some see between liberalism and democracy, arguing that democracy often challenges what they regard as the excessive emphasis placed by liberals on individual rights. Habermas shares this concern and examines how democracy might be reformed in such as way as to overcome some of the social and political problems that we confront today. And among contemporary pragmatists, perhaps the most ambitious political proposal is presented by Misak (Misak, 2000). Misak turns not to the work of Dewey but to that of Peirce, arguing that it contains the basis of an epistemic justification of democracy which sees it as the means for citizens to establish the truth of their beliefs.

By examining the work of these pragmatists, this book will consider how pragmatism calls into question many of the presumptions about men and women and their place in the world that have dominated modern philosophy. It will show that pragmatism is a contested tradition, indicating how different pragmatists have interpreted the insistence on attending to the practical. In doing so, however, it will also seek to identify points of commonality and agreement between them.

I

The Birth of Pragmatism: Charles Sanders Peirce and William James

Charles Sanders Peirce

Charles Sanders Peirce (1839–1914) trained as a chemist and worked intermittently as a scientist for much of his life. He saw no tension between philosophy and natural science, and indeed argues that philosophy should adopt the methods of the sciences. Peirce outlines the position which William James would later call pragmatism, but pragmatism is by no means the entirety of his philosophy; it is scarcely an exaggeration to say that there are few areas of inquiry about which he did not have something to say. His understanding of pragmatism is deliberately very narrow, conceived of exclusively as a theory of meaning. Yet, as such, it has important consequences for philosophy.

The spirit of Cartesianism

In 1868 Peirce published two essays in the *Journal of Speculative Philosophy* which form the background from which he was later to develop his understanding of pragmatism. The heart of these early papers is an examination of what he calls 'the spirit of Cartesianism' (Peirce, 1992: 28). In order to understand Peirce's argument, it needs to be considered in the context of Descartes' work. Descartes wrote in the intellectual climate forged by the emergence of the new sciences of the sixteenth and seventeenth centuries. The new sciences radically challenged the worldview of the Scholastics. The Scholastics had sought to harmonize Christianity with classical philosophy, in particular the work of Aristotle. The resulting picture of the world, which held that there was structure and purpose to nature, was one which the new sciences called into question. Descartes sought to demonstrate that, in overturning this image of the world, the new sciences could properly be seen as providing genuine knowledge.

Descartes offered a description of the mind as a private sphere separate from the external world, with knowledge understood as a matter of accurate representations of that world. This account of the mind generated a series of problems which have dominated modern philosophy. For, according to it, we are not in direct contact with objects in the world but only with our mental representations of those objects. We are imprisoned behind what Descartes called a 'veil of ideas' and must justify our confidence in thinking our mental representations correctly 'picture' the world. In this way, Descartes introduced into philosophy a radical form of scepticism by raising the question of whether we can know with certainty external reality. How might we be sure that we correctly represent the world? How indeed can we be sure of the existence of the external world at all?

In rejecting Scholastic accounts of scientific and metaphysical knowledge, Descartes identified certainty, understood as immunity from doubt, as a requirement of knowledge. If we can doubt a belief, any beliefs resting upon it for justification are undermined. Unless we can find a belief immune from doubt, we confront an 'infinite regress' which undermines our claims to knowledge. Such a belief must not rely on any other belief for justification, rendering it 'basic' (non-inferentially justified) and knowable 'immediately'. The assumption that sense-experience is beyond doubt fails when faced with the Arch Deceiver, leading to radical scepticism. Descartes claimed, however, that we can have knowledge *before* experience, in the form of 'clear and distinct perceptions' which rest upon the indubitable foundation of the *Cogito*. He employed these in deductive arguments to answer the radical sceptic, using God as a guarantor of the reliability of sense-experience. In doing so he introduced the notion that only foundationalism – the belief that we can locate indubitable beliefs which can be known 'immediately' – can block radical scepticism. As we will see, pragmatists reject the very idea of immediate knowledge, and of the Cartesian picture of the mind and its relation to the world which gave rise to radical scepticism. Peirce writes: 'Now without wishing to return to scholasticism, it seems to me that modern science and modern logic require us to stand upon a very different platform from this' (Peirce, 1992: 28).

In his early papers, Peirce allows that Cartesianism heralded an advance over medieval Scholasticism. However, he argues that it too needs to be questioned. Descartes had opened up an ontological dualism between mind and world, with knowledge seen as a matter of moving from the contents of our minds to construct a mental picture of the external world. Peirce's objection takes the form of arguing that this picture is untrue to how humans actually confront and experience the world. He does so by calling into question the very idea of direct, non-inferential knowledge of the kind Descartes thought provided a foundation for other kinds of knowledge. There is no knowledge given immediately to us – or, in Peirce's term, there is no 'intuitive' knowledge. Rather, knowledge presupposes interaction with the external world.

In the first of his essays, entitled 'Questions Concerning Certain Faculties Claimed for Man', Peirce begins by defining a 'cognition' as an object of thought, such as a concept or a judgement. Immediate cognitions, which Peirce calls 'intuitions', are objects of thought supposedly arrived at *independently of any previous knowledge and without reasoning from signs* (Peirce, 1992: 11). Simply enough, Peirce rejects the idea of immediate awareness of cognitions. His opening argument is empirical. He acknowledges that everyone thinks that they have intuitions, as evidenced by their preparedness to distinguish them from beliefs which they can trace to alternative sources, such as their education or prior experience. This, however, tells us nothing about whether those beliefs really are intuitions rather than being inferences from other beliefs. He supports this with the observation that, as a matter of fact, different people (not to say philosophers) take different ideas to be intuitions.

But what of the apparently obvious intuition that we have intuitive (immediate) knowledge of our selves? This was the intuition that most impressed Descartes in his argument that no one can doubt that they are thinking. Peirce thinks this an unwarranted assumption. His argument is once again empirical: he points out that young children do not manifest self-consciousness, and that their first thoughts are directed outwards to the external world. Although conscious, the child only becomes *self*-conscious through interaction with their environment. On Peirce's presentation, the child first builds up a picture of the world and only then develops a concept of themselves as individual selves. The notion of self stems in particular from the possibility of error, with the child's interaction with the world giving rise to an understanding of the difference between what is wished for and what is actually the case.

A child hears it said that the stove is hot. But it is not, he says; and, indeed, that central body is not touching it, and only what that touches is hot or cold. But he touches it, and finds the testimony confirmed in a striking way. Thus, he becomes aware of ignorance, and it is necessary to suppose a *self* in which this ignorance can inhere. So testimony gives the first dawning of self-consciousness. (Peirce, 1992: 20)

Peirce's understanding of these matters constitutes a complete reversal of the spirit of Cartesianism. For Descartes, the focus was upon one's inner states of mind to which one purportedly has privileged access, and how, from there, one might came to possess knowledge of the external world. Peirce's suggestion is that, despite its apparent plausibility, objects that might appear to be items of immediate awareness turn out to be the result of association between ideas and observations from the external world. This is not to deny that we are conscious beings, but is to say that our self-consciousness is built upon our knowledge of that world: '*our whole knowledge of the internal world is derived from the observation of external facts*' (Peirce, 1992: 22).

The question remains of the possibility of knowledge of things which are apparently immediately before the mind, such as the appearance of colours or the flavours of foods. Peirce takes up this question by making a distinction which would become of great importance in twentieth-century philosophy, between knowledge and mere sensory awareness. In the case of knowledge of the colour red, Peirce writes: 'If it be objected that the peculiar character of *red* is not determined by any previous cognition, I reply that that character is not a character of red as a cognition; for if there be a man to whom red things look as blue ones do to me and *vice versa*, that man's eyes teach him the same facts that they would if he were like me' (Peirce, 1992: 26). Knowledge of 'red', as distinct from awareness of the sensation of red, requires that one be in possession of the *concept* of red, and that capacity is one which is provided by one's interaction with other people in the light of the external world.

One important element of the view that knowledge depends upon interaction with the external world is Peirce's argument that all thought is in signs. Peirce claims that thought entails a three-way relationship, in which (i) a sign serves to represent (ii) an item or object to (iii) an 'interpretant'. This three-way, or triadic, relationship contrasts with the Cartesian view that the meaning is a two-way relationship, a matter of how signs represent items in the world. In turn, Peirce argues that the meaning of a particular sign is a function of its role in a *system* of such signs. As we will see below, Peirce thought of pragmatism as the way to clarify the meaning of signs.

Bringing these considerations together, Peirce's conclusion is that all cognitions are the result of previous cognitions. He acknowledges the attractiveness of the Cartesian belief in immediate knowledge, noting the apparent plausibility of the claim that 'since we are in possession of cognitions, which are all determined by previous ones, and these by cognitions earlier still, there must have been a *first* in this series' (Peirce, 1992: 25). However, despite its plausibility, he argues that there is no such thing as non-relational thought; there is no intuitive, or immediate, knowledge. Rather, knowledge is *inferential*:

> We must begin, then, with a *process* of cognition, and with that process whose laws are best understood and most closely follow external facts. This is no other than the process of valid inference, which proceeds from its premise, *A*, to its conclusion, *B*, only if, as a matter of fact, such a proposition as *B* is always or usually true when such a proposition as *A* is true. (Peirce, 1992: 30)

Fallibilist anti-scepticism

Peirce denies the existence of Cartesian intuitions, something immediately given to the mind, which might serve as an epistemic foundation for knowledge. This, however, raises a problem, which is that it generates an infinite regress of the sort Descartes claimed to block. Peirce sketches his own response to this problem in his paper 'Some Consequences of Four Incapacities', in which he develops his argument by engaging directly with Descartes. There he identifies several features which he labels Cartesian, and that he takes to be central to the history of modern philosophy.

The first of these features is that philosophy must begin with universal doubt. In Descartes' method everything is doubted in an effort to identify which beliefs (if any) can survive. Peirce argues that this is a wholly artificial requirement, one which is untrue to what it actually is to experience doubt. He points out that in our lives, doubt is only occasioned in response to specific circumstances:

> We cannot begin with complete doubt. We must begin with all the prejudices which we actually have when we enter upon the study of philosophy. These prejudices are not to be dispelled by a maxim, for they are things which it does not occur to us *can* be questioned. Hence this initial scepticism will be a mere self-deception, and not real doubt...A person may, it is true, in the course of his studies, find reason to doubt what he began by believing; but in that case he doubts because he has a positive reason for it, and not on account of the

Cartesian maxim. Let us not pretend to doubt in philosophy what we do not doubt in our hearts. (Peirce, 1992: 28–9)

Peirce, as we have seen, argues that there are no foundations for knowledge of the kind Descartes sought, namely basic beliefs which can be known with certainty. Yet he thinks that we *do* have foundations for knowledge, in the sense of beliefs that have been established in inquiry and that are presently not in question. These he calls 'prejudices', beliefs we rely upon for our current purposes even though they may come to be revised or relinquished at some point in the future. Peirce's argument effectively reverses the Cartesian burden of proof. Whereas Descartes granted the sceptic's premise that we can only have knowledge if it is based upon an indubitable foundation, Peirce argues that it rests with the sceptic to give us reason to question our settled beliefs. Doubt of the kind Descartes invoked is dismissed by Peirce as 'paper doubt'; for a doubt to be *real*, it must be one which we genuinely feel. In other words, Peirce sought an alternative to both dogmatism and scepticism, which he called 'fallibilism'. While any particular belief might, in the course of inquiry, be upset and overturned, they are unproblematically relied upon until reason to question them is given.

Peirce develops his argument against Descartes by challenging his understanding of certainty. Descartes identified certainty as residing within the individual consciousness, with the result that the individual is the final judge of truth. This Peirce dismisses, claiming in its place that knowledge is arrived at through collective inquiry. Only in a community of inquirers can those beliefs which we currently rest upon be subjected to scrutiny and found to be secure (or revised if not): 'We individually cannot reasonably hope to attain the ultimate philosophy which we pursue; we can only seek it, therefore, for the *community* of philosophers' (Peirce, 1992: 29). As we will see in the next section, Peirce thinks this community must be committed to a specific method of inquiry.

The proposal that knowledge is the result of collective endeavour leads Peirce to a further objection to Cartesianism. This is made in response to Descartes' claim that reasoning should be thought of as a single chain of inference leading back to epistemically basic intuitions (cognitions not inferred from other cognitions). Peirce argues that knowledge should be thought of rather as a collection of mutually supporting beliefs. Inquiry is not built up step by step from a single premise but is the result of many different findings: philosophy's 'reasoning should not form a chain which is no stronger than its weakest link, but a cable whose fibres may be ever so slender, provided they are sufficiently numerous and intimately connected' (Peirce, 1992: 29). The cable metaphor captures the combination of fallibilism and anti-scepticism that he thinks so important, for although any particular finding might be erroneous, this does not invalidate the entire structure of knowledge. Peirce's argument in support of this idea is once again empirical, which is that it captures the way inquirers actually proceed in their investigations.

Fixing belief through inquiry

The papers published in the *Journal of Speculative Philosophy* lay the groundwork for pragmatism without themselves mentioning the term. Peirce revisits these themes, again without reference to pragmatism, a decade later in essays published in the journal *Popular Science Monthly*. In 'The Fixation of Belief' (1877), he returns to the issue of the nature of belief and considers how it might be secured.

Peirce proceeds by contrasting belief with doubt. He adopts Alexander Bain's view that a belief is that which one would be prepared to act upon, with doubt defined as the uneasy sense of dissatisfaction caused when acting according to that belief does not result in the anticipated consequences: 'The feeling of believing is a more or less sure indication of there being established in our nature some habit which will determine our actions. Doubt never has such an effect' (Peirce, 1992: 114). Inquiry is provoked not by belief but by doubt, and is undertaken in order to attain a belief that will bring about an end to doubt. Recalling his earlier argument, Peirce writes that doubt must be *real*, the kind one genuinely feels, rather than the hypothetical doubt that animated Descartes.

Furthermore, Peirce maintains that inquiry is *exclusively* a matter of securing beliefs which are free from doubt. He writes that: 'the sole object of inquiry is the settlement of opinion. We may fancy that this is not enough for us, and that we seek, not merely an opinion, but a true opinion. But put this fancy to the test, and it proves groundless; for as soon as a firm belief is reached we are entirely satisfied, whether the belief be true or false' (Peirce, 1992: 114–15). That is to say, inquiry does not aim at truth but at security from doubt. If we reach a belief that answers doubt, we may call that belief true, but our doing so says nothing at all about whether the belief is in fact true: 'The most that can be maintained is, that we seek for a belief that we shall *think* to be true. But we think each one of our beliefs to be true, and, indeed, it is mere tautology to say so' (Peirce, 1992: 115).

In saying that the object of inquiry is to bring about an end to doubt, Peirce raises the question of how exactly it might do so. For there are many ways in which we might silence doubt, some of which do not lead to what can meaningfully be described as knowledge – one might, for example, arrive at a belief simply by ignoring evidence that counts against it. Accordingly, Peirce set about examining the merits of different methods of 'fixing belief'.

In 'The Fixation of Belief', Peirce claims that there are four methods of establishing belief or 'settling opinion'. The first is the 'method of tenacity', in which one holds fast to a belief irrespective of the weight of evidence for or against it. The tenacious believer does so by actively avoiding encounters which will lead to their beliefs being called into question. The second method is the 'method of authority', in which the declarations of an authority, such as a government or religious institution, are taken to be fixed and final. This method is similar to that of tenacity in that in both cases belief is protected from reasons and evidence that challenge it, though in this case this is done not by an individual act of will but by an authority through means such as censorship and repression.

The method of tenacity and the method of authority are importantly similar, and similarly flawed. Both might temporarily fix belief, but Peirce claims that both tend to be unsuccessful in the long term. The method of tenacity fails in the face of the fact that the tenacious believer will have their confidence shaken because they will inevitably confront people, as intelligent and well-informed as themselves, who believe contrary things. The method of authority is more successful, evidenced by the success of religious and political authorities in establishing orthodoxy and stifling dissent. Yet despite the superiority of the method of authority over that of tenacity, it too ultimately cannot fix belief, because no authority is able to regulate opinion on all topics. And it is weakened still more once we see that society will contain people with a diversity of beliefs, something which will threaten any easy confidence we have in our own beliefs:

> [People see] that men in other countries and in other ages have held to very different doctrines from those which they themselves have been brought up to believe; and they cannot help seeing that it is the mere accident of their having been taught as they have, and of their having been surrounded with the manners and associations they have, that has caused them to believe as they do and not far differently. (Peirce, 1992: 118)

The methods of tenacity and of authority contrast with a third, which Peirce dubs 'the *a priori* method', in which belief is adhered to on the basis of what seems 'agreeable to reason' (Peirce, 1992:

119). The *a priori* method is said by Peirce to be superior to both of the preceding alternatives, but he nevertheless finds fault in it for what he thinks of as its misplaced dependence on the tastes and inclinations of individual inquirers rather than a fidelity to facts. This objection can be linked to his earlier criticisms of intuitive knowledge. An idea being agreeable to reason relies upon intuitions and so, by demonstrating that we have no intuitions (that is, knowledge not determined by previous cognitions), the *a priori* method turns out to be something closer to intellectual taste or fashion.

The common failing of each of these methods is that none is able to secure lasting belief because, in their different ways, they all take personal attitudes alone to determine belief. Peirce argues that in order to secure lasting stability in belief we need to look beyond ourselves. If we do not, although we may temporarily allay our doubts, they will return (Peirce thinks this inevitable) when we encounter evidence that casts doubt on them. Something different is needed: 'To satisfy our doubts, therefore, it is necessary that a method should be found by which our beliefs may be caused by nothing human, but by some external permanency – by something upon which our thinking has no effect' (Peirce, 1992: 120). What Peirce calls 'the method of science' fits the bill. The method of science is the only method that takes inquiry to be answerable to the external world. Its 'fundamental hypothesis' is: 'There are real things, whose characters are entirely independent of our opinions about them' (Peirce, 1992: 120). The scientific inquirer embraces evidence, engaging with it by showing how existing beliefs can accommodate it or, if they do not, revising them accordingly.

This understanding of inquiry reflects Peirce's training as an experimental scientist. Its focus is on the conditions required to fix a belief so that it becomes accepted by a community of inquirers. Our understanding of reality unfolds due to the findings of prior researchers, which are then built upon in our own investigations, subject to the assessment and correction of others in the light of the evidence available.

Given its acceptance of the existence of 'real things', properly conducted inquiry will tend, Peirce claims, towards a consensus about them. He develops this thought in his second essay in *Popular Science Monthly*, entitled 'How to Make Our Ideas Clear' (1878). There he explains: 'Different minds may set out with the most antagonistic views, but the process of investigation carries them by a force outside of themselves to one and the same conclusion' (Peirce, 1992: 138). Scientific inquiry is public, and its experiments can be reproduced by different inquirers.

The claim that inquiry, if conducted properly, will tend towards a consensus is important for Peirce's understanding of truth. An abiding criticism of pragmatism, one which emerges repeatedly throughout its history, is that its forthright rejection of the correspondence theory of truth is intellectually irresponsible. Although, as we have seen, Peirce takes it that the purpose of inquiry is to secure fixed beliefs 'whether the belief be true or false', he insists that truth does exist. He connects truth and inquiry by proposing that the method of science is the only one that, if rigorously followed, will result in true belief. Peirce describes the truth in this way: 'The opinion which is fated to be ultimately agreed to by all who investigate, is what we mean by the truth, and the object represented in this opinion is the real' (Peirce, 1992: 139).

Peirce acknowledges objections to this account of truth. He notes that it may appear to identify the real with what is *thought* to be real. And he recognizes the problem of what he calls 'buried secrets', in which a truth may, on his understanding of the term, be beyond the means by which it might be established. In response to both points, he insists on the difference between what any particular community might happen to think and what inquiry in general will eventually conclude. A community might agree upon a belief but, in itself, this is no indication of its truth. Peirce's claim, rather, is that genuine inquiry, involving the rigorous testing of hypotheses and willingness to revise them if reason to do so is given, will result in the truth. If inquirers accept the constraint of 'real things, whose characters are entirely independent of our opinions about them', truth is not a matter of what a community happens to agree upon but is the conclusion which genuine inquiry will eventually uncover. Put otherwise, the real is not determined by the community; rather, the real is that to which the community is led (see Misak, 2004a: 135). And, if we acknowledge the difference between different forms of inquiry and appreciate the way in which genuine inquiry allows itself to follow the evidence wherever it leads, a response to the problem of buried secrets is available. This is that, although we may not currently be able to uncover the truth of certain questions, we cannot know what hidden truths might become accessible to us in the course of genuine investigation (Peirce, 1992: 139–40).

The pragmatic maxim

In his essay 'How to Make Our Ideas Clear', Peirce returns to the anti-Cartesian concerns that he had raised a decade earlier. He reminds us that Descartes refounded philosophy by subjecting traditional forms of authority to a radical form of scepticism, relocated the source of truth from religious authorities to the individual mind and, in so doing, passed from the method of authority to that of *apriority*. In so doing, Descartes made it a condition of the truth of ideas that they be *clear*. In 'How to Make Our Ideas Clear', Peirce objects that, in so doing, he overlooked the important difference between an idea seeming to be clear and its actually being clear.

The question, though, is how to make our ideas genuinely clear. Taking up the discussion of 'The Fixation of Belief', Peirce begins by inviting us to consider the nature of belief. Repeating his argument, a belief is said to be a habit of action. To establish the meaning of a belief, then, we must examine what habits it produces. Peirce argues that what is required for clarity is to see the meaning of a belief in terms of the empirical consequences that follow from it. In order to establish what these consequences are, he proposes the following maxim: 'Consider what effects, which might conceivably have practical bearings, we conceive the object of our concept to have. Then, our conception of these effects is the whole of our conception of the object' (Peirce, 1992: 132). This principle would subsequently become known as the 'pragmatic maxim'.

So presented, the pragmatic maxim raises the question of what is meant by a 'practical consequence'. Peirce's illustrations of the pragmatic maxim are straightforward and (appropriately enough) apparently clear. To say of an object such as a diamond that it is hard means that it is difficult to scratch it; if we say that something is heavy, we mean that it will, without opposing force, fall downwards. These cases illustrate that, for Peirce, the meaning of a concept is tied to the difference it makes to practice, with the pragmatic maxim explaining the meaning of an idea by identifying the courses of action which follow from it.

It is important for Peirce that the concepts clarified by the pragmatic maxim are of an entirely *general* character – the concept of hardness means, for instance, that certain consequences will follow from it, and others will be precluded, no matter who carries out an experiment. It does not matter whether I test a diamond or you do so; in both cases, we will discover that the diamond cannot be scratched. As we will see below, the issue of generality marks a significant difference from James' version of pragmatism.

A second point that Peirce insists on is that practical, experiential consequences constitute the *entirety* of the meaning of the concept. In the case of the concept 'force', he explains:

> The idea which the word force excites in our minds has no other func-
> tion than to affect our actions, and these actions can have no reference
> to force otherwise than through its effects. Consequently, if we know
> what the effects of force are, we are acquainted with every fact which
> is implied in saying that a force exists, and there is nothing more to
> know. (Peirce, 1992: 136)

The pragmatic maxim provides the criteria for meaning and, in so
doing, shows up ideas that are without meaning. Among the latter,
Peirce cites the doctrine of transubstantiation. For orthodox Catholics, bread and wine turn into the body of Christ during the Eucharist,
but do so without changing any of their sensible attributes. According
to the pragmatic maxim, transubstantiation is therefore meaningless:
'we can...mean nothing by wine but what has certain effects, direct
or indirect, upon our senses; and to talk of something as having all
the sensible characters of wine, yet being in reality blood, is senseless
jargon' (Peirce, 1992: 131).

In summing up, for Peirce pragmatism is conceived of as a method
for fixing the meaning of concepts. But, although consciously narrow,
this understanding is not a freestanding argument but was formulated
in response to the question of how meaning is to be fixed if we cannot
appeal to intuitions in the manner proposed by Descartes. Peirce
takes the pragmatic maxim to have significant implications for philosophy. By providing a criterion of meaningfulness, it demonstrates
that 'almost every proposition of ontological metaphysics is either
meaningless gibberish...or else is downright absurd' (Peirce, 1998:
338). However, metaphysics is not dismissed entirely by Peirce; he
takes some questions, such as the existence of free will, to be meaningful and important to address. The point is that these questions
ought to take their place as subjects to be examined by the experimental methods of the sciences.

William James

Pragmatism was introduced to the philosophical world in a lecture
given at Berkeley in 1898 by William James. In that lecture, which
was subsequently published with the title 'Philosophical Conceptions and Practical Results', James credits the invention of pragmatism to his friend Peirce. While Peirce was a trained natural scientist,
James (1842–1910) was a psychologist who, in his lifetime, was most
famous for his *Principles of Psychology* (1890). His philosophical
writings were, as he acknowledged, less systematic than his work in

psychology, with *The Will to Believe* (1897), *The Meaning of Truth* (1910) and *Essays in Radical Empiricism* (published posthumously in 1912) each a collection of essays. His fullest exposition of pragmatism was given in a series of lectures at the Lowell Institute and published in 1907 as *Pragmatism: A New Name For Some Old Ways of Thinking*. In these lectures, James provides a distinctive twist to Peirce's position, one significant in itself and one which would also give the latter cause to revisit his own formulation.

Extending the pragmatic maxim

In his essay 'What Pragmatism Means', published as part of his book *Pragmatism*, James presents the pragmatic maxim in the following terms:

> To attain perfect clearness in our thoughts of an object, then, we need only consider what conceivable effects of a practical kind the object may involve – what sensations we are to expect from it, and what reactions we must prepare. Our conception of these effects, whether immediate or remote, is then for us the whole of our conception of the object, so far as that conception has positive significance at all. (James, 1977: 377–8)

This formulation clearly resembles that offered by Peirce, with James identifying the meaning of an idea with its sensible effects. There is, however, a difference, one to which James alerts his audience when he writes that the pragmatic maxim 'should be expressed more broadly than Mr. Peirce expresses it' (James, 1977: 348).

Peirce's version of the pragmatic maxim anticipates the logical positivists' principle of verificationism, according to which meaningful statements are those (and only those) for which we can establish whether or not such statements are true. James' understanding of pragmatism is in contrast decidedly anti-positivist. For him the practical consequences of belief are not exclusively those which can be observed, but *any* kind of consequence in the life of the believer. The difference is illustrated if we return to the example of transubstantiation. Peirce holds that transubstantiation is meaningless because it produces no change in the bread or wine during the Eucharist. He concludes that there is in fact no difference between Catholics and Protestants on the matter: 'It is foolish for Catholics and Protestants to fancy themselves in disagreement about the elements of the sacrament, if they agree in regard to all their sensible effects, here or hereafter' (Peirce, 1992: 132). Helpfully, James also discusses transubstantiation, arguing in contrast to Peirce that it is meaningful should people find it so.

> Since the accidents of the wafer don't change in the Lord's supper, and yet it has become the very body of Christ, it must be that the change is in the substance solely. The bread-substance must have been withdrawn, and the divine substance substituted miraculously without altering the immediate sensible properties. But tho these don't alter, a tremendous difference has been made, no less a one than this, that we who take the sacrament, now feed upon the very substance of divinity. The substance-notion breaks into life, then, with tremendous effect, if once you allow that substances can separate from their accidents, and exchange these latter. (James, 1977: 391–2)

That is to say, James allows that the meaning of a belief can legitimately include the psychological consequences of holding that belief.

In *Pragmatism*, pragmatism itself is presented as answering a particular psychological need, one which James thought philosophy in the late nineteenth century unable to address. He holds that the traditional division between rationalist and empiricist philosophy reflects different temperaments, which he terms the 'tough-minded' and the 'tender-minded'. Tough-minded philosophers are empiricists, stressing fidelity to facts. In contrast, tender-minded philosophers are attracted to *a priori* principles. They tend, James claims, to be idealistic, optimistic and religiously minded, whereas the tough-minded adopt a materialistic and pessimistic outlook which combine in an opposition to religion.

Rationalism and empiricism are principally criticized by James not in narrowly philosophical terms but for their respective failures to answer human needs. He argues that non-philosophers tend to respect the natural sciences for their ability to explain the empirical world, but at the same time do not wish to give up on the comforts offered by religion. Neither the tough nor the tender-minded philosophers are able to accommodate this combination of needs. The tough-minded offer a materialistic description of the world which neglects important features of human experience, for example by thinking of values and religious ideals as nothing more than the by-product of physiological processes. The tender-minded fare no better though, for, in keeping with their sensibilities, they see the universe as a complete and rational whole, dismissing as unreal the contingencies and uncertainties that we confront. James takes this stand-off to reflect what he terms the 'present dilemma in philosophy'. He writes of this dilemma: 'You find empiricism with inhumanism and irreligion; or else you find a rationalistic philosophy that indeed may call itself religious, but that keeps out of all definite touch with concrete facts and joys and sorrows' (James, 1977: 368).

James urges that philosophy must address lived experience by combining respect for the facts discovered by natural science with space for moral conviction and religious belief. Such a philosophy would accommodate the needs and hopes that human beings have in their lives by respecting both tough and tender-minded temperaments. Pragmatism is presented as the means to do so: 'I offer the oddly-named thing pragmatism as a philosophy that can satisfy both kinds of demand. It can remain religious like the rationalism, but at the same time, like the empiricisms, it can preserve the richest intimacy with facts' (James, 1977: 373). James was excited by what he saw as the revolutionary potential of pragmatism. In a letter to his brother, the novelist Henry James, he went as far as expressing hopes that pragmatism in this broad sense might be a movement with consequences comparable in importance to the Protestant Reformation (cited in Dickstein, 1998: 3).

Peirce views pragmatism as breaking with many of the presumptions of modern philosophy and, in consequence, dispensing with large swathes of metaphysics. James, in contrast, remains attached to metaphysical questions, and is also sceptical of at least some versions of naturalism. He repudiates the idea that pragmatism entails 'shutting out all wider metaphysical views and condemning us to the most *terre-à-terre* naturalism' (James, 1977: 460). For him pragmatism addresses metaphysical questions by examining how, no matter how remote they may appear, they involve some practical concern. He gives the example of the dispute between materialist and theistic understandings of the universe. If we think, with both rationalists and empiricists, that 'the entire contents of the world [are] once for all irrevocably given', then it makes no difference to us whether we think of the world in materialist or theistic terms (James, 1977: 394). If, however, we look at the matter pragmatically, by examining the consequences of these different positions in our lives, we will come to appreciate the enormous differences between them.

> Materialism means simply the denial that the moral order is eternal, and the cutting off of ultimate hopes; spiritualism means the affirmation of an eternal moral order and the letting loose of hope. Surely here is an issue genuine enough, for any one who feels it; and, as long as men are men, it will yield matter for a serious philosophic debate. (James, 1977: 398)

In saying this, we see further how James broadened Peirce's maxim. He initially presents pragmatism as a method for identifying what is at stake in philosophical issues rather than offering solutions to them: 'at the outset, at least, it stands for no particular results. It has no dogmas, and no doctrines save its method' (James, 1977: 380). As his argument unfolds, however, it is clear that James thinks that pragmatism is a method that will answer metaphysical questions. Despite his desire to do justice to both tough and tender-minded philosophy, pragmatism is said to be a form of empiricism, one opposed to rationalism:

> It [pragmatism] is a method only. But the general triumph of that method would mean an enormous change in what I called in my last lecture the 'temperament' of philosophy. Teachers of the ultra-rationalistic type would be frozen out, much as the courtier type is frozen out in republics, as the ultra-montane type of priest is frozen out in protestant lands. Science and metaphysics would come much nearer together, would in fact work absolutely hand in hand. (James, 1977: 379)

Whereas Peirce holds that pragmatism will demonstrate that many metaphysical questions are without meaning, James thinks of it as offering alternative, and better, answers to these questions by casting them in terms of the effect they have for our behaviour.

The will to believe

In order to understand how James broadened the pragmatic maxim, we turn now to his essay 'The Will to Believe' (1896). As with his reformulation of the pragmatic maxim, 'The Will to Believe' focuses on the psychological states of believers by seeking to justify the claim that there are some circumstances in which one has the right to believe a proposition even if there is insufficient evidence to do so. His target is W. K. Clifford's essay 'The Ethics of Belief', which argued that one should never assent to a proposition without sufficient reason. James accepts that Clifford is correct in many instances. In the case of natural science, we should not make up our minds on a question until we have objective evidence – to this extent, he is in accord with Peirce's claim that scientists should be constrained by 'real things'. However, he disagrees with Clifford that it is *always* wrong to believe if one has insufficient evidence, arguing that sometimes it is not possible to postpone belief in this way. In these cases – once again, James has in mind religious belief – one has a right to believe in the absence of sufficient evidence.

The error that James thinks Clifford to have made is to have taken belief and conviction to be entirely matters of the intellect. But in fact, what we believe is often not something we have consciously considered but is rather an inheritance. Moreover, belief is constrained by circumstances which have been laid down for us. These factors give rise to very many beliefs for which we have no reason of the kind required by Clifford. 'The Will to Believe' was originally delivered as a lecture, and there James tells his audience: 'Here in this room, we all of us believe in molecules and the conservation of energy, in democracy and necessary progress, in Protestant Christianity and the duty of fighting for "the doctrine of the immortal Monroe," all for no reasons worthy of the name' (James, 1977: 721). This is not to say that intellectual reflection plays no part in deciding belief, only that it is but one part; also important are considerations such as one's hopes and fears, loyalties and passions.

James fleshes out his claim that belief is not purely a matter of the intellect and that one is sometimes justified in believing, in the absence of evidence, by making a series of distinctions. He begins by defining hypotheses which are candidates for belief as either *living* or *dead*. A live hypothesis is one which is a real possibility for belief, whereas a dead option is not. As with his discussion of practical consequences, James focuses upon psychological states of belief: what for one person is a live hypothesis is not for some others. For some people, for instance, the hypothesis that God exists is not a live option because they are either irreligious or convinced believers, but for those who are undecided it is very much a live option. Notice too the contingent nature of the difference between options which are alive and those which are not, evidenced in that some of the beliefs which James could confidently assume to be shared by the members of his audience in 1896 – faith in Protestant Christianity, to say nothing of the duty of fighting for 'the doctrine of the immortal Monroe' – could not be taken to be so today.

After establishing the nature of the distinction between living and dead hypotheses, James goes on to describe the choice of which hypothesis to believe as an *option*. Options are said to be of three kinds: living/dead, forced/avoidable and momentous/trivial. A *living option* is one where different possibilities are all candidates for belief. A *forced option* is one about which a person simply cannot postpone reaching judgement. And a *momentous option* is one where the choice taken is likely to be life-changing, notably when one has an option to do something which is unlikely to present itself again. An option that is living, forced and momentous is called a *genuine option*, with examples including questions of morality and religion.

For both devout believers and convinced atheists, religion is not a live option, but for others not so assured in their convictions, religious belief is living, forced and momentous because it offers rewards, such as comfort and consolation, which are lost by non-belief.

James came to see that his essay 'The Will to Believe' is importantly mis-titled. The idea of *willing* belief suggests volition; that one may decide whether or not to believe something. However, this is not his intention. The idea is rather that one sometimes has the *right* to believe, even if there is insufficient evidence to justify that belief. For this reason, James came to wish that he had entitled his essay 'The Right to Believe'.

'The Will to Believe' proved controversial, and among the criticisms two are particularly pertinent for pragmatism. First, James is talking about the psychological consequences of belief, something which critics have often interpreted to mean that individuals are free to believe whatever they like if it meets their particular needs. Second, his focus is on the role that belief plays in the life of an individual; what is for some people a genuine option will for others be closed. It can be objected that this opens the way to subjectivism and relativism about the truth of belief.

These objections are important, and James is not blind to them. He is, contrary to some interpretations, clear that in many cases one is not free to believe whatever one wishes. For he is speaking only of genuine options – and here, only those options which cannot be decided by the intellect. Furthermore, he is certainly attentive to the truth. One of his aims in making the various distinctions drawn in 'The Will to Believe' is to show that the attitude Clifford represents is, contrary to his intentions, unsuited to securing truth. This is because when the option at hand is a genuine one, suspending judgement because one has insufficient evidence *is itself* to adopt one of the hypotheses. While Clifford may claim that suspending judgement is very different from embracing one of the offered hypotheses, James points out that in practice this is not so. In the case of religious belief, 'We cannot escape the issue by remaining sceptical and waiting for more light, because, although we do avoid error in that way *if religion be untrue*, we lose the good, *if it be true*, just as certainly as if we positively chose to disbelieve' (James, 1977: 732).

The link between the argument of 'The Will to Believe' and James' pragmatism is that both place centre-stage the psychological consequences of belief. For him, Clifford's reason for thinking it better to have no belief rather than to risk having false beliefs stems from a particular desire, to 'Shun Error!' (This is also the Cartesian goal of which Peirce had complained.) The problem is that shunning error is not the only goal of inquiry, and against it James sets the disposition of those who wish to 'Believe Truth!' For people of this disposition, among whom James numbers himself, the pursuit of truth is sufficiently important for them to be prepared to run the risk of error: 'I can believe that worse things than being duped may happen to a man in this world; so Clifford's exhortation has to my ears a thoroughly fantastic sound' (James, 1977: 727). As we will now see, James' views on this matter inform his highly controversial theory of truth.

James' theory of truth

James presents pragmatism as an improvement upon both tough and tender-minded philosophy. Behind their differences, he discerns a common assumption, which is that they are committed to 'intellectualism'. It may sound odd for William James, variously professor of psychology and philosophy at Harvard, apparently to speak ill of the intellect, but by the term he means something very specific. 'Intellectualism', he writes, 'is the belief that our mind comes upon a world complete in itself, and has the duty of ascertaining its contents; but has no power of re-determining its character, for that is already given' (James, 1977: 735). This James rejects. The mind does not observe a world complete in itself but acts *in* the world and, in so doing, changes it. As we will now consider, this view has consequences for understanding truth.

In the sixth lecture in *Pragmatism*, James turns directly to the pragmatist understanding of truth. In presenting his theory he proceeds as he did before, showing how pragmatism constitutes an improvement upon currently dominant philosophical positions. He criticizes both coherence and correspondence (or as he calls it, 'copy') theories of truth for what he takes to be their shared assumption that truth is a fixed and static property. This he denies, arguing that it is inconsistent with the fluid and ever-changing reality that we confront. He insists on a point important to Peirce – that humans are not passive observers of the world but rather active participants within it, and that our understanding of truth must reflect this:

> I, for my part, cannot escape the consideration, forced upon me at every turn, that the knower is not simply a mirror floating with no foothold anywhere, and passively reflecting an order that he comes upon and finds simply existing. The knower is an actor, and coefficient on one side, while on the other he registers the truth which he helps to create. (cited in Putnam, 1995: 17)

The notion of a truth that one has played a role in creating may sound strange. James supports it, however, by treating it as a consequence of the latest findings and approach of the natural sciences, which by the nineteenth century had come to see that 'no theory is absolutely a transcript of reality, but that any one of them may from some point of view be useful' (James, 1977: 381).

In place of the static property presumed by both copy and coherence theories, James speaks of truths which we identify and use in our lives. As with his discussion of questions such as the controversy between materialist and spiritual understandings of the world, what matters for him is the role of truth for us. Against the abstractions of intellectualists, pragmatism returns the truth to us by asking of any idea what difference would be made were a belief true or false: 'Pragmatism...asks its usual question. "Grant an idea or belief to be true," it says, "what concrete difference will its being true make in anyone's actual life? How will the truth be realized? What experiences will be different from those which would obtain if the belief were false? What, in short, is the truth's cash-value in experiential terms?"' (James, 1977: 430).

His answer to these questions recalls Peirce's claim that a belief is a habit of action; for James, a true belief is a *reliable* habit of action, one which enables us successfully to pursue a course of action. True beliefs do not accurately represent reality but are rather tools which enable us to cope with it: *'ideas (which themselves are but parts of our experience) become true just in so far as they help us to get into satisfactory relation with other parts of our experience'* (James, 1977: 382).

James' primary motivation for defining truth in these terms was to effect a reconciliation between natural science and religious faith. In giving up the idea that a belief is true if it copies reality in favour of the view that beliefs can be true if they are useful in the lives of believers, he seeks to make room for truths of religion and morality: 'If theological ideas prove to have a value for concrete life, they will be true, for pragmatism, in the sense of being good for so much' (James, 1977: 387).

Pragmatism is sometimes said to have presented an alternative understanding of truth to the standard correspondence and coherence theories. It is, however, inaccurate to speak of a single pragmatist theory of truth, for James and Peirce hold very different views of the matter. Peirce connects truth to the method of science by holding that the scientific inquirer does not seek the good or expedient but rather takes herself to be answerable to the external world. James, in contrast, thinks of the truth in terms of what he calls its 'cash-value'. In other words, whereas Peirce maintains that the truth is independent of us and of our needs and interests, James thinks truth is tied to what, in some sense, we find useful to believe. As he anticipated, his understanding proved to be controversial. From a variety of perspectives, critics urged that it conflates the truth with whatever we think useful in order to meet particular needs. Bertrand Russell complained that James fails to allow for the distinction between what *is* true and what is *thought to be* true: 'The pragmatic account of truth assumes, so it seems to me, that no one takes any interest in facts' (Russell, 1910: 123).' This is an objection that has been raised many times since, including by several pragmatists. For W. V. O. Quine, James' view amounts to a 'defense of wishful thinking ... To argue this would be to confuse belief in God with existence of God' (Quine, 1981: 32). Richard Rorty remarks that James 'runs together the truth of a sentence (which, unless it contains a referent to a time, is eternally true or eternally false and cannot "become" true) with the expediency of believing a sentence to be true' (Rorty, 1998: 295).

James responded warmly to this line of criticism, arguing that attempts to characterize pragmatism as identifying the truth with that which is pleasant to believe are 'an impudent slander' (James, 1977: 442). The question remains, however, of why even sympathetic critics such as Rorty should read him in this way. The answer lies in James' attempt to provide 'cash-value' to the idea of truth by saying that something is true if it provides 'value for concrete life'. For, despite his protests, this does commit him to thinking of truth in terms of its utility, precisely what his critics complained of.

Pragmatism and radical empiricism

James' theory of truth is perhaps rendered more attractive when we see that he insists that success in questions of truth is a matter of enabling us to cope with the *whole* of experience. He writes:

> 'The true', to put it very briefly, is only the expedient in the way of our thinking, just as 'the right' is only the expedient in the way of our behaving. Expedient in almost any fashion; and expedient in the long run and on the whole of course; for what meets expediently all the experience in sight won't necessarily meet all farther experiences equally satisfactorily. Experience, as we know, has ways of boiling over, and making us correct our present formulas. (James, 1977: 438)

In other words, we cannot just think something true because we find it useful, for experience provides a check upon how useful we might find a belief: I might find it useful to believe that astrology provides a guide to the future, but experience will confound this belief. For James, truth is a matter of answering to experience in its entirety. As with Peirce, he emphasizes that inquiry builds upon what has gone before and has been established, with a true belief being one that inquirers are able to assimilate with existing knowledge. The inquirer:

> saves as much of it as he can, for in this matter of belief we are all extreme conservatives. So he tries to change first this opinion, and then that (for they resist change very variously), until at last some new idea comes up which he can graft upon the ancient stock with a minimum disturbance of the latter, some idea that mediates between the stock and the new experience and runs them into one another most felicitously and expediently. (James, 1977: 382)

The term 'experience', and our understanding of it, is one to which James frequently turns. He allies pragmatism with empiricism. But importantly, he distinguishes his position from earlier forms of empiricism.

James shares Peirce's view that the 'spirit of Cartesianism' has informed the history of modern philosophy, arguing that this includes even those canonically taken to be the opposite of Cartesian rationalists, the British empiricists. The empiricists held that knowledge of the world is derived not from *a priori* principles but from sensory experience. James agrees on the importance of experience, and yet objects that the empiricists had misrepresented the role that experience plays in our lives by taking us to be separate from, and passive observers of, the world. For the empiricists, the objects of our experience are individual perceptions. In its most radical form, in the work of Hume, this entailed the denial that we can experience causal relations between different objects; if we observe one billiard ball striking another, Hume claimed that we cannot see one cause the other to move, but only one movement followed by another. It was in order to address the scepticism of this view that Kant argued that there must be something which lies behind our experiences that holds them together. This response raises its own problems, however, for it invokes a self that stands apart from the empirical world and imposes what Kant called its categories of understanding upon it. James sought a different answer to the scepticism of empiricists like Hume without invoking the idea of a transcendental ego proposed by Kant. While James agrees that the empiricists were correct to view experience as the basic component of knowledge, they were mistaken in what this meant. We are not passive observers standing apart from the world but participants in the world who view experience in the context of our lives. This understanding of experience is said to avoid issues such as Humean scepticism by allowing that we do experience relations between events. James writes: 'Pragmatism represents a perfectly familiar attitude in philosophy, the empiricist attitude, but it represents it, as it seems to me, both in a more radical and in a less objectionable form than it has ever yet assumed' (James, 1977: 379).

James claims that lying behind the empiricists' understanding of experience is a particular conception of the mind. In James' term, they are committed to 'representationalism'. The empiricists (on this point following Cartesian rationalists) divided sharply between mind and world, so that the mind stands apart from the world and is the recipient of discrete impressions or pieces of sense data which purport to represent objects in that world. In contrast James argues that we confront the world *directly.* ' "Representative" theories of perception... violate the reader's sense of life, which knows no intervening mental image but seems to see [for instance] the room and book immediately just as they physically exist' (James, 1977: 173).

The term that James coined to describe this position is 'radical empiricism'. In *Pragmatism*, however, he is at pains to say that radical empiricism should be distinguished from pragmatism; in the Preface, he writes that one can reject the former while in no way compromising one's commitment to the latter. This is an accurate claim, but radical empiricism does connect to several theses which are important for James' understanding of pragmatism. The first is that a belief can only be counted as true if it is supported by the *entirety* of experience. Second, radical empiricism returns the world to us by holding that we experience it directly. And third, as we will now see, it connects to James' view of the significance of pluralism in human life.

Pluralism and the moral life

Today we are accustomed to the idea of pluralism; that different people, societies and cultures think different things true and important. For the most part we are prepared to tolerate those different from us. But this was not always so. The wars of religion of the sixteenth and seventeenth centuries divided Europe and led to bloodshed on a massive scale. One consequence of the wars of religion was the rise of liberalism, which emerged as an attempt to address the discovery that religious differences were here to stay and that the best (or at any rate, the least violent) response short of total victory to one side was mutual tolerance.

It is impossible to overstate the importance of liberal toleration for the history of modern Europe. But it rests on a compromise, a pragmatic (in the everyday sense of the term) accommodation to circumstance. James, in contrast, holds that pluralism should be *positively* embraced.

In his writings on morality, James questions the very idea of a single, universally valid way of life. His essay 'On a Certain Blindness in Human Beings' (1900) is motivated by the observation that lack of awareness of the needs and interests of others is the source of much misunderstanding and, often, strife. He provides an example from his own experience. Writing of a journey through rural North Carolina, he tells us that he came across what he thought a devastated landscape, one in which all natural life had been removed and all that remained was scarred and lifeless earth. For James, it was an appalling sight, but he then spoke to the settlers who had cleared the land, discovering that they had done so in order to cultivate it. For them, the sight was a sign of success and progress, of their triumph over nature. James writes of his own insensitivity: 'I had been as blind to the peculiar ideality of their conditions as they certainly would also have been to the ideality of mine, had they had a peep at my strange indoor academic ways of life at Cambridge' (James, 1977: 631).

The moral of James' essay is that it is all too easy to fail to see how others experience the world in ways different from ourselves. Our doing so carries with it the danger that we will be blind to legitimate differences (this underlines his insistence that pragmatists should not mock the temperaments which give rise to rationalism and empiricism). His hope is that we might become mindful that the ways in which we grasp and evaluate the world are peculiar to us and, in doing so, come to extend our sympathies and respect alternative perspectives. In particular, James hopes that we will come to recognize that there exists a plurality of goods which cannot be put together in a single way. Embracing pluralism means that we come to recognize that none of us is entitled to regard ourselves as in possession of the whole truth.

The blindness of which James thinks us all capable carries over into the way in which philosophers have approached morality. In an essay entitled 'The Moral Philosopher and the Moral Life' (1891), he criticizes those who have sought to identify a single formula for deciding moral questions. His approach, once again, is to address the psychological background to belief. He writes that different thinkers take it that their beliefs are justified by an independent moral realm: 'They imagine an abstract moral order in which the objective truth resides; and each tries to prove that this pre-existing order is more accurately reflected in his own ideas than in those of his adversary' (James, 1977: 616). James dismisses the very idea of such an order. Terms such as 'good' and 'right' do not represent items in such an order but express the attitudes of particular people and societies: 'They mean no absolute natures, independent of personal support. They are objects of feeling and desire, which have no foothold or anchorage in Being, apart from the existence of actually living minds' (James, 1977: 618). James maintains that moral philosophy should itself be seen as reflecting different needs and temperaments.

James' rejection of absolutes in morality led him to speak approvingly of the founders of utilitarianism. In 'The Moral Philosopher and the Moral Life' he applauds Bentham and James and John Stuart Mill for showing that moral ideals have arisen from the concern with bodily pleasures and pains, agreeing with them that '*the essence of good is simply to satisfy demand*' (James, 1977: 621). Moral philosophy should, he writes, be organized around the concern to satisfy as many such demands as possible. And yet he goes on to distinguish his position from utilitarianism. Utilitarianism shares with the proponents of 'an abstract moral order' a tendency to underestimate the complexity of the moral world in which we live. Different moral claims compete with each other, and it is not possible to settle such questions by appealing to abstract principles, even when (in the case of utilitarianism) those principles make reference exclusively to human interests.

James' own approach to morality centres on the idea of 'meliorism'. To explain it, he contrasts it with moral pessimism on the one hand and moral optimism on the other. The pessimist holds that the world is beyond saving, whereas the optimist thinks that salvation is not just possible but inevitable. Meliorism in contrast is characterized by hope, holding that salvation is possible but not inevitable. It thus requires purposeful action, undertaken in a spirit of hopefulness but without guarantee of success. James asks: 'Does our act then *create* the world's salvation so far as it makes room for itself, so far as it leaps into the gap?' His answer is the optimistic '*why not?*' (James, 1977: 467). He sees the responsibility to distinguish between good and bad, and to improve the world, firmly as our own. He is alive to the feelings that lead people to pessimism and hopelessness, and is equally aware that to tough-minded philosophers his recommendations will seem foolhardy. Yet he urges that this is no reason to give up the hope for a better future.

Pragmatism versus pragmaticism

James credits the invention of pragmatism to Peirce in his lecture of 1898, with Peirce himself coming to identify the position he worked out in his essay 'How to Make Our Ideas Clear' as pragmatism only as a result of that attribution. Yet James extends the term considerably beyond that proposed by Peirce by allowing it to include psychological states of belief. He also thinks that pragmatism's emphasis on the consequences of beliefs has implications for truth and for morality. Prompted in part by James, in his later writings Peirce took the opportunity to review his position. His attitude towards the use that James and others had made of pragmatism wavered between the cautiously appreciative and the downright hostile. In addition therefore to giving his philosophy a name, James provided a stimulus for Peirce to revisit and restate his position in order to distinguish it from what he took to be undesirable elements and applications.

In a letter written in 1907, the year in which James published *Pragmatism*, Peirce sets out what he understands by pragmatism and how his interpretation differs from other thinkers who have taken it up. He identifies two principles shared by all pragmatists: that it is a method of establishing the meaning of concepts, and that this method is the experimental approach of the natural sciences (Peirce, 1998: 400–1). However, how these two ideas are cashed out differs considerably from pragmatist to pragmatist, and Peirce proceeds to explain the differences and to establish the superiority of his own formulation.

In a series of lectures given at Harvard in 1898, Peirce addresses (in a phrase he took over, with no small degree of sarcasm, from James) 'matters of vital importance'. There he rejects the suggestion that philosophy should address the problems that men and women confront in their everyday lives. His reason for this stems from his view that philosophy can only be carried out successfully if it is aligned to natural science. He laments that this approach is only in its infancy. In large part, this is because philosophers have tended to be 'men who have not been nurtured in dissecting-rooms and other laboratories, and who consequently have not been animated by the true scientific Eros'. Rather, they have 'come from theological seminaries, and have consequently been inflamed with a desire to amend the lives of themselves and others' (Peirce, 1998: 29). The problem though goes deeper than the training of philosophers. For there is an important difference between practical and scientific matters, a difference which James is said not to recognize. Practical inquiry is driven by the aspiration to answer some particular human need. In contrast, scientific inquiry allows itself to be governed by an 'external permanency – by something upon which our thinking has no effect'. The scientist ought properly to have no interest in the needs of practical life: 'pure theoretical knowledge, or science, has nothing directly to say concerning practical matters, and nothing even applicable at all to vital crises. Theory is applicable to minor practical affairs; but matters of vital importance must be left to sentiment, that is, to instinct' (Peirce, 1998: 33).

In support of the distinction between practical and scientific matters and the corresponding difference between questions which are and are not properly philosophical, Peirce points out that when philosophers have addressed 'vital matters', they may claim for themselves the virtues of the dispassionate inquirer but, on inspection, their suggestions turn out to be rationalizations of prior convictions: 'Men many times fancy that they act from reason when, in point of fact, the reasons they attribute to themselves are nothing but excuses which unconscious instinct invents to satisfy the teasing "why's" of the *ego*. The extent of this self delusion is such as to render philosophical rationalism a farce' (Peirce, 1998: 32). Better then to acknowledge frankly that practical matters are unavoidably bound up with instinct, and to leave philosophy to its own narrow but important tasks.

Peirce's disdain here is in accord with James' claim that moral philosophers have often falsely assumed that their beliefs are supported by an 'abstract moral order'. The difference between them turns on how far *any* beliefs are free from personal and social interest. For Peirce, some beliefs, in particular those which result from the experimental methods of the natural sciences, are wholly separate from such things. James in contrast holds that they are not, and that *all* areas of human life are equally informed by particular interests. In his evocative image, 'The trail of the human serpent is...over everything' (James, 1977: 384).

Peirce's restatement of pragmatism is detailed most fully in three essays published in 1905 and 1906. The most important is his paper 'What Pragmatism Is'. There he reiterates his belief that pragmatism should be modelled on laboratory science, so that the meaning of a statement is one which would be experienced if an experiment is carried out correctly. Recalling his earlier account of the pragmatic maxim, Peirce writes:

a *conception*, that is, the rational purport of a word or other expression, lies exclusively in its conceivable bearing upon the conduct of life; so that, since obviously nothing that might not result from experiment can have any direct bearing upon conduct, if one can define accurately all the conceivable experimental phenomena which the affirmation or denial of a concept could imply, one will have therein a complete definition of the concept, and *there is absolutely nothing more in it.* (Peirce, 1998: 332)

In these papers, however, Peirce is concerned not only to distance himself from what he the thought misappropriation of pragmatism by others but also to correct misleading impressions created by his own work. His earlier writings were infected by what he came to see as nominalism. In 1878 he had written that the sensible effects of an object constitute the whole of that object, which carries with it the consequence that there is no difference between a hard and a soft object unless that object is actually tested. This, he came to see, lent itself to nominalist interpretation according to which meaning rests on the particularities of an individual experimenter and an individual experiment. This is a conclusion Peirce is anxious to avoid; nominalism in the form of the idiosyncrasies of personal belief is one of his objections to James' version of the pragmatic maxim. In a letter written in 1095, he argues that the law that diamonds are hard is a law which is of a general character and obtains whether or not a diamond happens to be tested.

> I myself went too far in the direction of nominalism when I said that it was a mere question of the convenience of speech whether we say that a diamond is hard when it is not pressed upon, or whether we say that it is soft until it is pressed upon. I *now* say that experiment will prove that the diamond is hard, as a positive fact. (Peirce, 1958, 8.208)

In his later writings, Peirce endorses what he calls 'scholastic realism', which holds that there are natural kinds of object existing independently of us, an idea which is, he argues, presupposed in his understanding of the method of science: 'Generality is, indeed, an indispensable ingredient of reality; for mere individual existence or actuality without any regularity whatever is a nullity. Chaos is pure nothing' (Peirce, 1998: 343). This claim connects to the argument of 'The Fixation of Belief', in which the virtue of laboratory experimentation was held to be that the same result would occur regardless of whoever carried it out. For without 'real generals', the scientific enterprise cannot be conducted, because the ability of scientists to make testable predictions is only possible against a background of general laws existing independently of them.

Despite entering these caveats, Peirce insists on the consistency of his overall presentation of pragmatism, and that in returning to his earlier work his aim is clarification rather than revision. In particular, he holds fast to the idea that pragmatism is exclusively a theory of meaning. He recognizes however, and to his obvious distaste, that the term had come to be used in different ways and that the original meaning had been challenged:

> at present, the word begins to be met with occasionally in the literary journals, where it gets abused in the merciless way that words have to expect when they fall into literary clutches. Sometimes the manners of the British have effloresced in scolding at the words as ill-chosen, – ill-chosen, that is, to express some meaning that it was rather designed to exclude. (Peirce, 1998: 334)

In response, he renamed his position 'pragmaticism', a term 'ugly enough to be safe from kidnappers' (Peirce, 1998: 335). (It should be noted that in this particular passage, he is not referring to James.) The ensuing history of pragmatism would see further departures from Peirce's understanding of the nature of the pragmatic maxim. Its broadest application is provided by John Dewey, to whom we now turn.

2

John Dewey on Philosophy and Democracy

The writings of John Dewey (1859–1952) span some sixty years, with his first papers written as a graduate student at Johns Hopkins in the 1880s and the last shortly before his death in 1952. As might be expected from such a long intellectual life, his ideas developed and changed. His early writings were informed by Hegel, in particular by an understanding of the organic relationship between individuals and their society, as well as an unwavering belief that philosophy issues from particular historical circumstances. But as his thought matured, his Hegelianism came gradually to be supplemented by an interest in natural science, and he moved closer to the thinking that animated Peirce's writings. Dewey suggests that many of the presumptions that are central to philosophy are hangovers from concerns of earlier periods in history and as such can safely be set aside. However, he remains within the philosophical tradition by seeking to offer new understandings of its central concepts – notably experience and truth – in the light of the new sciences.

Philosophy as the quest for certainty

Philosophy inquires into questions such as the nature of knowledge, truth and justice. It has often done so by offering systematic analyses which purport to offer an account of their essential nature, rather than empirical investigation into particular instances. For this reason, it may seem that the historical emergence of philosophy itself, though perhaps of interest to intellectual historians, is not of relevance to philosophical inquiry proper. Dewey thought differently. In works such as *Reconstruction in Philosophy* (1919) and *The Quest for Certainty* (1929), he examines the circumstances in which philosophy emerged with a view to helping his readers appreciate how they have determined its function.

Dewey proposes that philosophy finds its origins not in an idealized love of wisdom but in the context of the concrete struggle for survival. Life has always been marked by uncertainties such as disease, flood and famine. Early humans had no grasp of the natural causes of such things and interpreted them as the work of unseen supernatural forces. Many of them responded by adopting a deferential attitude towards these forces in an effort to placate them. Dewey argues that this accounts for the rise of myth and ritual, and of early religious belief.

Such things became central to the culture of early societies, providing meaning and a structure around which their members might live their lives. In particular, they gave rise to moral codes, collected together in religious texts. However, this deferential approach understandably met with limited success in helping those societies deal with the problems they confronted. Thus arose a second, more confrontational, approach. This was the development of arts which enabled men and women to alter their environment in an effort to make it more hospitable. Tools were developed which aided endeavours such as hunting and the cultivation of land. Whereas the first approach attempted to adapt human attitudes to the environment, this second sought to mitigate that environment by transforming it.

Practical knowledge proved to be extremely useful by enabling humans to acquire a degree of control over the world around them. However, because the world of practice is one of change and uncertainty, success in dealing with it is never assured. Dewey claims that for all its practical value, humans thus continued to long for something more fixed and certain. In his memorable phrase, they quest for certainty: 'The quest for certainty is a quest for a peace which is assured, an object which is unqualified by risk and the shadow of fear which action casts' (Dewey, *LW* 4: 7).

The empirical world is subject to contingencies and thus cannot guarantee certainty. Certainty was thus taken to be achievable only in matters untouched by empirical circumstances. Dewey writes that, as a result, belief emerged in two different realms of existence. One was the empirical world which humankind could to an extent understand but never fully control. It is characterized by practical activity, undertaken out of necessity, usually by poorer members of society.

The other was the apparently supernatural world beyond our experience and immediate understanding, a realm which became the concern of the noble and leisured classes, free from the need to engage in practical affairs. Together, these factors led to the elevation of spiritual over worldly matters. Dewey speaks of: 'the conception of two distinct realms. The inferior was that in which man could foresee and in which he had instruments and arts by which he might expect a reasonable degree of control. The superior was that of occurrences so uncontrollable that they testified to the presence and operation of powers beyond the scope of everyday and mundane things' (Dewey, *LW* 4: 11).

The separation between the lowly material and higher spiritual realms was, however, unsustainable. For as practical knowledge grew, it came more and more to be involved with matters that had hitherto been deemed spiritual and the sole concern of ecclesiastical authorities. Traditional beliefs were undercut as science came to address issues which previously were the concern of religion. This, Dewey claims, heralded the birth of philosophy. It led thinkers such as Plato to seek out alternative means to defend beliefs previously justified by reference to the authority of the past. Rather than appealing to the past, philosophy grew out of the attempt to provide traditional beliefs with rational justification. Dewey claims: 'Metaphysics is a substitute for custom as the source and guarantor of higher moral and social values' (Dewey, *MW* 12: 89).

Dewey is clear that the advances that philosophy brought about over ritual and primitive religion should be celebrated. More exactly, the requirement that custom be answerable to reason rather than tradition signalled a significant stage in human progress. Yet he thinks we should also notice the ways in which philosophy carries over much of the content of these earlier beliefs. As he remarks, 'The belief that the divine encompasses the world was detached from its mythical context and made the basis of philosophy' (Dewey, *LW* 4: 13). Philosophy and religion share an emphasis upon the eternal, and one of philosophy's recurrent themes is the identification of the real with the unchanging and a correspondingly low view of the mutable and contingent. Dewey claims that this is because change is assumed to indicate imperfection, and that only the eternal can be perfect.

Philosophy, therefore, can be seen to have taken over from religion a metaphysical dualism between two realms of existence, the imperfect and contingent and the eternal and changeless. This in turn led to an epistemological dualism, between knowledges of these two different realms: the everyday world was the subject of scientific inquiry whereas the higher world provided the material for rational speculation. Dewey argues that, from the ancients onwards, philosophy has taken its task to be contemplation of eternal truth, truth which exists above the contingencies and concerns of everyday life: 'the office of knowledge is to uncover the antecedently real, rather than, as is the case with our practical judgements, to gain the kind of understanding which is necessary to deal with problems as they arise' (Dewey, *LW* 4: 14).

Reconstructing philosophy

Dewey shares Peirce's view that pragmatism will show that many philosophical problems can safely be set aside. But he offers a much fuller diagnosis of why this should be the case. In his work he seeks to show that such problems result from particular historical contingencies and that, owing to changes in social and intellectual circumstances, the need to address them may have passed. Works such as *Reconstruction in Philosophy* and *The Quest for Certainty* claim that philosophy reflects not timeless questions but rather the need to provide a rational justification for beliefs which had in earlier times been taken to stem from custom and tradition: 'It had its task cut out for it from the start. It had a mission to perform, and it was sworn in advance to that mission. It had to extract the essential moral kernel out of the threatened traditional beliefs of the past' (Dewey, *MW* 12: 89).

Dewey identifies several problems with belief in a conception of philosophy as the timeless pursuit of wisdom. One is that, in maintaining this self-image, philosophers have removed themselves from the everyday world and rendered philosophy irrelevant. The difference between the philosophical focus on the 'antecedently real' and the need to solve particular problems has led to the unfortunate situation in which philosophy has nothing to say about the latter: 'While in its own context the philosophy of ultimate reality entered into the vital concerns of men, it now tends to be an ingenious dialectic exercised in professorial corners by a few who have retained ancient premises while rejecting their application to the conduct of life' (Dewey, *MW* 10: 41). A second concern with philosophy so understood is that philosophers have contributed to an unfortunate conservatism in which the present is legitimized by being presented as an aspect of eternity rather than regarded as a contingency that, whatever its benefits, might have to be revised. For philosophy is prone to stick to problems even when the need to answer them has long passed: 'it is unusually conservative – not, necessarily, in professing solutions, but in clinging to problems' (Dewey, *MW* 10: 3).

The conservatism that Dewey thinks characterizes much philosophy is evident in its response to the scientific revolutions of the seventeenth century. The image of the world presented by the new sciences was one of change, not fixity, the exact opposite of the one which, as we have seen, he thinks gave rise to philosophy as a discipline. Modern philosophy was thus torn: it 'could neither be frankly naturalistic, nor yet fully spiritualistic to the disregard of the conclusions of physical science. Since man was on one hand a part of nature and on the other hand a member of the realm of spirit, all problems came to a focus in his double nature' (Dewey, *LW* 4: 43).

From the seventeenth until the late nineteenth century, philosophers reached an uneasy compromise with modern science. Modern philosophy 'accepts the conclusions of scientific inquiry without remaking the conceptions of mind, knowledge and the character of the object of knowledge that are involved in the methods by which these conclusions are reached' (Dewey, *LW* 4: 58). Typically, it did so by accepting that science provides an accurate description of the non-human physical world, but excluded it from human life by instituting a metaphysical dualism, such as Kant's distinction between phenomenal and noumenal worlds. For Dewey, a 'recovery in philosophy' would involve first and foremost a wholehearted acceptance of the implications of modern science.

Late in his life, Dewey spoke of his gradual drift from Hegelianism, and this was in the direction of a thoroughgoing naturalism. As he saw it, this meant attending to the work of Darwin. *On the Origin of Species* was published in 1859, the year of Dewey's birth, and he was among the first to appreciate its importance for philosophy. Whereas Newtonian science sought the immutable physical laws which underlie all areas of life, Dewey took from Darwin a focus on the importance of the temporary and contingent. As Robert Brandom puts it:

> Understanding whose paradigm is Newton's physics consists of universal, necessary, eternal principles, expressed in the abstract, impersonal language of pure mathematics. Understanding whose paradigm is Darwin's biology is a concrete, situated narrative of local, contingent, mutable practical reciprocal accommodations of particular creatures and habitats. (Brandom, 2004: 2)

Darwin did not, of course, emerge from nowhere, but was made possible by precursors such as Copernicus, Kepler and Galileo, men who encouraged a shift away from thinking about permanent states of affairs. Building upon them, Darwin's insight is that this approach should apply fully to our own lives. Dewey uses Darwin to naturalize Hegel, giving up on the latter's idea that there is an inevitable progression in history and focusing instead on the suggestion that there is nothing that transcends our particular human purposes. Accordingly, philosophy must in Dewey's view turn its attention from the immutable to the concrete: 'The influence of Darwin upon philosophy resides in his having conquered the phenomena of life for the principle of transition, and thereby freed the new logic for application to mind and morals and life' (Dewey, *MW* 4: 7–8).

Dewey was not the first philosopher to examine the consequences of Darwin's ideas for our understanding of the world. Unlike figures such as Herbert Spencer, however, he does not attempt to read off from Darwin any particular political conclusion. The influence of Darwin lies rather in his understanding of our location in the transitory and shifting nature of the world. He tells us that humans are animals which, however complicated, share with all species the overriding need to adapt to their environment. Beliefs are what Peirce called 'habits', robust and stable enough to rely upon but always open to revision, not least because they have to adapt themselves to other changes in the environment. Dewey writes: 'conceptions, theories and systems of thought...are tools. As in the case of all tools, their value resides not in themselves but in their capacity to work shown in the consequences of their use' (Dewey, *MW* 12: 163).

Reconstructing philosophy along the lines he proposes will, Dewey hopes, help to encourage it to be more open to new problems and thus contribute towards their solution. He argues that philosophy should proceed not by addressing perennial questions but by turning to the problems that confront people in particular times and places. He commends a more workaday – or, as he calls it, 'experimentalist' – philosophy, one which takes as its task contributing to the issues that occupy men and women: 'Philosophy recovers itself when it ceases to be a device for dealing with the problems of philosophers and becomes a method, cultivated by philosophers, for dealing with the problems of men' (Dewey, *MW* 10: 46). He acknowledges that asking philosophers to relinquish concern with ultimate reality amounts, for many, to giving up philosophy itself, but he regards this as an unjustified inference, and thinks that a reconstructed philosophy will increase its social relevance: 'Philosophy which surrenders its somewhat barren monopoly of dealings with Ultimate and Absolute Reality will find a compensation in enlightening the moral forces which move mankind and in contributing to the aspirations of men to attain to a more ordered and intelligent happiness' (Dewey, *MW* 12: 94).

The benefits of adopting this new, experimentalist, view of philosophy would, Dewey thinks, be considerable. In addition to making philosophy more socially relevant, he holds out the hope that it would contribute towards a more just and tolerant society. Philosophy could no longer lay claim to higher knowledge of an immaterial world, but would take its place as one more discipline answerable to the contingencies of experience: 'The change would do away with the intolerance and fanaticism that attend the notion that beliefs and judgements are capable of inherent truth and authority; inherent in the sense of being independent of what they lead to when used as directive principles' (Dewey, *LW* 4: 221).

Dewey's re-description of experience

In *Reconstruction in Philosophy* and *The Quest for Certainty*, Dewey argues that philosophical problems press upon us only if we accept their premises, and that, if we trace them back to the circumstances of their emergence, we might better understand them and become free of them. This therapeutic element is an important part of his writings, but it is not the only part. In works such as *Experience and Nature* (1925) and *Logic: The Theory of Inquiry* (1938), Dewey's message is not that of a therapist but of a practitioner offering re-descriptions of philosophical concepts in the light of accepting the findings of modern science. One such re-description is that of the concept of experience.

Dewey describes himself as an empiricist, but joins James in presenting an understanding of experience different from that of earlier British empiricists. The British empiricists held that knowledge is derived from experience, itself seen as a matter of sense perception from which the mind builds up accurate impressions, or representations, of the world. Dewey thinks this understanding, although it perhaps seems obvious, problematic. In particular, it institutes a dualism between subject and object, between the external world and the mind which seeks to represent it: 'mental life originated in sensations which are separately and passively received, and which are formed, through laws of retention and association, into a mosaic of images, perceptions, and conceptions' (Dewey, *MW* 12: 128). This gives rise to a set of issues that have become central to modern philosophy, and which, as we have seen, animated Peirce. These problems turn on answering the sceptic, for example regarding how we can know that the images in our minds accurately represent the objects in the world, or indeed whether there is an external world at all.

According to Dewey, such questions are the result of a particular, and mistaken, conception of experience. It treats experiences in isolation, both from each other and from their role in our lives. The empiricists viewed experiences as discrete sensations which are then put into sequence by the human mind, but Dewey denies that we experience the world in this way. We do not consciously associate and conjoin separate experiences, for the world we experience is itself one of relationships – we see objects moving in relation to other objects, people interacting with each other and the world, etc. Such relationships are not experienced passively but are rather seen in a given context – for instance, we see a person waving to another in context, as a form of greeting.

This understanding of experience is located by Dewey in the context of modern philosophy. He notes that Kant identified the difficulty with the British empiricist conception of experience as discrete episodes, and complained that the empiricists ignored the contribution of the mind in organizing it. For Kant, understanding involves the application of *a priori* categories, categories which are both fixed and unverifiable in experience and yet exert a constraint upon it. According to Dewey, Kant should be applauded for taking this step, yet he criticizes him for maintaining the dualism of subject and object. Although he identified the problem with traditional empiricism, Kant remained within the framework which they had set out, that of a dualism between mind and world in which the mind passively receives sense data from the external world: 'Kantianism...accepted the particularism of experience and proceeded to supplement it from non-empirical sources. A sensory manifold being all which is really empirical in experience, a reason which transcends experience must provide synthesis' (Dewey, *MW* 10: 13).

Dewey's writings are motivated by different concerns from those which prompted James. James sought to provide space for religious faith, while Dewey is animated by a view of the significance of a biological and experimentalist approach to human life. However, the resulting account of experience is very similar, both in terms of its understanding of the nature of experience and in its anti-representationalism. Dewey writes:

> If the things of experience are produced, as they are according to my theory, by interaction of organism and environing conditions, then as

Nature's own foreground they are not a barrier mysteriously set up between us and nature. Moreover, the organism – the self, the 'subject' of action, – is a factor *within* experience and not something outside of it to which experiences are attached as the self's private property. According to my view a characterization of any aspect, phase, or element of experience as *mine* is not a description of its direct existence but a description of experience with respect to some special problem for some special purpose, one which needs to be specified. (Dewey, *LW* 14: 17)

He insists that philosophy must recognize that humans do not stand apart from their world, and give up entirely the subject–object dualism that has marked philosophy since Descartes and which have given rise to various 'problems of philosophers'. In a response to George Santayana, he writes: 'I cannot refrain from once more asking how those who hold a purely "subjectivistic" idea of experience provide means for ever getting outside of its charmed circle' (Dewey, *LW* 14: 17). On Dewey's view, in contrast, this problem simply does not arise, because we do not start from the individual mind and work outwards, but are rather social beings interacting with our environment.

British empiricism took over the Cartesian view that the mark of the mental is the immediacy with which we have representations. Dewey holds in contrast that even our seemingly private experiences depend upon our relations to the external world: 'everyday experience...is saturated with the result of social intercourse and communication' (Dewey, *LW* 1: 6). The mind itself is a product of social interaction, because our thoughts are given meaning by the role they play in social life: 'every meaning is generic or universal. It is something common between speaker, hearer and the thing to which speech refers' (Dewey, *LW* 1: 147). Although our minds contain thoughts and ideas, they are not the creation of a private consciousness but presuppose meanings which have their origin in social life. Quine was to point out that, here, Dewey develops a theme central to twentieth-century philosophy: 'Dewey long preceded Wittgenstein in insisting that there is no more to meaning that is to be found in the social use of linguistic facts' (Quine, 1981: 36–7).

The errors of modern epistemology are taken by Dewey to be an expression of an assumption that can be traced back to Plato. They rest on what he calls the 'spectator theory of knowledge'. The idea is that reality possesses an intrinsic nature and that knowledge is a matter of seeking to represent it accurately; that, as he put it, 'what is known is antecedent to the mental act of observation and inquiry, and is totally unaffected by these acts' (Dewey, *LW* 4: 19). The spectator theory of knowledge has at its heart the mistaken distinction between the world and our experience of it, one which modern science has shown to be false. Dewey's alternative holds that:

> Wherever there is life, there is behaviour, activity. In order that life may persist, this activity has to be continuous and adapted to the environment. This adaptive adjustment, moreover, is not wholly passive; it is not a mere matter of the moulding of the organism by the environment...In the interests of maintenance of life there is transformation of some element in the surrounding medium. (Dewey, *MW* 12: 128)

Dewey sees the concern to draw an absolute distinction between 'means' and 'ends' as a hangover from ancient societies, in which members of lower classes undertook instrumentally important tasks whereas aristocrats were free to pursue the good for its own sake. But, following Hegel, he points out that, as we strive to secure our ends, we find that we revise our view of what we want. Together, these considerations led him to speak of the relation between means and ends as a 'temporal and relational' continuum (Dewey, *LW* 13: 229).

Warranted assertibility as the goal of inquiry

One of the consequences the development of the modern sciences has for our understanding of the world is the manner in which it impacts on our techniques of inquiry. Dewey's theory of inquiry is detailed most fully in his *Logic: The Theory of Inquiry*. There he argues that inquiry should be seen in naturalistic terms, as in that of an organism seeking to secure equilibrium with its environment. Inquiry is prompted when we confront a situation in which there is some issue or problem that must be resolved. This he calls an 'indeterminate situation'. We try to transform an indeterminate situation into one which is determinate by examining possible solutions, tentatively adopting a hypothesis which we then investigate to see whether it answers our needs. If a hypothesis succeeds in answering need by transforming an indeterminate situation into one which is determinate, it is said to be 'warranted': 'If inquiry begins in doubt, it terminates in the institution of conditions which remove the need for doubt. The latter state of affairs may be designated by the words *belief* and *knowledge*...I prefer the words "warranted assertibility"' (Dewey, *LW* 12: 15).

In the course of developing his position, it can be seen how close Dewey comes to much in Peirce. Like Peirce, he challenges the Cartesian quest for certainty. Descartes persuaded philosophers that in order for a claim to be warranted it must be based upon indubitable foundations, with the ensuing history of modern philosophy declaring one or other candidate for that role. Dewey's diagnosis of how foundations are erected is that inquirers are prone to singling out some particular beliefs and treating them as the basis for all else: 'An episode in a series of operational acts is fastened upon, and then in its isolation and consequent fragmentary character is made the foundation of the theory of knowing in its entirety' (Dewey, *LW* 4: 150). This is to be expected; if the pragmatists are correct, knowledge is a web of belief, and it is natural for inquirers mistakenly to take those beliefs which are *currently* fixed and stable and think of them as permanent, Cartesian, foundations. For Dewey, however, there are no absolute first principles or foundational beliefs. There are, rather, beliefs which we steer by, and our confidence in them is provisional. But, like Peirce, he emphasizes that questioning them requires reasons: 'Unless there is some reason to doubt whether presumptive knowledge is really knowledge, we take it as a net product.... Such objects, until we have occasion to doubt them, are settled, assured' (Dewey, *LW* 4: 149).

As with Peirce's concern with 'fixing belief', Dewey's focus on warranted assertability raises the question of exactly how beliefs are to be reliably secured. And, like Peirce, he is clear that not just anything will do. One cannot say that a belief is warranted just because it brings about an end to our doubts: 'The commonest fallacy is to suppose that since the state of doubt is accompanied by a feeling of uncertainty, knowledge arises when this feeling gives way to one of assurance. Thinking then ceases to be an effort to effect change in the objective situation and is replaced by various devices which generate a change in feeling or "consciousness"' (Dewey, *LW* 4: 181). Rather, warranted assertibility is a matter of arriving at well-grounded beliefs, which answer to our objective situation rather than to our individual needs. Dewey shares Peirce's view that this requires attending to the methods by which beliefs are arrived at.

Dewey calls the method of inquiry which provides well-founded beliefs the 'method of science', the method of testing hypotheses by reference to evidence. He outlines it as follows:

[The method of science] (1) regards all statements as provisional or hypothetical till submitted to experiential test; (2) endeavours to frame its statements in terms which will themselves indicate the procedures required to test them; and (3) never forgets that even its assured propositions are but the summaries of prior inquiries and testings, and therefore subject to any revision demanded by further inquiries. (Dewey, *MW* 6: 38)

The method of science locates normative authority within communities of inquiry, with scientists treating claims as addressed to them in their capacity as members of a social practice governed by shared norms. They cannot simply appeal to habit or to the past but are required to test their claims through experiments, and are expected to give up a hypothesis if evidence requires it: 'No scientific inquirer can keep what he finds to himself or turn it to merely private account without losing his scientific standing. Everything discovered belongs to the community of workers. Every new idea and theory has to be submitted to this community for confirmation and test' (Dewey, *LW* 5: 115). Significantly, Dewey thinks experimentalism, although modelled on laboratory science, is of relevance to *all* areas of human life in order to address the 'problems of men'. Whatever the question might be, the way to address it is to propose hypotheses and attempt to test them with a view to determining the utility of adopting them.

We can see that, although they agree on much, Dewey thinks pragmatism has application in more areas than Peirce was prepared to accept. He commends the application of the method of science to every part of life. The scientific enterprise itself is not freestanding, but is rooted in social life more generally. Its methods and techniques – open-mindedness, flexibility, preparedness to be swayed by the findings of our fellow inquirers – are those which Dewey felt ought to be shared to a greater or lesser degree by everyone and should be adopted everywhere, including in political and social matters. 'While it would be absurd to believe it desirable or possible for every one to become a scientist when science is defined from the side of subject matter, the future of democracy is allied with spread of the scientific attitude' (Dewey, *LW* 13: 168).

In viewing inquiry in instrumental terms, as the attempt to inquire into specific 'indeterminate situations' rather than to identify the 'antecendently real', Dewey is reluctant to identify its goal as truth. With James, he rejects both the correspondence and coherence theories for thinking of the pursuit of truth as attempting to represent an antecedent state of affairs. In contrast, Dewey holds that truth concerns hypotheses that relate to future action: 'The "truth" of any present proposition is, by the definition, subject to the outcome of continued inquiries; its "truth", if the word must be used, is provisional; as near the truth as inquiry has as yet come, a matter determined not by a guess at some future belief but by the care and pains with which inquiry has been conducted up to the present time' (Dewey, *LW* 14: 56–7).

It should be noted, however, that Dewey does not identify truth with warranted assertibility. Bertrand Russell understood Dewey to be saying that warranted assertibility is equivalent to truth, which entailed that truth is relative, being determined by its particular effects (Russell, 1991: 780). This is, however, not the case. In *Logic: The Theory of Inquiry*, the only reference to truth is in one footnote in which he agrees with Peirce's definition of truth as 'the opinion which is fated to be ultimately agreed to by all who investigate' (Dewey, *LW* 12: 343n6). Dewey's preference for speaking not of truth but of warranted assertibility is because he is hostile to the notion that truth is some fixed state, and prefers to speak instead of the *process* of securing truth: 'To say that a man seeks health or justice is only to say that he seeks to live healthily or justly. These things, like truth, are adverbial. They are modifiers of action in special cases' (Dewey, *MW* 12: 175).

The social construction of the good

The challenge that Dewey takes natural science to present to philosophy ought, he argues, to produce a radical change in its presumptions and aspirations. Rather than contrast philosophy's concern with immutable with empirical inquiry, his naturalism, as we have seen, led him to propose that the experimental method of science be incorporated into *all* areas of human inquiry. In his work, questions that had been taken to concern the fixed and eternal are returned to the everyday world, where scientific methods might be employed to answer them.

Dewey followed this suggestion into every area of philosophy, including his thinking about morality, the area of life which is the most resistant to employing the methods of the natural sciences. Philosophers and non-philosophers alike typically think that morality requires some form of foundation; Dewey writes that, although philosophers tend to assume foundations can be known by reason whereas most others believe them to be divinely revealed, they agree that foundations exist, and in both cases this is because of the belief that everyday moral attitudes are, by themselves, inadequate. Dewey takes this to be an assumption that has carried over from the dualism of an immaterial realm accessible to reason and a material and contingent realm suited for investigation by empirical science, and that can be traced back to the distinction between the life of contemplation and that of practice. This is, however, an optional distinction born of specific social conditions: 'If men had associated their ideas about values with practical activity instead of with cognition of antecedent Being, they would *not* have been troubled by the findings of science' (Dewey, *LW* 4: 34).

If we conceive of morality as a form of practical activity, in Dewey's view we will see that the worth or validity of moral beliefs and judgements stems from the actions they bring about, and thus that the supposedly problematic relationship between morality and natural science 'is wholly artificial' (Dewey, *LW* 4: 34). Why does he think this? According to Dewey, philosophers have sought to protect morality from the vicissitudes of everyday experience by identifying a single principle upon which to ground it (this includes even Aristotle, a philosopher who also thought that morality should be viewed in terms of practical activity). Surveying the history of moral philosophy, he concludes that it has done so by abstracting some particular good from the role it plays in our lives and proclaiming it to be of universal validity. Against this he insists that morality should be understood in the context of our being organisms seeking to respond to features of our environment. We find ourselves needing to act but being uncertain about which course of action to select from among a range of possibilities. Inquiry into morality should thus be carried out in precisely the same way as that into scientific questions: as the experimental testing of hypotheses. Moral principles should be treated pragmatically, as tools to help silence doubt by resolving problematic situations:

> Instead of being rigidly fixed, they would be treated as intellectual instruments to be tested and confirmed – and altered – through consequences effected by acting upon them…A moral law, like a law in physics, is not something to swear by and stick to at all hazards; it is a formula of the way to respond when specified conditions present themselves. (Dewey, *LW* 4: 221–2)

It might be thought that there is an important difference between inquiry in natural science and inquiry in questions of morality. Natural science describes facts in the physical world, whereas morality concerns what *ought* to be the case. Dewey questions the firmness of this distinction, arguing that all areas of life are subject to the 'continuum of means and ends'; just as the questions asked by natural science change as a result of the conclusions of previous investigations, so too do those of moral life. He cautions against unreflective reliance upon tradition, commending reading from the history of philosophy in order to remind ourselves of the different assumptions that men have unreflectively taken for granted. Many will, of course, resist any suggestion that scientific methods should be introduced into discussion of morality, but Dewey thinks this a further instance of the felt need to anchor beliefs to something immutable, a need he hopes his writings might help set aside.

We should be clear, however, that Dewey does not wish to reduce morality to a mechanical process. He carefully distinguishes naturalism and materialism, the loose identification of which, he complains, enables anti-naturalists 'to charge naturalists with reduction of all distinctive human values, moral, esthetic, logical, to blind mechanical conjunctions of material entities – a reduction which is in effect their complete destruction' (Dewey, *LW* 15: 47–8). Pragmatism sees human behaviour as thoroughly naturalistic without allowing the descriptions of natural science to drive out all others. Dewey agrees with the attempt to connect morality to interests and desires, but resists the suggestion that the fact that something is *taken* to be desirable leaves no remaining question of whether that thing *ought* to be desired: 'Values (to sum up) may be connected inherently with liking, and yet not with *every* liking but only with those that judgement has approved, after examination of the relation upon which the object liked depends' (Dewey, *LW* 4: 211).

Dewey's concern to avoid reductionism is evidenced in his refusal to specify too fully a standard by which moral beliefs might be measured. Instead, he speaks in somewhat general terms, writing: 'Growth itself is the only moral "end"' (Dewey, *MW* 12: 181). By 'growth' he means the capacity to develop as a human being, something which is not a merely mechanical process but requires reflection rather than mere stimulus-response to one's surroundings. Equally, growth stands opposed to uncritical acceptance of tradition or social class. Dewey, as we have seen, opposes the idea of 'fixed ends'; one should not, he argues, rest content with the social role that circumstances and history dictated but re-weave the resources of one's circumstances in order to develop as a person. The importance of the individual revising his or her beliefs in this way explains why Dewey leaves the direction of growth unspecified: to specify for all time what constitutes human growth would violate his experimentalist belief that the criteria for growth can only be discovered through inquiry and not fixed in advance by the philosopher. He argues that what matters, rather, are the social conditions within which growth might be fostered, something which leads him to address questions in political philosophy – in particular, to a discussion of the importance of democracy.

Democracy as a way of life

Democracy lies at the heart of Dewey's writings, but is also a topic that was central to his own life. His role in progressive social causes – he helped to found both the American Civil Liberties Union and

The National Association for the Advancement of Colored People – led him to be regarded as America's 'philosopher of democracy' (see for example Westbrook, 1999). However, he laments the fact that, for the most part, philosophers have discounted democracy. The reason for this is readily appreciated: democracy is the realm of interests and trade-offs, the kind of messy contingency that philosophy seeks to transcend. Dewey regrets that, on the rare occasions when philosophy has attended to democracy, it has been unsuccessful. In particular, it has proceeded by assuming an unattractive idea of human nature: 'it has clothed itself in an atomistic individualism, as full of defects and inconsistencies in theory as it was charged with obnoxious consequences when an attempt was made to act upon it' (Dewey, *MW* 11: 52). Part of his attempt to reconstruct democracy is accordingly to offer a revised account of individuality.

In the writings of thinkers such as Locke, Dewey glimpses a connection between individualism and empiricism. Empiricism has a political dimension, that of challenging the power of ecclesiastical and political institutions. It affirms individual rights and maintains that social institutions cannot be justified by reference to tradition but rather in terms of how far they meet the tests posed by experience (see Bernstein, 1966: 52–3). Dewey claims that this emancipatory aspect of empiricism served a valuable purpose, standing central to the European Enlightenment: 'The enlightenment, the *éclaircissement*, the *Aufklärung* – names which in the three most advanced countries of Europe testified to the widespread belief that at last light had dawned, that dissipation of the darkness of ignorance, superstition, and bigotry was at hand, and the triumph of reason was assured' (Dewey, *LW* 14: 100). Yet Dewey argues that the project of the Enlightenment has, as yet, not been carried through as far as it ought to be. Locke and others mistakenly regarded the relationship between the individual and society as being an antagonistic one, in which the former is protected against the latter by a set of rights which guarantee her or his freedom. Dewey thinks the classical liberals were correct to emphasize individual freedom, but mistaken in identifying it exclusively as a matter of non-interference by others. That identification stemmed from a particular understanding of the individual and his or her relation to society, one which takes the individual to exist prior to society: 'the individual is regarded as something *given*, something already there' (Dewey, *MW* 12: 190). The classical liberals took it that the individual has a character that can be realized only by the removal of externally imposed obstacles. This carries through into an important strain in political theory, the social contract, in which men and women 'are mere individuals, without any social relations *until* they form a contract' (Dewey, 1969–90, *Early Works* – hereafter in text references *EW* – 1: 231). For Dewey, this is to get things exactly the wrong way around. Individuality is a social creation, and can only be realized within a community, one that provides both an individual's identity and a range of meaningful choices.

In his earliest writings, Dewey followed Hegel in thinking society an organic unity, with the individual an abstraction: 'Society, as a real whole, is the normal order, and the mass as an aggregate of isolated units is the fiction' (Dewey, *EW* 1: 232). Dewey wrote these words in 1888, but his view of individuality came to change somewhat, largely in reaction to political events. In an essay entitled 'I Believe' (1939), he writes that: 'I should now wish to emphasize more than I formerly did that individuals are the finally decisive factors of the nature and movement of social life' (Dewey, *LW* 14: 91). The reason for this change was the rise of totalitarian states in Eastern Europe, seen by Dewey to be present in nascent form in the calls for political collectivism in the United States as a response to concerns about the inequities of capitalism (concerns which he shared).

Dewey remained consistent throughout his life, however, of the view that individuals can develop only when certain social conditions are present. Though a liberal, he is clear that classical liberalism does not sufficiently provide for such development. It provides freedom for those who possess sufficient material resources, but not for those lacking those things. And, indeed, it leaves these others open to being exploited by those with the means to do so. For this reason, Dewey concludes that rights, in the absence of the resources needed to take advantage of them, cannot be said to be equal, no matter their formal standing in the law.

> Since actual, that is, effective, rights and demands are products of interactions, and are not found in the original and isolated constitution of human nature, whether moral or psychological, mere elimination of obstructions is not enough. The latter merely liberates force and ability as that happens to be distributed by past accidents of history. This 'free' action operates disastrously as far as the many are concerned. The only possible conclusion, both intellectually and practically, is that the attainment of freedom conceived as power to act in accord with choice depends upon positive and constructive changes in social arrangements. (Dewey, *LW* 3: 100–1)

While classical liberalism was an important force for reform in the seventeenth and eighteenth centuries, Dewey finds it to have come to stand in the way of further progress. For it sought to justify a minimal state, something which in practice precludes many people from participating as equals in public life by denying them the resources necessary to do so. The answer to the excessive focus on individual rights and the related problem of material inequality was to be found, Dewey argues, in democracy.

Dewey was an enthusiastic supporter of democracy, but democracy in the fullest sense of the term. He speaks of it not simply as a political arrangement but as a 'way of life'. In his essay 'Creative Democracy – The Task Before Us' (1939), Dewey argues that democracy is a matter of the conduct of daily life. Democracy at the level of the state and its institutions is, of course, important, but just as important are local communities. He writes: 'I am inclined to believe that the heart and final guarantee of democracy is in free gatherings of neighbors on the street corner to discuss back and forth what is read in uncensored news of the day, and in gatherings of friends in the living rooms of houses and apartments to converse freely with one another' (Dewey, *LW* 14: 227).

Dewey's understanding of democracy as a way of life is clearly a departure from democracy as it was practised in the 1930s – and as it continues to be practised today. In defence of this view, he entered into a series of discussions with his former student Walter Lippmann. Lippmann criticized democracy out of fear of the way in which public opinion can be distorted and, more generally, for the lack of knowledge of many citizens and their unwillingness to participate in politics. This led him, in *Public Opinion* (1922), to argue in favour of a governing class comprised of dedicated experts. Dewey is not unsympathetic to the claim that democracy in his time was inadequate, but his response was to call for a reinvigorated public life. In *The Public and Its Problems* (1926), he argues that, despite the complexity of modern society, citizens could come together and learn about matters of public concern.

At their best, Dewey held that democracies provide the conditions for the development of different ways of living, whilst at the same time providing the mechanisms by which citizens can mutually recognize each other's interests and consider their own in relation to them. In this way, as Hilary Putnam points out, Dewey provides a 'political turn' to Peirce's conception of epistemic inquiry (discussed in chapter 4). Democracy is a method of social inquiry, of applying social intelligence to public and political questions. In contrast, non-democratic forms of life fail to do so. When citizens are affected by a particular problem, they have an interest in involving themselves in participating in the solution to this problem.

Dewey argues that for democracy to become a way of life requires the cultivation of peculiarly democratic attitudes, such as a willingness to engage in a democratic dialogue, offer reasons in support of one's views, and listen respectfully to one's fellow citizens. This appeal to democracy as protecting self-interest is not an original idea, but it was important in refuting Lippmann's call for rule by an elite. For Dewey argues that elites simply cannot know what is in the interests of other groups in society. They would come to govern in their own good, ignoring those of the wider society: 'A class of experts is inevitably so removed from common interests as to become a class with private interests and private knowledge, which in social matters is not knowledge at all' (Dewey, *LW* 2: 364).

Dewey's writings on democracy have been widely criticized, and two objections stand out. The first is that in his keenness to model democracy on the methods of the natural sciences, he ignores important differences between them. Politics is a realm of conflict between different groups, and political solutions tend to be the result of compromise between them. In the light of the ethnic and religious diversity that marks the United States, as well as limits to material resources, Dewey can be criticized for being overly optimistic about the prospects for harmonizing different interests. The second objection is that Dewey did not give any indication of how democracy as a way of life might be realized at the national level. He emphasizes the importance of direct, face-to-face communication, but the question arises of how anything like this might be achieved in a country the size of the United States.

Insofar as Dewey recognized these issues, his responses did not satisfy his critics. And, as is indicated in chapters 4 and 5, those who undertake to defend Deweyan democracy have tended to go beyond his writings in addressing them. However, it should be noted that Dewey did not maintain that democracy as a way of life will result in an easy harmony between different groups within society. Indeed, he criticizes the presumption that it would, thinking it stemmed from the quest for certainty which held that there is a single purpose or meaning to human life. This he denies; it is precisely because of the differences between people that democracy is a necessary part of modern life.

3

Pragmatism and Analytic Philosophy: W. V. O. Quine, Wilfrid Sellars and Donald Davidson

Willard Van Orman Quine

Willard Van Orman Quine (1908–2000) is widely regarded as one of the most important philosophers of the twentieth century. His reputation was established with the publication of his paper 'Two Dogmas of Empiricism' in 1951. There Quine describes his position as a form of pragmatism. However, the background to his thought is not the work of Peirce, James and Dewey but rather logical positivism (or as it is sometimes called, logical empiricism). In 1932–3 as part of his graduate work at Harvard, Quine travelled in Europe, spending time in Vienna, Prague and Warsaw. In Prague he participated in meetings of the Vienna Circle and was introduced to Rudolf Carnap, the most influential exponent of logical positivism. His understanding of pragmatism can only be understood in the context of logical positivism, which he initially supported but became increasingly critical of.

Two dogmas of empiricism

In the Introduction we saw that the standard account of pragmatism holds that it was eclipsed during the 1930s and 1940s by the work of the logical positivists. Like the classical pragmatists before them, logical positivists such as Carnap and Hans Reichenbach were impressed by the successes of the natural sciences. At the same time, they were critical of philosophy, which seemed incapable of demonstrating anything like the equivalent success. They observed that throughout its history, different philosophers have drawn on their own assumptions and reached their own conclusions, and yet there seemed to be no prospect of reaching the kind of result routinely achieved in the natural sciences. So, like Peirce, they thought that the task of philosophy must be rethought. The positivists argued that philosophy does not have its own subject matter, but is rather a method of analysing statements with the aim of identifying those that are meaningful. Their key move was to say that, in order to be meaningful, a statement had either to be answerable to empirical testing or to be analytic. Analytic statements are true by virtue of the meaning of the linguistic terms of which they are comprised, and so do not require empirical testing; for example, the sentence 'All bachelors are unmarried men' is true in virtue of the meaning of the constituent terms 'unmarried man' and 'bachelor'. In contrast, synthetic (or empirical) statements are true not only in virtue of their meaning but also because of the nature of the empirical world. For the positivists, the distinction between analytic and synthetic statements was reflected in a distinction between different domains of inquiry. Analytic truths, or truths of meaning, are the subject matter of philosophy, whereas synthetic truths are the subject matter of empirical science. This entailed that statements of ethics and religion are strictly without meaning, because they are neither analytic nor empirically verifiable or refutable.

For a few years after returning from Europe, Quine accepted a version of this picture. However, he came to express doubts, outlining them in his paper 'Two Dogmas of Empiricism'. The logical positivists' picture presupposed what Quine came to see as a false relationship between language and experience. He argues that, for all its intuitive appeal, the distinction between analytic and synthetic truths could not finally be drawn, because no statement is devoid of empirical content.

Quine identifies the first dogma of empiricism as the distinction between analytic and synthetic truths. He begins 'Two Dogmas' by distinguishing two kinds of analytic statement. The first is those that are logically (that is, formally) true, for example 'All unmarried men are unmarried'. This is true irrespective of the meaning of the terms 'unmarried' and 'men'. The second is analytic statements such as 'All bachelors are unmarried men'. The truth of this sentence, unlike the first, depends on the meaning of the term 'bachelor': if it is not a synonym for 'unmarried man', the statement is not true. It is with this second class of analytic statement that Quine thinks we can see how empirical considerations impinge. 'Bachelor' is a synonym for 'unmarried man' because those terms are defined as they are. However, this does not show that 'All bachelors are unmarried men' is an analytic statement (a statement without empirical content) because definitions are themselves established in a particular empirical context. Of the example of defining 'bachelor' as 'unmarried man', Quine asks: 'Who defined it thus, and when?' (Quine, 1980: 24). If we appeal to a dictionary, this merely postpones the question, for the lexicographer has recorded accepted usage rather than defined it. We still need to ask who defined it, and when, in order to generate the fact of its accepted use.

What is lacking in this account is an explanation of synonymy. One is suggested by the logical positivists' verificationist theory of meaning, according to which the meaning of a statement is established by the empirical methods by which it might be confirmed or refuted. This position seems to provide an account of synonymy: 'statements are synonymous if and only if they are alike in point of method of empirical confirmation or infirmation' (Quine, 1980: 37).

Quine objects to the form given to the verificationist theory by the logical positivists. Their claim is that a statement, taken on its own, can be confirmed or refuted by experience. This he identifies as the second dogma of empiricism, that of 'reductionism'. Quine's claim is that it founders because sentences are not open to being confirmed or refuted individually. This idea is captured in what has become known as the Duhem–Quine thesis. According to this thesis, originally propounded by the mathematician and physicist Pierre Duhem, theories of the world are under-determined by the evidence because, whenever an inquirer comes across data that seem not to support her hypothesis, there are two options open to her. She might choose to reject that hypothesis, but equally she might revise other assumptions which form the background to her inquiries. Quine argues that any claim can be maintained in the face of experience if we make adjustments to other beliefs, but, at the same time, no statement is immune to revision.

Quine proposes that knowledge be thought of as a 'web of belief'. Some beliefs lie at the centre of that web, in the sense that they are implicated in all forms of knowledge; he has in mind specifically knowledge of logic and mathematics. We are unwilling to relinquish such beliefs because, given their centrality to our understanding of the world, upsetting them would impact upon too many of our other beliefs. In this way, Quine accounts for analytic truths by redefining them; 'analytic' is used as a descriptor of a belief's place in the web rather than as a description of what determines its truth value. If evidence tells against such beliefs, rather than give them up we will cast around and seek to accommodate them by revising other beliefs. Those nearer the edge of our web of belief, which we can more readily imagine relinquishing in the face of contrary evidence, are empirical truths. The difference between them is however one of degree, not of kind.

The classical pragmatists challenged the Cartesian sceptic by embracing fallibilism, arguing that there must be reason to cast doubt on beliefs which we currently rely upon. Quine agrees, but thinks that the relationship between our beliefs is more complicated than they took it to be. Peirce's metaphor is of a cord wound together out of different strands, but Quine in effect shows that that cord is woven together in a highly complicated manner, and that there is no single way in which it might be rewoven. Leaving aside this metaphor, there is no simple way in which beliefs might be held or revised. We can preserve any belief, even in the face of doubt, if we are prepared to make revisions to other beliefs. Quine writes: 'Conservatism figures in such choices, and so does the quest for simplicity...Each man is given a scientific heritage plus a continuing barrage of sensory stimulation; and the considerations which guide him in warping his scientific heritage to fit his continuing sensory promptings are, where rational, pragmatic' (Quine, 1980: 46).

Quine's naturalism

In 'Two Dogmas', Quine does not reject empiricism but seeks to show that the logical positivists did not fully carry through on their commitment to it. This is, he thinks, evident in the work both of Lewis and of Carnap. Lewis and Carnap took the distinction between true and false statements to be one that operates within 'conceptual schemes' (ways of organizing and understanding the world). So, for example, questions about mathematics are answerable within a framework of certain ways of speaking about numbers (addition, subtraction, etc). The truths that operate within conceptual schemes are either analytic or synthetic: they are empirical in the case of science, analytic in the case of philosophy. But the question of whether to use a particular conceptual scheme at all is not one that can be answered by appeal to its truth; it is rather a practical question about the benefits of employing that scheme. By holding that some questions are not empirical ones, Carnap is said by Quine to be inconsistent, and it is his rejection of the purported distinction between questions which are asked *within* conceptual schemes and those asked *about* the utility of such schemes which frames Quine's understanding of himself as a pragmatist: 'Carnap, Lewis, and others take a pragmatic stand on the question of choosing between language forms, scientific frameworks; but their pragmatism leaves off at the imagined boundary between the analytic and the synthetic. In repudiating such a boundary I espouse a more thorough pragmatism' (Quine, 1980: 46).

Quine's 'more thorough pragmatism' holds that there are no strictly analytic truths of the kind which the logical positivists had taken it to be the task for philosophy to explain. The distinction between questions asked within a conceptual scheme and those asked about such schemes is given up and replaced with the view that all statements answer to experience. Inquiry is itself holistic, with beliefs hanging together and no straightforward connection holding between an individual belief and the experience which will confirm or refute it. Quine underlines that this conclusion repercusses upon philosophy itself. All truths are empirical truths, and thus are the subject of the natural sciences.

Quine's naturalism became more evident in writings published after 'Two Dogmas'. In a series of lectures given in 1968 entitled 'Ontological Relativity', Quine highlights his naturalism with reference to similarities with Dewey:

> Philosophically I am bound to Dewey by the naturalism that dominated his last three decades. With Dewey I hold that knowledge, mind, and meaning are part of the same world that they have to do with, and that they are to be studied in the same empirical spirit that animates natural science. There is no place for a prior philosophy. (Quine, 1969: 26)

By saying there is no role for a prior (or 'first') philosophy, Quine means to deny the existence of propositions which might be justified without reference to experience. As he sees it, traditional epistemology from Descartes through to Carnap is the history of failed attempts to carry through on the project of first philosophy. His own view is that philosophy does not stand apart from and provide a foundation for empirical science but must rather be consistent with that science, for the sciences provide the only legitimate authority in inquiry (as Peirce had argued).

This raises the question of what gives rise to that authority. Quine's answer is a pragmatic one: the natural sciences are successful, helping us cope with the world by providing the means to predict and control it: 'As an empiricist I continue to think of the conceptual scheme of science as a tool, ultimately, for predicting future experience in the light of past experience' (Quine, 1980: 44).

What then is left for epistemology? Quine argues for the replacement of 'traditional' with what he calls 'naturalized' epistemology.

The task of traditional epistemology is to identify basic or foundational beliefs in order to justify our empirical beliefs about the world. Quine argues that all attempts at such derivation have failed, but this does not mean giving up on epistemology. He proposes a naturalized epistemology, the purpose of which is to study the psychological processes by which we form beliefs about the world from the stimulation of our sense organs: 'Th[e] human subject is accorded a certain experimentally controlled input – certain patterns of irradiation in assorted frequencies, for instance – and in the fullness of time the subject delivers as output a description of the three-dimensional external world and its history' (Quine, 1969: 82–3). One consequence of adopting Quine's naturalized epistemology is that the reason for distinguishing between internal and external questions in the manner of Carnap and Lewis disappears. People build up understandings of the world as a result of sensory input, but there is no pragmatic necessity to divide these into questions *about* different conceptual schemes and questions about the truths operating *within* those schemes. Naturalized epistemology also entails a rejection of the dogma of reductionism for, in responding to the sensory stimulation of the world, we do so holistically and not one belief at a time.

Without foundations of the kind sought by traditional epistemology, many think that we are implicated in an empty-headed relativism, according to which there is no rational reason to prefer one conceptual scheme over another. Quine, however, insists that we are not. The impossibility of standing outside of the domain of natural science does not mean that we are unable to improve upon it from within.

> We can improve our conceptual scheme, our philosophy, bit by bit while continuing to depend on it for support; but we cannot detach ourselves from it and compare it objectively with an unconceptualized reality. Hence it is meaningless, I suggest, to inquire into the absolute correctness of a conceptual scheme as a mirror of reality. Our standard for appraising basic changes of conceptual scheme must be, not a realistic standard of correspondence to reality, but a pragmatic standard. (Quine, 1980: 79)

Quine illustrates the epistemic situation he takes us to find ourselves in with reference to the metaphor of Neurath's boat. According to Neurath, the philosopher is not in the position of a shipwright building a boat from scratch in dry dock but is instead like a sailor, repairing it whilst at sea by standing on one plank in order to replace another. At times different planks may come to need replacement – they may not function as they should in order to keep the boat afloat.

In this case, however, the only way of effecting a repair is by standing on still others.

Quine's considered view of pragmatism

Quine takes pragmatism to be the result of purifying empiricism of the two dogmas he identifies. However, his allegiance to pragmatism was rather selective. In his paper 'The Pragmatists' Place in Empiricism', he remarks of the classical pragmatists: 'I have found little in the way of shared and distinctive tenets' (Quine, 1981: 37). There he objects to some elements found in Peirce and James, but his attitude towards pragmatism is less one of criticism than of perplexity; he claims that there are few ideas shared by the classical figures and few which can genuinely be taken to have originated with them. (Although he doesn't say so, here he recalls James, who described pragmatism as a 'new name for some old ways of thinking'.) Quine concludes his paper with the suggestion that there are two positions which can meaningfully be taken to be central to pragmatism: 'The two best guesses seemed to be behavioristic semantics, which I so heartily approve, and the doctrine of man as truth-maker, which I share in large measure' (Quine, 1981: 37).

Behaviouristic semantics holds that there is no meaning lying behind our words which determines how they should be employed. Rather, the meaning of words is purely a matter of how people actually use them. In this way, behaviouristic semantics opposes mentalistic accounts according to which meanings lie behind our use of words, with words paired off with bits of the world. Quine describes this as the 'myth of the museum': 'Uncritical semantics is the myth of a museum in which the exhibits are meanings and the words are labels. To switch languages is to change the labels' (Quine, 1969: 27). Mentalistic semantics takes it that words have determinate meanings over and above those that can be observed in people's behaviour. The problem with mentalistic semantics, Quine argues, is that behavioural evidence is all that we have to go on. We cannot get inside another person's mind; all we can know of them is what we observe in their behaviour.

The most important consequence of behaviourism is that it calls into question the idea of determinate meanings of our words. This thought is captured in Quine's thesis of the 'indeterminacy of translation', detailed in his book *Word and Object* (1960). There, Quine undertakes to explain how we successfully communicate with each other without assuming that the meaning of our words is transparent or explainable in terms such as analyticity. He does so with reference to a thought experiment, in which a field linguist has to translate the word 'gavagai'. He has no translation manual, and so must do so by observing the behaviour of the community who use that word. As a rabbit scurries past, a member of that community utters 'gavagai'. The field linguist tentatively translates this as 'Lo, a rabbit', a conclusion seen to be justified when the situation repeats itself (Quine, 1960: 29).

This is an illustration of behaviouristic semantics. But Quine uses it to make the point that translating 'gavagai' as 'rabbit' is not the only option available. For 'gavagai' can mean 'rabbit' but, based on the behavioural evidence (the only resource available to the field linguist), it might equally mean 'brief temporal segments' of rabbits, or 'undetached rabbit parts'. The point is that it is indeterminate which translation is correct. One cannot say that 'gavagai' both means 'rabbit' and 'undetached rabbit parts' since those two meanings are distinct, but on a behaviourist account both meanings are consistent with the way in which the word is used. Quine writes: 'manuals for translating one language into another can be set up in divergent ways, all compatible with the totality of speech dispositions, yet incompatible with one another' (Quine, 1960: 27).

The question for behaviouristic semantics then is: how can we ever manage successfully to communicate with each other? How do you and I know that we mean the same thing by our words? Quine's response is that we manage to communicate with each other with a degree of success because we operate within a context of shared belief and assumption. He writes: 'begin by picturing us at home in our language, with all its predicates and auxiliary devices...This network of terms and predicates and auxiliary devices is, in relativity jargon, our frame of reference, or coordinate system. Relative to *it* we can and do talk meaningfully and distinctively of rabbits and parts, numbers and formulas' (Quine, 1969: 48).

Underlying Quine's doctrine of the indeterminacy of translation is the idea of 'ontological relativity'. Ontological relativity holds that all of our theories about the world are underdetermined by the data: some will be ruled out as not fitting the data, but Quine's claim is that there will remain theories, all of which are justifiable and yet different. He makes this point starkly in the case of different scientific worldviews. The ancient Greeks believed in Homeric gods, whereas we of course do not, but in both cases the explanation is posited in order to explain the data. Quine remarks that: 'For my part I do, qua lay physicist, believe in physical objects and not in Homer's gods; and I consider it a scientific error to believe otherwise. But in point of epistemological footing the physical objects and the gods differ only in degree and not in kind. Both sorts of entities enter our conceptions only as cultural posits' (Quine, 1980: 44). Quine thinks the language of physics privileged, but the reasons for that privilege are pragmatic. He continues: 'The myth of physical objects is epistemologically superior to most in that it has proved more efficacious than other myths as a device for working a manageable structure into the flux of experience' (Quine, 1980: 44).

The second element in pragmatism to which Quine is sympathetic is what he calls the idea of 'man as truth-maker'. Initially, this might appear to conflict with his naturalism, according to which humans seem responsible to (rather than makers of) the physical world. Quine denies that there is a conflict: 'Despite my naturalism, I am bound to recognize that the systematic structure of scientific theory is manmade. It is made to fit the data, yes, but invented rather than discovered, because it is not uniquely determined by the data. Alternative systems, all undreamed of, would have fitted the data, too' (Quine, 1981: 33). Just as different translations can be given of the events that prompt us to utter 'rabbit', so more generally can different theories fit the available evidence. Those theories are manmade and, if they successfully fit the data, can be held to be true.

But although Quine takes himself to agree with the classical pragmatists on the issue of 'man as truth-maker', he departs from Peirce about precisely what this entails. Quine claims that different systems, or theories, might all fit the data, something which Peirce seems to deny in his belief that inquiry will ultimately converge upon a single truth. In response, Quine argues that this assumes that we know what it means to compare theories in order to ascertain which of them most accurately approximate that truth. However, Peirce nowhere offers us a criterion or method to establish the degree of comparative success in approximating the truth, and for Quine this is for the reason that no such criteria are available. Even if inquiry were to be conducted indefinitely, different theories would all equally fit the data: 'Scientific method is the way to truth, but it affords even in principle no unique definition of truth. Any so-called pragmatic definition of truth is doomed to failure equally' (Quine, 1960: 23). As we will see, Quine's objection to Peirce's understanding of truth is one which other pragmatists have come to share.

Wilfrid Sellars

It is fair to say that the work of Wilfrid Sellars (1912–89) has not been accorded the same importance as that of Quine. That being said, his writings have recently come to receive greater attention. Sellars did not identify himself with pragmatism, but his ideas have strong affinities with the classical pragmatists, especially Peirce, and are also important for writers such as Rorty and Robert Brandom. Sellars is best-known for his critique of what he calls 'the Myth of the Given', set out in his essay 'Empiricism and the Philosophy of Mind' (1956). The Myth of the Given is the idea that simply by virtue of having a sensation or impression one therefore *knows* something. For Sellars this is an unwarranted inference, and ignores the conceptual component of knowledge. Sellars labels his own position 'psychological nominalism', which places the ability to use language at the heart of human life by seeing normativity in terms of social practices.

The Myth of the Given

Sellars' principal philosophical hero is Kant, and his many essays engage, directly or implicitly, with Kantian themes. Kevin Scharp and Robert Brandom report that Sellars once said that he sought in his work to usher philosophy from its Humean into its Kantian stage (Scharp and Brandom, 2007: x). By this he means to offer an account of human beings as continuous with the natural world but also as distinct in our ability to bring understanding to the world through the employment of *concepts*.

To explain the central importance of the conceptual in Sellars' work, let's turn to his most famous essay, 'Empiricism and the Philosophy of Mind'. In his essay, Sellars reminds us that the classical empiricists inherited the Cartesian assumption that the mind is an inner arena. On this account, something is presented (in Sellars' word, 'given') to the mind – for the empiricists this is raw experience – from which the individual constructs a picture of the outside world. What is given to us is immediate, by which two things are meant. First, such knowledge is non-inferential; it 'presupposes no learning, no forming of associations, no setting up of stimulus-response connections' (Sellars, 1997: 20). Second, it is not subject to error: one might be mistaken that one is seeing a triangle, but one cannot be mistaken that one *thinks* one is seeing a triangle. Immediate knowledge of this kind is said to be important because it provides our beliefs with an indubitable foundation, with knowledge of the external world derivative, inferred from this basic or foundational knowledge of our inner states. (Notice that this is in contradistinction to *rationalist* foundationalism, but is nonetheless foundationalist in its intention.)

Empiricism is the target of 'Empiricism and the Philosophy of Mind', but the essay is not limited to challenging empiricism and targets all proposals for 'the given'. Sellars outlines various candidates for the role of the given, which include sense contents, material objects objects, and propositions. Acknowledging that many modern philosophers have sought to attack the given, he claims that they have only carried their attack so far, focusing in particular on sense data. In its place, however, they have tended to substitute other items, for example first principles or physical objects, to fulfil its role. Sellars proposes to go further. While he focuses on sense data, he means to show that his argument is entirely general, constituting 'a general critique of the entire framework of givenness' (Sellars, 1997: 14).

Sellars' key insight is that our immediate awareness is not cognitive. He argues that there is an all-important distinction between sensual awareness and propositional knowledge. Sensual awareness does not constitute knowledge; in Brandom's illustration, a parrot might be trained reliably to identify colours when they are brought into its visual field, but it cannot be said to *know* what colours are (Brandom, 1997: 140, 2002a: 349–51). Sellars argues that knowledge requires conceptual awareness. Concepts are linguistic entities, and knowledge, he claims, thus depends upon one's knowledge of a language. The resulting position he calls 'psychological nominalism', the view that awareness is linguistic: '*all* awareness of *sorts, resemblances, facts*, etc., in short, all awareness of abstract entities – indeed, all awareness even of particulars – is a linguistic affair' (Sellars, 1997: 63).

The claim that all knowledge is linguistic seems clearly false; after all, a baby is certainly aware of its immediate environment. To demonstrate its plausibility, Sellars begins by challenging the confidence – in his opinion, misplaced – we have in the idea of the given. The Myth of the Given holds that sensations alone provide knowledge, but Sellars complains that the issue of how they might do so is typically left unanswered. His own suggestion is that for something to count as knowledge it must occupy a *normative* role by virtue of its function in legitimate inference. Crucially, the given cannot serve this function; although it can *cause* us to believe something, it cannot *justify* us in so doing. Justification depends rather upon taking one's place in what he calls 'the game of giving and asking for reasons'. Sellars writes: 'The essential point is that in characterizing an episode or a state as that of *knowing*, we are not giving an empirical description of that episode or state; we are placing it in the logical space of reasons, of justifying and being able to justify what one says' (Sellars, 1997: 76). The space of reasons is central to Sellars' argument. Moving around in that space is not a causal matter, the kind of thing studied by the natural sciences, but is a normative affair in which people make assertions about what they think is the case and seek to justify their assertions to others. By asserting 'That's a triangle', one undertakes the commitment to offer reasons for that claim, knowing for example that it has three sides, that its angles add up to 180 degrees, and so forth. Only the ability to do so confers the entitlement to claim that one possesses knowledge, something which a parrot, squawking in response to the sight of a red triangle, does not have.

According to psychological nominalism, to grasp even something as simple as a triangle requires the concept of 'triangle' in order for one to be able to classify it as such: *'instead of coming to have a concept of something because we have noticed that sort of thing, to have the ability to notice a sort of thing is already to have the concept of that sort of thing, and cannot account for it'* (Sellars, 1997: 87). To become aware of something in the first place is to respond to it by applying a concept to it. In this regard, Sellars rejects outright the theory of concept acquisition propounded by both Locke and Hume. This is, however, not to say that there are no non-inferential beliefs. Once one has acquired language, one is able to use it to make non-inferential claims; one might, for example, know that the object one is looking at is a triangle just by observation. Sellars' point, however, is that the ability to make such non-inferential judgements requires the conceptual resources brought into existence by the learning of language, so that one can only notice a triangle if one possesses the concept of 'triangle' and can apply it to particular instances.

What is the relation of psychological nominalism to pragmatism? In an essay entitled 'Some Reflections on Language Games' (1954), Sellars briefly explains that, in his view, the classical pragmatists came close to recognizing the importance of the conceptual resources offered by language, but misconceived precisely what that resource might be. For they tended to think of language merely as a tool to address problems:

> Now I would hold that Pragmatism, with its stress on language (or the conceptual) as an instrument, has had hold of a most important insight – an insight, however, which the pragmatist has tended to misconceive as an *analysis* of 'means' and 'is true.' For it is a category mistake...to offer a definition of 'S means p' or 'S is true' in terms of the role of S as an instrument in problem solving behavior. (Sellars, 2007: 40)

The problem as Sellars sees it is that the classical pragmatists viewed the conceptual solely in terms of the use to which those concepts might be put. What he thinks this misses is that the use of concepts is not simply a means to help us pursue antecedent ends but is constitutive of language's basic structure and not something that can be grasped after initial formulation. This is intimated in the work of the pragmatists, but Sellars thinks it needs to be emphasized and placed at the centre of our attention:

> if the pragmatist's claim is reformulated as the thesis that the language we use has a much more intimate connection with conduct than we have yet suggested, and that this connection is intrinsic to its structure as language, rather than a 'use' to which it 'happens' to be put, then Pragmatism assumes its proper stature as a revolutionary step in Western Philosophy. (Sellars, 2007: 40)

A further point on which Sellars makes common cause with the classical pragmatists is in his denial of foundations for knowledge. Psychological nominalism directly challenges Descartes' claim that there must be some class of epistemically basic beliefs (beliefs not inferred from other beliefs). Knowledge and understanding is inferential, and one can only be said to have a belief if one is able to locate that belief within the space of reasons. But the result is not, as might be feared, that we cannot confidently lay claim to knowledge, for knowledge is seen to be a matter of the relationship between beliefs. As with each of the classical pragmatists, Sellars views inquiry as a self-supporting, self-corrective process: 'For empirical knowledge, like its sophisticated extension, science, is rational, not because it has a foundation but because it is a self-correcting enterprise which can put any claim in jeopardy, though not all at once' (Sellars, 1997: 79).

The Myth of Jones

Sellars argues that knowledge of our inner mental states requires that we possess awareness of the public, conceptually structured world. Knowledge that what we are seeing is a red triangle is only possible when one becomes a member of a linguistic community and is able to utilize the conceptual resources it provides (in this case, 'redness' and 'triangle'). However, the difficulty that Sellars faces is that by denying that sensory awareness constitutes knowledge, psychological nominalism seems to leave no room for subjective, inner, episodes. The conflict arises out of Sellar's rejection of the notion of pre-linguistic concept *acquisition* (as propounded by Locke and Hume) in favour of linguistic concept *formation*, coupled with the fact that language is a primarily social endeavour. The task then is to account for inner episodes of the kind many, following Descartes, take to be immediate.

We saw in chapter 1 that one of the ways in which Peirce takes pragmatism to challenge the 'spirit of Cartesianism' is in its rejection of the idea of direct or immediate knowledge. Peirce argued that, in giving up on that idea, we can nevertheless account for our privileged access to the contents of our own minds. In giving up on immediacy, Sellars also examines how we can account for knowledge of our mental states. He writes: 'In short, we are brought face to face with the general problem of understanding how there can be *inner episodes* – episodes, that is, which somehow combine *privacy*, in that each of us has privileged access to his own, with *intersubjectivity*, in that each of us can, in principle, know about the other's' (Sellars, 1997: 87). His response to this problem is developed by recourse to a second myth, 'The Myth of Jones'. Sellars uses this myth to explain both how a community which does not possess the concept of inner episodes comes to acquire that concept, and, furthermore, how individuals within that community come to have direct (non-inferential) knowledge of such episodes.

'Sellars' argument presents a hypothetical community, one which does not possess the idea of inner mental episodes'. The members of that community behave exactly like us, the only difference being that they lack the concepts, such as thought, sensation and desire, which are traditionally associated with mental states. One day, Jones sets about trying to explain some forms of behaviour among the members of that community. The behaviour in question occurs when he observes people behaving in an apparently rational manner but without speaking. Jones hypothesizes that a process is going on inside their heads, a process which is hidden, but nevertheless postulated as an explanation of their behaviour. Jones sees this behaviour as akin to an internal conversation:

> Suppose, now, that in the attempt to account for the fact that his fellow men behave intelligibly not only when their conduct is threaded on a string of overt verbal episodes – that is to say, as we would put it, when they 'think out loud' – but also when no detectable verbal output is present, Jones develops a theory according to which overt utterances are but the culmination of a process which begins with certain inner episodes. (Sellars, 1997: 102–3)

Having postulated the existence of inner episodes, Jones then teaches the members of his community how to use that concept in order to explain each other's behaviour. They come to understand that behaviour by seeing each other as engaged in inner speech, analogous to the process of public discourse. In the third part of the story, Jones teaches people how to apply the theory to their *own* behaviour. Once they have done so and have become familiar with the concept of inner episodes, they are able to make non-inferential reports about themselves, just as they are able to make such reports about items and events in the world. Speaking of the learning process of one man, Dick, Sellars writes: 'Dick can be trained to give reasonably reliable self-descriptions, using the language of the theory, without having to observe his overt behavior' (Sellars, 1997: 106). That is to say, Dick is able to make reports of what he is thinking, and do so in a way which does not rely on Cartesian assumptions about his starting with immediate knowledge of his own mind.

In sum, Sellars uses The Myth of Jones to show how we can make claims about the contents of our own minds, and how it is that we can rightly claim to be in a better position to do so than other people, in a way which is consistent with psychological nominalism. We acquire the concept of inner episodes via dialogue and communication with other language-users such that we are made able to imagine the concept operational in others before internalizing it to our own selves. And, once we have the concept of 'inner episode', we are able to use it to make reports of those episodes directly (without inference). Sellars writes:

> As I see it, this story helps us understand that concepts pertaining to such inner episodes as thoughts are primarily and essentially *intersubjective*, as intersubjective as the concept of a positron, and that the reporting role of these concepts – the fact that each of us has a privileged access to his thoughts – constitutes a dimension of the use of these concepts which is *built on* and *presupposes* this intersubjective status. (Sellars, 1997: 107)

In his critique of the given and his account of The Myth of Jones, Sellars can be seen to have carried through on lines of thought identified by Peirce. Both attack the idea of immediate knowledge and of epistemic foundationalism. And both reconceptualize 'immediacy' to presuppose competent language use; we can have immediate non-inferential knowledge of our mental states, but only once sufficient mastery of language is in place.

The manifest and scientific images

Sellars concludes 'Empiricism and the Philosophy of Mind' with the following reflection:

> I have used a myth to kill a myth – the Myth of the Given. But is my myth really a myth? Or does the reader not recognize Jones as Man

himself in the middle of his journey from the grunts and groans of the cave to the subtle and polydimensional discourse of the drawing room, the laboratory, and the study, the language of Henry and William James, of Einstein and of the philosophers who, in their efforts to break out of discourse to an *arché* beyond discourse, have provided the most curious dimension of all. (Sellars, 1997: 117)

In reference to those who strive to break out of discourse, Sellars neatly calls attention to the fact that their so doing is *itself* part of the process of human development explained by psychological nominalism; their seeking to break out of language is an aspiration only made possible as a result of induction into it. Sellars here intimates a view of humanity's place in the universe, a view he develops in his essay 'Philosophy and the Scientific Image of Man'.

In his essay, Sellars discusses the emergence of personhood, locating it within a quasi-historical framework. He writes that today we confront two images of the world and our place within it. The first, the 'manifest image', is a philosophical conception of personhood which can be traced from the ancient Greeks through to the present day, according to which human beings are viewed as being both sentient creatures and agents capable of rational action: 'It is the framework in terms of which, to use an existentialist turn of phrase, man first encountered himself – which is, of course, when he first came to be man' (Sellars, 1963: 6). The second, 'scientific image', emerged from the scientific revolutions of the seventeenth century. It developed out of the manifest image, but regards that image merely as a first approximation at understanding reality which is now more adequately offered by the sciences: 'From its [the scientific image's] point of view the manifest image on which it rests is an "inadequate" but pragmatically useful likeness of a reality which first finds its adequate (in principle) likeness in the scientific image' (Sellars, 1963: 20).

We saw in chapter 2 that Dewey sketches an account of how natural science emerged and came into conflict with older forms of knowledge. Sellars is less concerned with offering a history than with calling attention to the manifest and scientific images as different categories of understanding. The manifest image focuses upon the category of *personhood*, in which the world is conceived in terms of *intentionality*, whereas the scientific is the domain of the description of physical objects and events. The issue as Sellars sees it is how to bring these two images together. The problem to be confronted is that they are two *rival* images, which make competing claims and thus encourage the temptation to elevate the one over the other. Thus, some philosophers have argued that the categories of personhood might be reduced to a vocabulary of physical phenomena (prioritizing the scientific image) whereas others hold that intentionality cannot be reduced in this manner (prioritizing the manifest image). Sellars argues that both positions are inadequate. He agrees that human intentionality and agency cannot be reduced to the language of physical phenomena, but, unlike many opponents of reductionism, he also thinks it necessary to account for intentionality within a naturalistic account of the world. The aim then is to join the images without attempting to reduce one to the other: 'the task of showing that categories pertaining to man as a *person* who finds himself confronted by standards (ethical, logical, etc.) which often conflict with his desires and impulses, and to which he may or may not conform, can be reconciled with the idea that man is what science says he is' (Sellars, 1963: 38).

Sellars thinks that such a reconciliation can be effected. He is clear that the scientific image is best suited for describing and explaining the physical world. This might seem to leave no room for the manifest image, but Sellars argues that this is not the case. This is because natural science cannot explain intentionality. In principle at least, the scientific image offers a complete description of man's place in the world, but a complete *description* is not fully to exhaust what is needed, for it does not take account of the *normative* dimension of human thought and action: 'To say that a certain person desired to do A, thought it his duty to do B but was forced to do C, is not to *describe* him as one might describe a scientific specimen. One does, indeed, describe him, but one does something more. And it is this something more which is the irreducible core of the framework of persons' (Sellars, 1963: 39).

The framework of personhood is a normative framework within which individuals are regarded as persons, with personhood understood by Sellars to be a matter of membership of a norm-governed community: 'Now, the fundamental principles of a community, which define what is "correct" or "incorrect", "right" or "wrong", "done" or "not done", are the most general common *intentions* of that community with respect to the behaviour of members of the group' (Sellars, 1963: 39). Sellars continues:

> A person can almost be defined as a being that has intentions. Thus the conceptual framework of persons is not something that needs to be *reconciled with* the scientific image, but rather something to be *joined to* it. Thus, to complete the scientific image we need to enrich it *not* with more ways of saying what is the case, but with the language of community and individual intentions, so that by construing the actions we intend to do and the circumstances in which we intend to

do them in scientific terms, we *directly* relate the world as conceived by scientific theory to our purposes, and make it *our* world and no longer an alien appendage to the world in which we do our living. (Sellars, 1963: 40)

To unpack this a little, Sellars' claim is that personhood is a matter of intentionality. We hold beliefs about the world, and those beliefs are intentional in the sense that they are *about* something; a person has beliefs about triangles, ice cubes, etc. The intentional is therefore the domain of the normative, not the descriptive, since intention implies motivation to act, believe, behave, think, etc. This will involve giving reasons to justify why one should do/believe/act as one does, something which returns us to Sellars' claim about the space of reasons and its centrality to knowledge. Intentionality is normative since the very nature of action is to effect change in the world, not merely to describe it but to do things to ensure things are the way they should be (whether or not action involves ensuring a situation remains the same, or involves ensuring a situation ceases to be as it is). And, for Sellars, reason-giving in support of such results of intention, by playing the game of giving and asking for reasons, is of central importance.

One reservation that might be offered regarding Sellars' view is whether he has successfully achieved the reconciliation he attempts, or whether he has simply emphasized the importance of the manifest image rather than telling us how intentionality can be understood within a naturalistic framework. What is clear though is his hope of overcoming the limitations of those who seek to reduce intentionality to physical states without going on to install a dualism between mind and world, offering as the way to do so an account in which different discourses all have their place. Rather than say (with Quine) that one language, that of physics, is epistemically privileged, Sellars provides room for different discourses as being necessary for different purposes. The scientific image is employed in order to describe and explain the physical world, whereas the manifest image (the language of intentionality) is used to account for normativity, the giving and responding to reasons.

Donald Davidson

Donald Davidson (1917–2003) was a student of Quine, whose influence is clear and acknowledged throughout his work. He follows up on Quine's thought in many areas, often extending it in ways of which the latter disapproved. Davidson's claim to pragmatism stems largely from Richard Rorty's efforts to read him into the pragmatist tradition, but that interpretation is not without basis. If we agree with Quine that pragmatism is what is left over from empiricism once it is rid of the two dogmas he identifies, then Davidson too is a pragmatist. But the point can be pressed further, for Davidson sets aside empiricism in its entirety. In urging us to give up on what he calls the third dogma of empiricism, he shares with the classical pragmatists, and with Sellars, the view that thought and knowledge are only possible in the context of shared communication.

The third dogma of empiricism

Davidson is not an uncritical disciple of Quine, and issues his most direct challenge to him in his influential paper 'On the Very Idea of a Conceptual Scheme' (1974). There Davidson accepts Quine's criticisms of the empiricist dogmas of the analytic–synthetic distinction and of reductionism, but goes on to object to what he calls 'the dualism of scheme and content, of organizing system and something waiting to be organized' (Davidson, 1984: 189). James and Dewey offered revised accounts of empiricism; in 'Two Dogmas of Empiricism', Quine argued that pragmatism is a form of empiricism once the dogmas of the analytic–synthetic distinction and of reductionism have been vanquished. Davidson is more radical, giving up completely on empiricism. The scheme–content distinction is said to be a further dogma of empiricism: 'The third, and perhaps the last, for if we give it up it is not clear that there is anything distinctive left to call empiricism' (Davidson, 1984: 189).

The third dogma is the view that there are two parts to our picture of the world. First, there is the raw or uninterpreted material given to us in experience. The second part is the mind, which organizes what is given by imposing a structure upon it. In modern philosophy, various candidates have been proposed as such a component, with examples including Kant's intuitions and Hume's operations of the mind. They are united in the assumption that different conceptual schemes *organize* empirical content.

The idea of a conceptual scheme gives rise to conceptual relativism. For, if we are able to distinguish the conceptual structure of knowledge from its empirical content, then it is possible that this content might be organized in different ways. Conceptual relativism was made famous by Thomas Kuhn, who wrote that scientists in different traditions work within 'different worlds'. As Davidson's argument unfolds, though, it is clear that it is targeted as much at Quine as it is at Kuhn. Quine challenged the first and second dogmas of empiricism but, according to Davidson, continued to distinguish between scheme and content. Quine held that we build up a picture of the world from the stimulation of our sense organs, allowing for the possibility that we might have made different things from the sensory input given to us. Quine is thus committed to conceptual relativism, allowing for different but equally correct interpretations of the given.

Davidson's argument against the idea of a distinction between scheme and content begins by identifying conceptual schemes with languages: the question of whether different conceptual schemes exist is for him the same as whether different non-translatable languages could exist, such that the terms of one language could not be translated into those of another. The issue of different conceptual schemes thus is that of whether or not we can make sense of the idea of non-translatable languages. Davidson argues that we cannot. To say that one language cannot be translated into another requires that we be able to specify a criterion which both shows that another person's utterances amount to a language (rather than just being sounds and noises) *and* that they cannot be translated into our own. Davidson's claim is that these two requirements cannot both be met: we cannot make sense of the untranslatability of a language and yet judge a person to be speaking a language. We *can*, he continues, make sense of partial untranslatability, but doing so only makes sense in a context of more general understanding: 'We can be clear about breakdowns in translation when they are local enough, for the background of general successful translation provides what is needed to make the failure intelligible' (Davidson, 1984: 192). The idea of different points of view makes sense, but in order to make sense there must be a shared basis upon which to compare them. And, if there is such a basis, then radical untranslatability is shown up as unintelligible.

What follows from this? Davidson's conclusion is that if there are no such things as different conceptual schemes, no sense can be made of there being a single conceptual scheme. As he puts it, 'if we cannot intelligibly say that schemes are different, neither can we intelligibly say that they are one' (Davidson, 1984: 198). We should, that is, give up the very idea of conceptual schemes giving shape and meaning to empirical content.

According to Davidson, the reason why some are attracted to the idea of the scheme–content distinction is that it offers a foundation for our beliefs, with different schemes anchored to immediate, uninterpreted reality. As an illustration, he cites Lewis' claim that: 'There are, in our cognitive experience, two elements; the immediate data, such as those of sense, which are presented or given to the mind, and a form, construction, or interpretation, which represents the activity of thought' (Lewis, 1929: 38; cited in Davidson, 2001: 40). Davidson acknowledges, and embraces, the consequences of rejecting this position: 'empiricism is the view that the subjective ("experience") is the foundation of objective empirical knowledge. I am suggesting that empirical knowledge has no epistemological foundation, and needs none' (Davidson, 2001: 46). That is, empirical knowledge requires nothing outside of itself for justification.

At one point, Davidson presented himself as offering a *coherence* theory of truth and knowledge, which holds that 'nothing can count as for holding a belief except another belief. Its partisan rejects as unintelligible the request for a ground or source of justification of another ilk' (Davidson, 1990a: 123). On this point he disagrees with Quine. Experience is non-propositional, yet Quine presents it as evidence for our beliefs. Davidson denies this, holding that nothing non-propositional justifies belief. He came to regret calling his account of truth and knowledge a coherence theory, recognizing that one might secure coherence between beliefs and yet those beliefs be untrue. However, he continued to insist that, although sensory stimulation plays a *causal* role in our coming to have beliefs, it plays no part in *justifying* those beliefs: 'sensory stimulations are indeed part of the causal chain that leads to belief, but cannot, without confusion, be considered to be evidence, or a source of justification, for the stimulated beliefs' (Davidson, 1990a: 132). Knowledge is wholly a matter of using some of our beliefs in order to justify others. In saying this, Davidson makes common cause with Sellars' critique of the given, of something which provides the raw material upon which our claims to knowledge are founded.

The problem, though, is that without some foundation in what is given to us, do our beliefs not become arbitrary? What can we say to the Cartesian sceptic? For Davidson, one will only be exercised by these questions if one thinks of knowledge as the attempt to represent some independent thing. But if we give up on the scheme–content distinction, we give up the idea that representations may or may not accurately represent the world, for we set aside any sense in which we are separated from the rest of the world in the manner posited by Descartes. Davidson thinks that doing so has the further beneficial consequence of avoiding the relativism which follows from the idea of alternative conceptual schemes: 'It is good to be rid of representations, and with them the correspondence theory of truth, for it is thinking there are representations that engenders intimations of relativism' (Davidson, 2001: 46). By giving up on representation-alism, we simultaneously give up on the correspondence theory of truth, for the idea that representations may or may not accurately represent reality is a question which is no longer seen to make sense. In place of representations, he argues that our words and thoughts are about the objects in the world that cause them, something which precludes the possibility that the contents of our minds might be radically different from the world around us (a point we will return to in the next section).

'On the Very Idea of a Conceptual Scheme' is one of Davidson's most famous papers, but its argument points to a larger picture of the mind and its relation to the world. In a later essay entitled 'The Myth of the Subjective', Davidson argues that the scheme–content distinction is aligned to that which is taken to hold between the sub-jective and objective, and that underlying both is a distinctive, and optional, conception of the mind. He writes: 'Instead of saying it is the scheme-content dichotomy that has dominated and defined the problems of modern philosophy, then, one could as well say it is how the dualism of the objective and the subjective have been conceived. For these dualisms have a common origin: a concept of the mind with its private states and objects' (Davidson, 2001: 43). This picture of the mind is of course one which can be traced back to Descartes, to whom is owed the problem of how such a mind might come to possess knowledge of the external world.

Cartesianism holds that we start with the mind and attempt to work our way from there to knowledge of the external world. David-son argues that Cartesianism has carried over into contemporary philosophy, including even Quine's work. Quine's naturalized episte-mology, as we have seen, rests on the idea that knowledge of the world stems from the stimulation of our retinas or from some other sensory surface. The problem is that the sceptic can always question the grounds we have for moving from knowledge of the contents of our own minds to knowledge of the external world by pointing out that the external world could be very different from how it appears to us: 'The familiar trouble is, of course, that the disconnection creates a gap no reasoning or construction can plausibly bridge. Once this starting point has been chosen, there is no saying what the evi-dence is evidence for, or so it seems. Idealism, reductionist forms of empiricism, and skepticism loom' (Davidson, 2001: 43). Davidson grants that in these terms, the sceptic cannot be answered, but also points out that one need only accept this conclusion if one is per-suaded by the way in which Descartes has framed the assumptions which give rise to scepticism in the first place. The sceptic starts with the subjective and asks how one might move to knowledge of the external world. Davidson's alternative suggestion, which we will now examine, is that three kinds of knowledge are equally important; in addition to knowledge of what is going on in our own minds, these are knowledge of other minds and knowledge of the external world: 'the acquisition of knowledge is not based on a progression from the subjective to the objective; it emerges holistically and is interpersonal from the start' (Davidson, 2004: 18).

Three varieties of knowledge

We all of us possess what Davidson calls three varieties of knowledge. We have knowledge of ourselves, our wants, intentions and sensations. We also know something about the world around us. And we know, at least sometimes, what other people are thinking and feeling. These varieties of knowledge have different characteristics. One knows one's own beliefs and desires without evidence, whereas knowledge of items and events in the world depends upon evidence provided by our senses. And knowledge of what is going on in the minds of other people requires evidence too, which we typically observe in their behaviour.

All of this is fairly clear, but what Davidson finds interesting in it is that philosophers are often tempted to assert that one of these varieties of knowledge has conceptual priority over the others. Those who take their lead from Descartes take self-knowledge as conceptually prior, and attempt to derive knowledge of other minds and of the external world from it. Davidson's proposal is different. He argues that none of these three forms of knowledge is conceptually prior, and that none can be reduced to one of the others. Rather, all three are equally important and equally necessary for explaining the others.

How does Davidson explain them and the relation between them? He begins by asking the apparently simple question of what it is for a person to have a thought. Like Sellars, he claims that being able to discriminate among different objects in the world is not sufficient for having a thought. Non-human animals discriminate between sources of food which will sustain them and those which are poisonous, but this does not mean that they think. The difference is that we, and not they, have an understanding of *concepts*. Davidson argues that knowledge of concepts requires that one is aware that one might misapply them:

> I should...like to reserve the word 'concept' for cases where it makes clear sense to speak of a mistake, a mistake not only as seen from an intelligent observer's point of view, but as seen from the creature's point of view. If an earthworm eats poison, it has not in this sense made a mistake – it has not mistaken one thing for another: it has simply done what it was programmed to do. (Davidson, 2004: 8)

The key concept is that of truth, an understanding that one's thoughts can be correct or incorrect. In particular, one must possess the concept of *objective* truth, meaning that one is aware that a state of affairs exists which is wholly distinct from one's beliefs about it. That is to say, first-personal knowledge requires that one appreciate the difference between true and false belief: 'Someone who has a belief about the world – or anything else – must grasp the concept of objective truth, of what is the case independently of what he or she thinks' (Davidson, 2001: 209).

The mark of thought is that it can be true or false, but the question then is where our understanding of the truth comes from. Davidson's answer is that it comes from communication. The claim is that knowledge of the minds of other people is a condition for our having thoughts of our own, and *that* requires that we communicate with each other: 'The source of the concept of objective truth is interpersonal communication....We have no grounds for crediting a creature with the distinction between what is thought to be the case and what is the case unless the creature has the standard provided by a shared language; and without this distinction there is nothing that can clearly be called thought' (Davidson, 2001: 209–10).

In order for communication between two people to succeed there must be a shared understanding of what they mean by their words. How is such understanding to be attained? Central to Davidson's argument is the idea of 'radical interpretation', an idea that owes much to Quine's account of translation (discussed above). As with Quine's translator, Davidson's interpreter has no prior knowledge of the meaning of another person's utterances, and goes about trying to understand them by seeking to assign propositional content to those utterances. When trying to interpret others, the aim is to make sense of their behaviour, and to do so the interpreter necessarily attributes to them beliefs about the world to which they are observed responding. The interpreter does so by employing what Davidson calls the 'principle of charity'. In his paper 'A Coherence Theory of Truth and Knowledge', he explains that: 'the principle directs the interpreter to translate or interpret so as to read some of his own standards of truth into the pattern of sentences held true by the speaker. The point of the principle is to make the speaker intelligible, since too great deviations from consistency and correctness leave no common ground on which to judge either conformity or difference' (Davidson, 1990a: 129).

The process of radical interpretation yields what Davidson calls an *interpersonal* standard in which the speaker and his or her interpreter come to understand each other. Why though should that standard also be seen as an *objective* one? This is a pressing question for Davidson, given his concern to avoid the sceptical consequences of Cartesianism. In response, Davidson argues that objectivity is generated by reference to the causal impact of the world upon us *and* our shared responses to it. It requires a third variety of knowledge, knowledge of the world:

> Until a base line has been established by communication with someone else, there is no point in saying one's own thoughts or words have a propositional content. If this is so, then it is clear that knowledge of another mind is essential to all thought and all knowledge. Knowledge of another mind is possible, however, only if one has knowledge of the world, for the triangulation which is essential to thought requires that those in communication recognize that they occupy positions in a shared world. (Davidson, 2001: 213)

That is to say, knowledge is a product not of a two-way relation between speaker and interpreter, but of a three-way relation between speaker, interpreter and their shared environment. The three varieties of knowledge are interrelated, and none can be had without the other two. Knowledge of the propositional content of our minds depends upon communication because that is the only way to identify the truth or falsity of our thoughts. But we can only attribute thoughts to others if we know our own thoughts, because that attribution is a matter of matching their behaviour with our own. And both require a third element, namely knowledge of our shared environment. Only with all three working simultaneously can we be said to possess knowledge at all.

One consequence of Davidson's account of knowledge and its acquisition is to rule out radical scepticism. The triangular relationship between interpreter, speaker and world means that large-scale error is not possible, for we are each of us responding to the same world (remember that conceptual relativism disappears along with the third dogma of empiricism, the scheme–content distinction). The attempt to interpret another person will inevitably involve some mistakes, but recognizing those mistakes itself presupposes a background of correct belief. It is that background which frames our understanding of the world and which provides the only content for our beliefs, whether or not any particular one of those beliefs is in fact true: 'any particular belief or set of beliefs about the world around us may be false. What cannot be the case is that our general picture of the world and our place in it is mistaken, for it is this picture which informs the rest of our beliefs and makes them intelligible, whether they be true or false' (Davidson, 2001: 213–14).

By arguing that knowledge stems from interpersonal communication, rather than the subject correctly apprehending the object, Davidson has a response to the sceptic. We should be clear, however, that his response does not entail answering the sceptic in her own terms, but rather re-describing the process of acquiring knowledge so that scepticism is not a possibility. This re-description might seem to come at a cost though, that of appearing to deny the subjective element of thought, the fact that we are each of us in a better position to report upon our own mental states than is anyone else. Davidson claims that his position allows for this. He calls attention to the difference between our *having* a thought and the *content* of that thought. If we have a thought, it is indeed our own, but its content is given by concepts which are in the public domain. In a comment with clear echoes of Peirce and of Sellars, Davidson writes: 'though possession of a thought is necessarily individual, its content is not. The thoughts we form and entertain are located conceptually in the world we inhabit, and know we inhabit, with others. Even our thoughts about our own mental states occupy the same conceptual space and are located on the same public map' (Davidson, 2001: 218).

Is Davidson a pragmatist?

Rorty claims that Davidson, in arguing for the intimate relationship between thought and communication, should be thought of as part of the pragmatist tradition. However, Davidson resisted the association of his writings with pragmatism. In the introduction to his collection of essays entitled *Inquiries Into Truth and Interpretation* (1984), he denies that the consequence of abandoning empiricism brings him into the pragmatist tradition (Davidson, 1984: xxi). He writes there that pragmatism is a form of relativism, and relativism, as a consequence of the third dogma, is of course what he objects to in empiricism. Precisely what he means by 'relativism' in the context of pragmatism is not specified there, but in other places

Davidson spells out his disagreement more fully. This centres upon objections to his understanding of what the classical pragmatists took truth to be.

In the title of one of his papers, Davidson speaks of the 'folly' of trying to define truth, the folly of trying to reduce the concept of truth (along with other philosophical concepts, such as 'belief' and 'knowledge') to something more basic (in Davidson, 2005). This is a folly for the reason that the concept of truth is one of the most basic we possess and cannot be analysed in some other terms. In his Dewey Lectures, entitled 'The Structure and Content of Truth' (1990c), Davidson draws out the consequence of this view: 'We should not say that truth is correspondence, coherence, warranted assertability, ideally justified assertability, what is accepted in the conversation of the right people, what science will end up maintaining, what explains the convergence on single theories in science, or the success of our ordinary beliefs' (Davidson, 1990c: 309). In giving up both correspondence and coherence theories of truth, Davidson is in agreement with the classical pragmatists. He also shares the importance they placed on seeking to examine the role that the concept of truth plays in our lives. However, he strongly dissents from what he thinks the pragmatists understood this role to be: 'Dewey thought that once truth was brought down to earth there were philosophically important and instructive things to say about its connections with human attitudes, connections partly constitutive of the concept of truth. This is also my view, though I do not think Dewey had the connections right' (Davidson, 1990c: 281). Where Davidson takes himself to differ from Dewey is in what he infers from the failure of the correspondence and coherence theories. As Davidson understands them, the classical pragmatists concluded that one can give up on objectivity and simply identify truth with usefulness or practical success, something he thinks importantly mistaken: 'I agree with the pragmatists that we can't consistently take truth to be both objective and something to be pursued. But I think they would have done better to cleave to a view that counts truth as objective, but pointless as a goal' (Davidson, 2005: 7).

The claim that truth is pointless as a goal of inquiry might strike some as outrageous. After all, when physicists, historians, geographers, etc., pursue their inquiries, what are they doing if not seeking to establish the truth of some question? Davidson recognizes that his is a counter-intuitive claim, but argues that it is nevertheless correct. Truth cannot be said to be a goal of inquiry for the reason that we are unable to distinguish it from justified belief. But we cannot simply identify truth with justified belief; a belief may meet all of our standards of evidence, and have persuaded all who have inquired into the matter, and yet not be true. As he remarks, 'We know many things, and will learn more; what we will never know for certain is which of the things we believe are true. Since it is neither visible as a target, nor recognizable when achieved, there is no point in calling truth a goal' (Davidson, 2005: 6).

And yet Davidson is clear that, although truth cannot be taken to be a goal of inquiry, it remains a centrally important concept. As we saw above, he takes it to be essential to the idea of belief to know that beliefs can be true or false. It is on the matter of the objectivity of truth that Davidson takes himself to differ markedly from the classical pragmatists, and why he resists being classified as one.

Two things can be noted about Davidson's view of the classical pragmatists. The first is that it is not clear that his is an accurate account of the considered views of Peirce, James and Dewey on the issue of truth. Each of these pragmatists sought to bring the truth back to us by examining it in terms of the role it plays in our lives but, at their best, were careful to avoid any simplistic equation of truth with practical success. Moreover, Davidson seems rather closer to the pragmatists here than he realizes. His claim that truth is not a goal of inquiry recalls Dewey's argument that the aim of inquiry is to secure 'warranted assertibility'. In saying this, Dewey did not give up on the notion of objective truth and did not reduce it to what is warranted. Rather, his claim was that truth is not a goal we can steer by, and that in our inquiries we should instead pursue the practical and tangible goal of securing beliefs that are warranted. Davidson recognizes some similarities with Dewey on this matter, for example when he writes that: 'The best we can do is test, experiment, compare, and keep an open mind. But no matter how long and well we and coming generations keep at it, we and they will be left with fallible beliefs' (Davidson, 2005: 6).

If we turn to contemporary pragmatism, a second point to make in relation to Davidson is that few pragmatists are, as we will see in later chapters, happy with the accounts of truth offered by (or attributed to) the classical figures. As indicated in chapter 2, James' suggestion that truth be assimilated to practical success is challenged by both Quine and Rorty, and, as we will see, Peirceans such as Cheryl Misak have revised Peirce's understanding of truth as that which awaits us at the end of inquiry. Nevertheless, philosophers such as Rorty and Misak think that one can remain a pragmatist even while dispensing with these unfortunate elements found (however accurately) in the work of the classical writers.

Perhaps for this second reason, Davidson came to accept that he could legitimately be taken to be a pragmatist. In his 'Afterthoughts' to his paper 'A Coherence Theory of Truth and Knowledge', he writes: 'Rorty urges two things: that my view of truth amounts to a rejection of both coherence and correspondence theories and should properly be classed as belonging to the pragmatist tradition, and that I should not pretend that I am answering the skeptic when I am really telling him to get lost. I pretty much concur with him on both points' (Davidson, 1990b: 134). The slight hint of equivocation at the end of this passage does not concern Davidson's view of truth or his relationship to pragmatism, but rather the second issue, of what his dismissal of the sceptic amounts to. For Davidson does not simply ignore the sceptic but, like Peirce before him, offers an alternative account of truth and knowledge, and in so doing shows how the sceptic's concerns simply do not arise.

4

Neo-Pragmatism: Richard Rorty and Hilary Putnam

Richard Rorty

Richard Rorty's (1931–2007) book *Philosophy and the Mirror of Nature* is widely credited for having revived interest in pragmatism. Published in 1979, the book mounts a challenge to many of the presuppositions of modern philosophy, targeting its image as the discipline that lays bare the foundations of knowledge. It opens with the claim that the three most important philosophers of the twentieth century are Wittgenstein, Heidegger and Dewey. And, of the three, Dewey is the closest to Rorty's heart. He shares Dewey's targets of the correspondence theory of truth and the spectator theory of knowledge. He also, like Dewey, folds his understanding of pragmatism into a larger narrative which locates it in culture more generally. Rorty's highly influential, sometimes idiosyncratic, and often controversial understanding of pragmatism combines a reading of the work of the classical pragmatists with that of more recent philosophers such as Quine, Sellars and Davidson, and addresses issues in the philosophy of mind and philosophy of language, as well as in moral and political theory.

The mirror of nature

Rorty traces the origins of modern philosophy to the development of the new sciences in the seventeenth century and their clash with Greek and Christian worldviews. The materialistic and mechanistic picture provided by the new sciences directly conflicted with the immaterial view of the world that Christianity took over from Plato and Aristotle (Rorty, 2007: 163). The problem for the new sciences was that while they provided empirical knowledge, they did not offer an account of the basis for that knowledge. Accordingly, the aim of philosophers such as Descartes and Locke was to provide a way of justifying the legitimacy of the new sciences.

The starting point to Rorty's account of the emergence of modern philosophy is Descartes' description of the mind in epistemic terms. Descartes offered a description of the mind as a private sphere separate from the external world to which we have privileged access. Knowledge is conceived of as a matter of accurate representations, with mental ideas 'mirroring' the contents of the world. Rorty writes: 'In Descartes's conception – the one which became the basis for "modern" epistemology – it is *representations* which are in the "mind". The Inner Eye surveys these representations hoping to find some mark which will testify to their fidelity' (Rorty, 1979: 45).

In *Philosophy and the Mirror of Nature*, Rorty describes how the image of mind as mirror was retained by subsequent philosophers. Locke differed from Descartes in denying that rational reflection alone can establish knowledge, arguing rather that knowledge is derived from sense experience. And yet Locke retained Descartes' central revolutionary point, the picture of the mind as an inner arena which strives to describe accurately the outside world. For Locke, knowledge results from the mind having been impressed in the correct way by the object before it: 'knowing a proposition to be true is to be identified with being caused to do something by an object' (Rorty, 1979: 157).

Kant was to complain that Locke had not grasped exactly how radical was the form of scepticism that Descartes' view entailed. This is because Locke simply assumed that we are entitled to count the deliverances of our senses as knowledge. In other words, he conflated *causation* with *justification*, providing an explanation of what gives rise to our beliefs but running it together with an account of the reasons which justify them. Kant's response, transcendental idealism, sought to overcome the problems with both Cartesian rationalism and British empiricism by holding that the mind *constructs* the objects it experiences. The thought is that our 'inner' representations of the world are less like a mirror and more like a painting, so that any representation of the world necessarily involves interpretation in accordance with the concepts that we have in virtue of being minds. Rorty argues that by holding that we constitute the world according to the categories of our minds rather than being compelled to represent the world according to its causal impact upon us, Kant took an important step forward. But he thinks this only a first step, for Kant retained the Lockean view of knowledge as a matter of perception, examining it, as he puts it, 'within the framework of causal metaphors – "constitution," "making," "shaping," "synthesizing," and the like' (Rorty, 1979: 161).

According to Rorty, Kant's key move, one which remained central to philosophy through to the twentieth century, was to distinguish between scheme and content. Knowledge is the result of two separate elements, *concepts* (of the mind) and *intuitions* (empirical content derived from sense experience). Kant believed concepts to be innate, in the sense that they are a requirement for the ability to perceive or experience. He argued that the mind uses its concepts to organize intuitions, with knowledge the resultant product of these two kinds of representation. To this view, Kant added a further distinction, that between analytic and synthetic knowledge. Here, he extended a distinction already leveraged by Hume between truths of demonstration (*a priori*, usually analytic truths) and truths of experience (*a posteriori*, and usually synthetic). Accordingly, some statements were said to be true by virtue of the meaning of concepts: the sentence 'That triangle has three sides' needs no empirical validation but is true by virtue of the meaning of the component terms. Others, such as 'That triangle is red', require empirical investigation.

Kant originated an image of philosophy as the discipline which purports to display the underlying structure of knowledge, with epistemology the non-empirical discipline which establishes the cognitive status of different areas of inquiry, determined by whether they are responsive to reason or whether they merely express taste or opinion. Rorty describes Kant as having thereby invented a discipline which is both separate from, and possesses epistemic authority over, not only natural science but all areas of empirical inquiry: 'the Kantian picture of concepts and intuitions getting together to produce knowledge is needed to give sense to the idea of "theory of knowledge" as a specifically philosophical discipline, distinct from psychology' (Rorty, 1979: 168). In the late nineteenth and early twentieth centuries his picture was taken over by analytic philosophers such as Frege and Russell. They did this under the auspices of the study of language, but retained distinctions which are owed to Kant, notably between *a priori* and empirical questions, and between statements which are cognitive and those which are taken merely to be expressive. Rorty remarks that: 'Even when they claim to have "gone beyond" epistemology, they have agreed that philosophy is a discipline which takes as its study the "formal" or "structural" aspects of our beliefs, and that by examining these the philosopher serves the cultural function of keeping the other disciplines honest, limiting their claims to what can be properly "grounded" ' (Rorty, 1979: 162).

Rorty's objection to the representationalism common to Descartes, Locke and Kant is that it invites us to question the status of different representations. To answer the Cartesian sceptic, representationalists take it that some representations are *privileged*. The two central forms of privileged representation in twentieth-century philosophy are that which is given to us immediately in experience (Sellars' target) and truths of meaning (Quine's target). These privileged representations provide indubitable foundations upon which to ground knowledge-claims. In the fourth and central chapter of *Philosophy and the Mirror of Nature* Rorty brings together arguments from Quine and Sellars to mount a thoroughgoing critique of the representationalist picture of philosophy. He reads them as together having shown that neither kind of representation will do the work asked of it: Sellars calls into question the idea that something given in experience constitutes knowledge, and in his work Quine shows that there are no statements which are true by virtue of meaning alone. Furthermore, if Quine is correct to say that there are no statements that are true just in virtue of the meaning of words, we must also give up on the Kantian idea of first philosophy, for there are no meanings for philosophy to clarify. Rorty writes:

> if we do not have the distinction between what is 'given' and what is 'added by the mind,' or that between the 'contingent' (because influenced by what is given) and the 'necessary' (because entirely 'within' the mind and under its control), then we will not know what would count as a 'rational reconstruction' of our knowledge. We will not know what epistemology's goal or method could be. (Rorty, 1979: 169)

When the analytic–synthetic distinction is discarded along with the notion of the given, there is no scope for the philosopher standing over the rest of culture in order to judge the epistemic status of different areas of inquiry.

According to Rorty, however, the break with epistemology made by Quine and Sellars was incomplete. Rorty accepts Davidson's view that Quine continued to adhere to a form of the given, in thinking that a naturalistic successor to empiricism could be found in the idea that we constitute the world as a result of the stimulation of our senses. For his part, Sellars invoked distinctions, such as the necessary and contingent, which Quine had overcome. The result is that they both showed a part, but only a part, of the way to move beyond the foundationalist concerns of epistemology. Rorty claims that it is only with Davidson's rejection of the dualism of an organizing scheme and a content awaiting organization that these limitations are fully overcome. Combining the insights of these three philosophers is to get 'the visual, and in particular the mirroring, metaphors out of our speech altogether' (Rorty, 1979: 371).

In *Philosophy and the Mirror of Nature*, Rorty identifies the position he outlines as 'epistemological behaviorism'. Epistemological behaviourism seeks to understand thought and behaviour from a public standpoint, with differences in belief which make no difference to behaviour discarded. Quine had shown, for instance, that the difference between supposed analytical and synthetic truths is not one that can be made if we examine how humans actually behave in the world. At that stage Rorty eschewed the label 'pragmatism', a word which he feared 'a bit overladen' (Rorty, 1979: 176). Pragmatism is, however, the word, and the tradition, with which he came to identify. He came to argue that the moral of the pragmatism common to Peirce, James and Dewey, and to Quine, Sellars and Davidson, is that knowledge is not a matter of a relation between words and the world but rather between participants in conversation: 'The crucial premise of this argument is that we understand knowledge when we understand the social justification of belief, and thus have no need to view it as accuracy of representation' (Rorty, 1979: 170). The emphasis upon social practice means that the distinctions that representationalist philosophers have insisted on since Descartes – between scheme and content, necessary and contingent truths, etc. – ought to be set aside. Inquiry is rather, as Quine and Sellars saw it, a matter of re-weaving a web of beliefs, a web in which any belief may be put into question but not all at the same time.

Pragmatism as anti-representationalism

Philosophy and the Mirror of Nature criticizes the idea that knowledge is a matter of mental or linguistic representation of the external world. Essays published throughout the 1970s and 1980s develop this line of criticism by bringing out its connections with the work of the classical pragmatists, in particular by presenting it, somewhat contentiously, as 'continuous with Dewey's' (Rorty, 1991: 16).

Rorty has offered several different characterizations of pragmatism, but the one which looms large in his concerns is the view that it amounts to *anti-representationalism*. The immediate context for pragmatism as anti-representationalism is the contemporary debate between realists and anti-realists. Rorty seeks to undercut this debate by presenting realists and anti-realists alike as committed to representationalism; the disagreement between them concerns which areas of culture – if any – represent items in the world. For him, pragmatism is neither realist nor anti-realist because it rejects representationalism in its entirety.

But exactly what is it to reject representationalism? Rorty recognizes that the world exists independently of us, in the sense 'that most things in space and time are the effects of causes which do not include human mental states' (Rorty, 1989: 5). His point is that those causes do not have to be *represented* in any particular way – for example, 'the pressure of lightwaves of Galileo's eyeball' did not, in itself, cause Galileo to describe the solar system in the way that he did (Rorty, 1991: 81). Following Davidson, the point is to reject the idea that we can divide between the activities of the mind and the contribution of the world, and in consequence make distinctions such as those between disciplines which can obtain objectivity, for example mathematics and physics, and those, for example ethics and literary criticism, which can only amount to subjective expression of preference. If we give up representationalism, Rorty hopes that we will allow that different areas of culture will serve different needs and interests but that none is epistemically privileged. For this reason, he criticizes Quine for his belief that science is best suited to serve the purposes it was once hoped philosophy would fulfil: 'Quine, after arguing that there is no line between science and philosophy, tends to assume that he has thereby shown that science can replace philosophy. But it is not clear what task he is asking science to perform. Nor is it clear why natural science, rather than the arts, or politics, or religion, should take over the area left vacant' (Rorty, 1979: 171).

According to Rorty, anti-representationalists see language not as mirroring nature but rather as a set of tools developed to cope with it. It might be objected to this view that its purpose *is* to represent the world. Rorty denies that the purpose of language can be reduced to that of representing items in the world, arguing that it can also be used to construct new things, such as objects or models of interaction and interpretation. He presents this idea as following on from a Darwinian account of human behaviour. All human behaviour, including higher forms of behaviour such as composing operas or philosophical treatises, is continuous with that of the non-human animals. Darwin, Rorty writes, called into question the idea that human beings stand in representational relationship to the world; Rorty interprets him as having raised the question of at which point in evolution organisms stop coping with the environment and start trying to represent it accurately. He writes: 'To pose the riddle is to suggest the answer: Maybe they never *did* start representing it. Maybe the whole idea of mental representation was just an uncashable and unfruitful metaphor' (Rorty, 1999: 269). Rather than seeking to represent the world, Rorty claims that it is more fruitful to see ourselves as attempting to cope with it.

Understood in anti-representationalist terms, Rorty seeks to account for the difference between, say, the levels of agreement reached in physics and that which obtains in literary criticism. Different claims to knowledge are distinguished not by reference to their epistemic status but by their reception by one's peers in inquiry. If we drop the metaphor of representationalism, the difference in degrees of confidence in our beliefs and thus (as we will see below) objectivity, turns on our capacity to secure agreement about them. Whereas natural scientists are often agreed both on goals and on what counts as the means to secure them, such agreement rarely exists in questions of aesthetics or ethics. While there have been systematic attempts to establish conditions of 'good' inquiry in science so that standards exist and are widely accepted, no attempts have been successful in securing the same outcome in less evidentially based areas of discourse. But for Rorty this does not render the latter any less legitimate.

Rorty argues that different vocabularies have different tasks and answer to different needs, but none is epistemically privileged over any other. However, he came slightly to amend this position. In a paper examining some key differences between Rorty and Davidson, Bjørn Ramberg argues that Rorty misunderstands what Davidson meant by insisting on the inescapability of normative vocabulary (Ramberg, 2000: 366–7). Rorty had taken Davidson's view that normative vocabulary is privileged to be apiece with the privilege that Quine grants to the language of physics. Ramberg argues that this is not the case. As we saw in chapter 3, Davidson rejects the Cartesian account of knowledge in which we construct a mental image of the external world, in favour of an understanding of knowledge as resulting from communication. This process, which Davidson calls 'triangulation', is, as Ramberg points out, inescapably normative, because we have to recognize each other *as participants* in a norm-governed practice in order to ascribe beliefs and commitments to each other. In response, Rorty accepts Ramberg's argument, and revises his position accordingly. Normativity *is* privileged: 'We cannot stop prescribing, and *just* describe, because the describing counts *as* describing only if rule-governed, only if conducted by people who talk about each other in the vocabulary of agency' (Rorty, 2000: 372).

The very fact that a discourse is governed by rules implies normativity, since the application of rules depends upon our acknowledging each other as beings who are responding to those rules, and who are answerable for their responses.

If pragmatism is conceived of as anti-representationalism, two differences between Rorty and the classical pragmatists emerge. The first is the shift from talking about experience to talking about language. Despite his admiration for Dewey, Rorty argues that Dewey's desire to re-describe experience amounts to a failure to grasp the consequences of his own best insights. His essay 'Dewey's Metaphysics' criticizes Dewey's attempt to create a metaphysics based on a notion of experience (in Rorty, 1982). Rorty objects that any account of experience will inevitably blur together sensation and cognition (as Locke had done three centuries earlier). He is thus pleased to note that Dewey came to regret seeking to rehabilitate the notion of experience. By dropping reference to experience and thinking instead of language, Rorty takes Dewey to have come, in his later works, to anticipate the importance of Sellars' distinction between the space of causes and the space of reasons.

The second difference that Rorty identifies between the classical pragmatists and more recent figures is that philosophers such as Davidson do not emphasize 'the method of science'. The idea that science exemplifies a distinctive method has been called into question by work in the philosophy of science, most famously in Thomas Kuhn's book *The Structure of Scientific Revolutions*. Rorty writes that: 'Although Kuhn did not explicitly attack the notion of "scientific method" (as Feyerabend later did), the effect of his book was to let that notion quietly fade away' (Rorty, 1999: 35). We must be careful to be clear what Rorty means here. He is denying that science is inherently more rational or objective than other areas of inquiry, but not that scientists at their best do not exhibit particular virtues, namely the virtues of the conscientious investigator. These are the virtues to which Peirce and Dewey called attention, and the only substantive difference between them and Rorty is in respect to the suitability of singling out 'science' as the label for them. For the virtues of science are those which, at their best, are said by Rorty to be held by *all* those who investigate.

Objectivity, relativism and truth

Insisting on Sellars' distinction between the space of causes and the space of reasons helps us to understand better Rorty's most controversial suggestion, which is that philosophers should radically revise the notion of objectivity. In *Philosophy and the Mirror of Nature*, he claims that 'our only usable notion of "objectivity" is "agreement" rather than mirroring' (Rorty, 1979: 337). In subsequent works, he makes this point by proposing that objectivity should be thought of as a matter of securing solidarity among participants in conversation.

Objectivity is typically invoked as a normative standard which exists independently of individual or cultural beliefs and which can be used to judge those beliefs. By denying any authority to the non-human world, Rorty seems to many critics to be guilty of irrationalism. This he denies. The attempt to secure solidarity is a matter of Davidsonian triangulation, addressing the causal input from the world *and* the reasons offered by our fellow inquirers (themselves arising in response to their own attempts to cope with the world). The causal pressures of the world lead us to create vocabularies to cope with them, but Rorty's claim is that the *authority* of those vocabularies is a matter of the reception they receive from our conversational peers. Authority depends upon the social practice of reason giving, or conversation, and we cannot enter into a conversation with brute causal pressures. Robert Brandom summarizes the argument in this way: 'The target is philosophical invocations of representations supposed to be epistemically privileged solely by their relations to certain kinds of *things* – perceptible facts and meanings – apart from the role those things play in practices of acknowledging them as authoritative' (Brandom, 2000a: 159).

Rorty generalizes the Sellars–Quine rejection of empirical and analytic foundations by rejecting all forms of knowledge outside of culture and history. In this sense, he thinks of pragmatism as *anti-authoritarian*, entailing a rejection of any 'source of normativity other than the practices of the people around us' (Rorty, 2007: 107). We treat a claim as addressed to us, in our capacity as members of a social practice governed by shared norms. Scientists are required to test their claims through experiments and are expected to give up a hypothesis in the face of conflicting evidence; judges decide cases based on case law and precedent; poker players take the pot depending on who has the best hand (Rorty, 1991: 80). In all cases, the decisions of communities of inquiry constitute the last word: 'Empiricism's appeal to experience is as inefficacious as appeals to the Word of God unless backed up with a predisposition on the part of a community to take such appeals seriously' (Rorty, 2007: 11).

To be sure, the constraints imposed by communal norms are contingent, local and, as Rorty accepts, *ethnocentric*. In a comment which invokes James' discussion in 'The Will to Believe', he remarks, one consequence of antirepresentationalism is the recognition that no description of how things are from a God's-eye point of view, no skyhook provided by some contemporary or yet-to-be-developed science, is going to free us from the contingency of having been acculturated as we were. Our acculturation is what makes certain options live, or momentous, or forced, while leaving others dead, or trivial, or optional. (Rorty, 1991: 13)

Ethnocentrism seems to entail relativism, but this Rorty also denies, arguing that his position in no way commits him to believing there is nothing to choose between alternative beliefs. The issue as he sees it concerns rather the ground upon which it is possible to stand in order to decide between those alternatives. In casting doubt on the availability of *neutral* ground, philosophers like himself are attacked for denying the very possibility of making that choice. But for Rorty, to draw that conclusion is to be guilty of what he calls 'silly relativism', 'the bad inference from "no epistemological difference" to "no objective criterion of choice"' (Rorty, 1991: 89). He spells out the difference in the following illustration:

> *Our* moral view is, I firmly believe, much better than any competing view, even though there are a lot of people whom you will never be able to convert to it. It is one thing to say, falsely, that there is nothing to choose between us and the Nazis. It is another thing to say, correctly, that there is no neutral, common ground to which an experienced Nazi philosopher and I can repair in order to argue out our differences. That Nazi and I will always strike one another as begging all the crucial questions, arguing in circles. (Rorty, 1999: 15)

In the absence of a neutral, common ground, what remains are different views, and arguments about which should prevail. We have to work with the particular settled beliefs we have, accepting all the while (with Peirce) that they are fallible, and might need to be revised in the course of inquiry if reason to do so emerges.

Having rejected traditional accounts of objectivity, what then of Rorty's view of truth? Rorty joins the classical pragmatists in rejecting the correspondence theory of truth, although his particular objections point us towards how he will come to view pragmatism in larger cultural terms. One objection is that the notion of correspondence is motivated by the desire to be constrained by something beyond ourselves, a desire Rorty provocatively views as analogous to the need to humble ourselves before God. A second objection is that it encourages invidious comparisons between different areas of inquiry, for, unlike the findings of the natural sciences, there seems to be nothing to which moral and aesthetic statements might correspond.

Rorty's positive view of truth changed, however. Thinking that he had to substitute an alternative for the correspondence theory, for a time he adopted Peirce's account of truth as what would be agreed upon at the end of inquiry. He gave up this idea, however, because he came to think that no sense can be given to the idea of the end of inquiry, and that Peirce's view represents a halfway measure which recognizes the problems of the correspondence theory and yet could not entirely set it aside. Rorty's considered view of truth is to take from Davidson the idea that truth cannot be defined, and he credits him with showing how one might remain within the pragmatist tradition whilst giving up on the accounts of truth offered by Peirce and James.

To say that truth cannot be defined is, importantly, not to give up on the idea of truth itself; examples of propositions Rorty claims to be true cited on the first page of *Consequences of Pragmatism* include 'Bacon did not write Shakespeare', 'Love is better than hate' and '2 + 2 = 4'. It does, however, mean agreeing with Davidson that truth is not a goal of inquiry. Rorty takes up Davidson's view that there is no way to identify whether one has reached that goal. We can tell when we have justified our beliefs – we can justify them in the light of the available evidence to the relevant audience. But we have no further way of establishing whether or not such beliefs are true, and Rorty joins Davidson in arguing that, because of this, there is no good reason to make the additional claim that truth is a separate goal of inquiry.

By saying that truth is not a goal of inquiry, Rorty has been widely criticized for apparently reducing truth to justification. One particular sentence from *Philosophy and the Mirror of Nature* seems to support this interpretation, where he writes that truth is 'what our peers will, *ceteris paribus*, let us get away with saying' (Rorty, 1979: 176). Rorty later described this sentence as 'incautious and misleading hyperbole' (Rorty, 2010a: 45). Keeping in mind his Davidsonian refusal to define truth, and his objection to James' theory (of conflating what is true with what is thought useful – see chapter 1), that sentence should be read not as a *definition* of truth but as a *description* of what is taken to be true by a community of inquiry. However, Rorty emphasizes that the fact that something is taken to be true is in no way indicative of whether it is in fact true. In order to make this point as vivid as possible, he emphasizes the difference between truth and justification, explicated in what he calls 'the cautionary use of truth', an idea captured in the phrase 'justified, but maybe not true'.

Even if we accept that the goal of inquiry is to secure justification for our beliefs and that there is no further question as to their truth, the issue remains of what happens if we secure justification for a false or dangerous belief. It was in order to guard against inquirers fixing upon mistaken beliefs that Peirce distinguished different forms of inquiry and emphasized that only the method of science – that inquirers should be attentive to the evidence and to the reasons offered by their peers – genuinely yields knowledge. As we've seen, Rorty thinks the methods of inquiry characteristic of science are not limited to natural scientists but characterize *any* kind of well-conducted inquiry. Insisting on the importance of such inquiry leads to his suggestion that we shift from a focus on epistemology and metaphysics to what he calls 'cultural politics'. This suggestion focuses on the importance of the conditions required to facilitate inquiry in all relevant domains (not just science). Importantly, one of those conditions is the freedom to put ideas forward – in particular, that we can speak freely and seek to defend whatever it is we take to be true in virtue of having good justification for belief by submitting it to our conversational partners in open inquiry: 'In other words, what matters is your ability to talk to other people about what seems to you true, not what is in fact true. If we take care of freedom, truth can take care of itself' (Rorty, 1989: 176). What motivates the shift of focus to cultural politics is that, without such a focus, we stay in the relatively inert land of having identified the conditions required for good inquiry but without having done anything to ensure that such conditions hold in the world so that good inquiry can take place.

Pragmatism's contribution to the Enlightenment project

In papers written after *Philosophy and the Mirror of Nature*, Rorty came to focus more and more on an understanding of pragmatism which locates it in cultural and historical terms. He thinks of pragmatism 'not just as clearing up little messes left behind by the great dead philosophers, but as contributing to a world-historical change in humanity's self-image' (Rorty, 1998: 132). Alongside his view of pragmatism as anti-representationalism, he also describes it as anti-authoritarian, refusing to see authority as owed to anything other than freely arrived at human agreement. As we will now examine, he locates pragmatist anti-authoritarianism as a successor to the Enlightenment of the eighteenth century.

For Rorty, the Enlightenment's contribution to Western culture cannot be overstated. Its importance lies in challenging the belief that respect and obedience are owed to traditional forms of authority such as that of revealed religion – for the philosophers of the Enlightenment, all forms of authority need to be validated through the exercise of reason. Rorty, however, believes that the process of anti-authoritarianism and secularization begun by the Enlightenment is incomplete. Enlightenment philosophers such as Locke and Kant took their anti-authoritarianism and reliance on reason to legitimize philosophical inquiry into the justifications for political authority, emphasizing the way in which political authority ought to be justifiable to the individual through argument, rather than via some *de facto* subordinate relation to God-given authority. During the seventeenth and eighteenth centuries, opposition to the established religious authorities came primarily from the newly emerging natural sciences, and it was therefore natural for these philosophers to utilize its language and methodology. However, this rhetoric retained forms of the religious need for human projects to be answerable to a non-human reality: 'the Enlightenment ran together the ideal of the autonomy of science from theology and politics with the image of scientific theory as Mirror of Nature' (Rorty, 1979: 333).

Although committed to the project of the Enlightenment, Rorty thinks it important to distinguish between what he regards as two different legacies: the philosophical and the political. These concern two different sets of question. Philosophical questions are a matter of the foundations of liberalism, specifically whether liberal institutions are justified by a source such as natural right or human nature. Political questions, in contrast, concern the desirability of liberal institutions and their advantages when compared to alternatives. Rorty proposes that we can give up Enlightenment philosophy without endangering liberal institutions: 'abandoning Western rationalism has no discouraging political implications. It leaves the Enlightenment political project looking as good as ever' (Rorty, 1997a: 36). For him, the fact that the two projects are taken to be interwoven is a historical contingency, and he argues that giving up on the one has no implications for the continued pursuit of the other; the political project is one which Rorty thinks stands alone without any need of philosophical back-up.

By setting aside the idea that science, or any other area of life, mirrors nature, Rorty aligns pragmatism with Romanticism. Rather than seeking something to obey – be it the will of God or the categorical imperative – the Romantics emphasized the role of the imagination, prioritizing the attempt to make the future different from the past. By focusing on that which one has created rather than upon that which one has inherited, Rorty thinks that the Romantics should be commended for paving the way to a form of what he calls 'romantic polytheism', the view that there are different but legitimate ways of life. On this point he associates pragmatism with pluralism, an association that had earlier been made by James; polytheism is consistent with the romantic idea of inventing our purposes rather than living out an antecedent plan. These different purposes cannot be combined on a single scale, or ranked according to a single standard.

Rorty argues, however, that, just as the Enlightenment is an unfinished project, so too do we need to move beyond the Romantics. The Romantics mistakenly focused exclusively on individual self-creation, ignoring the responsibilities that we owe to each other. Pragmatism is presented as a successor to Romanticism in its combination of the romantic sense of the importance of self-creation with an awareness of public commitment. Rorty's suggestion is to provide each its own sphere, which he hopes will allow for peaceful co-existence between them: 'talk of universal validity is simply a way of dramatizing the need for intersubjective agreement, while romantic ardor and romantic depth are simply ways of dramatizing the need for novelty, the need to be imaginative. Neither need should be elevated over, or allowed to exclude, the other' (Rorty, 2007: 85). The balance between private perfection and social responsibility is struck in what he calls 'the ideally liberal society'.

Private irony and liberal hope

The ideally liberal society is sketched in *Contingency, Irony, and Solidarity*, published in 1989. That book presupposes the account of knowledge presented in *Philosophy and the Mirror of Nature* but is of wider compass, drawing not only upon figures in analytic and Continental philosophy but also on novelists such as Proust, Nabokov and Orwell. In it Rorty argues that there is no need to weave together one's individual passions and one's social responsibilities. As he remarks, 'J. S. Mill's suggestion that governments devote themselves to optimizing the balance between leaving people's private lives alone and preventing suffering seems to me pretty much the last word' (Rorty, 1989: 63).

The aim of leaving people's private lives alone is a form of what Isaiah Berlin called 'negative liberty', the absence of obstacles which interfere with one's actions. In conceiving of freedom in this way, Rorty departs from Dewey, for whom freedom required active involvement in communal life. Rorty expresses no attraction to a life of civic engagement, distancing himself from Dewey's defence of participatory democracy. Although he describes himself as a Deweyan, he nowhere attends to the details of Dewey's political writings, and looks to other philosophers, notably Nietzsche, to exemplify the kind of freedom he has in mind. Nietzsche is said to be a philosopher of self-creation, one who identified the importance of appropriating and re-describing experiences rather than accepting inherited descriptions. As Rorty writes, 'To create one's mind is to create one's own language, rather than to let the length of one's mind be set by the language other human beings have left behind' (Rorty, 1989: 27).

The importance accorded by Rorty to freedom through re-description is central to his claim that the citizens of the ideally liberal society will be 'ironists'. The ironist places self-creation at the heart of her identity by acknowledging the contingency of what Rorty calls her 'final vocabulary'. Such a vocabulary is final because the words of which it consists – 'good', 'right', 'kindness', etc. – cannot be backed up by non-circular argument. If the use of those words is questioned, the only response is to appeal to other beliefs whose justification depends at least partly on the belief being questioned. Rather than seeking to purify herself of doubt, the ironist embraces the inescapability of contingency. She undertakes self-creation though re-description, recognizing all the while that there is no way to move beyond description to what Rorty calls 'Reality as It Is in Itself' (Rorty, 1998: 72).

Self-creation is one of the aims of ideal liberal society. The second concerns one's responsibilities to one's fellow citizens. Rorty captures this relation of responsibility with reference to Judith Shklar's definition of liberals as people for whom 'cruelty is the worst thing we do'. For Shklar, cruelty contrasts with sin: whereas sin is transgression against God, cruelty is a matter of inflicting pain upon another human being. There is, Shklar says, no inherent conflict between sin and cruelty, but someone who regards cruelty as the worst thing we do necessarily relegates sin to at most a secondary concern. Rorty takes up Shklar's distinction between sin and cruelty by presenting liberals as people who take their duties as being owed exclusively to themselves and to their fellow human beings.

In itself, the injunction to avoid cruelty says nothing about what cruelty might be or how it is to be avoided. For this reason, some commentators have pressed Rorty to provide a definition of cruelty. This is, however, to miss the point. To specify the necessary and sufficient conditions of cruelty implies that we are able to give a final account of what is and is not cruel, but Rorty's claim is that we are never in this position (just as we can never say that we have reached the end of inquiry). His argument here recalls that of Dewey, who was troubled that rights might enshrine forms of injustice and who in response proposed that the task for philosophy should be to 'break the crust of convention' (cited in Rorty, 1989: 167). Like Dewey, Rorty argues that liberal societies need to be constantly reminded of the ways in which the current arrangements of rights and freedoms impact negatively upon certain people. He is accordingly sceptical of the attempt to ground rights on something beyond social norms and practices (for example, natural rights theory) because the acceptance of such rights leads us away from a concern with cruelty and back towards a concern with transgression against some higher authority, be it God or human nature. The trouble with rights is that they address predetermined forms of cruelty without leaving space for novel descriptions yet to be discovered, and can trick us into thinking that we have already identified all the forms of cruelty that we need be concerned about.

Throughout his work, Rorty holds that imagination rather than argumentation is the chief source of moral improvement. In saying this, he criticizes what he takes to be the conservatism of many philosophers. He writes that: 'Universalist philosophers assume, with Kant, that all the logical space necessary for moral deliberation is now available – that all important truths about right and wrong can not only be stated but be made plausible, in language already to hand' (Rorty, 1998: 203). Rorty takes reformist movements such as feminism to have shown that sometimes that language does not presently exist, and that the purpose of philosophy should be to help create it. Rorty argues that philosophers such as Mill and Dewey have a role to play in doing so, but more useful are those who sensitize us to the particular details of suffering, whom he calls 'the specialists in particularity – historians, novelists, ethnographers, and muckraking journalists' (Rorty, 1991: 207). Such people bring into focus the details of different lives. Novelists are said to be especially helpful in this regard, with writers such as Nabokov and Dickens providing details of forms of cruelty (committed either by individuals or by institutions) that we had not previously considered, on people with whom we may hitherto not have concerned ourselves.

Hilary Putnam

Although he sometimes expresses reluctance to describe himself as a pragmatist, Hilary Putnam (b. 1926) is one of its most significant contemporary exponents. In the course of his intellectual life Putnam has traversed a wide philosophical territory, frequently revising his views in the light of encounters with different thinkers and ideas.

Since the 1980s, he has turned repeatedly to the classical pragmatists, each of whom he has written about in detail. Rorty, as we have seen, attempts to bring the insights of Peirce, James and Dewey together with those of more recent philosophers in order to develop an account of pragmatism which might benefit both philosophy and culture more generally. Putnam too mines the work of the classical pragmatists, drawing on them to support arguments against targets in analytic philosophy. Like Rorty, he has sought to connect philosophy to political questions, arguing that it must return to the problems of men and women. Unlike Rorty, he thinks it important that pragmatism retain the idea that our responsibilities are not exhausted by those owed to particular communities of inquiry.

The supremacy of the agent point of view

'The heart of pragmatism', Putnam proposes, is 'the insistence on the supremacy of the agent point of view'. The classical pragmatists helped us to see that we are not spectators looking at the world from the outside but rather agents operating within it. They held that we should recognize that there are many different descriptions of the world, to be evaluated by how far they are useful in achieving specific ends, there being no description of the world available apart from that from some particular standpoint. Putnam continues: 'If we find that we must take a certain point of view, use a certain "conceptual system", when we are engaged in practical activity, in the widest sense of "practical activity", then we must not simultaneously advance the claim that it is not really "the way things are in themselves" ' (Putnam, 1987: 70).

Putnam interprets the pragmatists' emphasis on the supremacy of the agent point of view as helping to illuminate his own long-standing doubts about what he calls 'metaphysical realism'. For the metaphysical realist, 'the world consists of some fixed totality of mind-independent objects. There is exactly one true and complete description of "the way the world is". Truth involves some sort of correspondence relation between words or thought-signs and external things and sets of things' (Putnam, 1981: 49). Metaphysical realism is an *externalist* position in that it seeks to anchor knowledge claims to what Putnam calls the 'God's-eye point of view', the view of the world independent of any particular description that might be given of it. His principal objection to metaphysical realism is that it removes the world from us; for the metaphysical realist, it is possible that we are entirely out of touch with the world, so that even our best-supported theories might turn out to be untrue.

For Dewey, the question of a determinate world existing entirely independently of human agents hamstrung philosophy by diverting attention away from the problems of men. At the same time, while focusing on problems arising in particular circumstances, Putnam argues that Dewey successfully avoided the kind of relativism that (as we will see below) he finds in Rorty. Putnam is happy to note that his own concern with metaphysical realism was shared by the pragmatists. In his Dewey Lectures, published as *The Threefold Cord: Mind, Body, and World*, he writes: 'I am convinced that my concern in these lectures – the search for a middle way between reactionary metaphysics and irresponsible relativism – was also one of Dewey's concerns throughout his exemplary philosophical career' (Putnam, 1999: 5).

For a time, Putnam attempted to find that middle way by arguing for a form of what he called 'internal realism'. His argument against metaphysical realism concerns the incoherence of externalism, the idea that there is a perspective outside of all human descriptions. As an illustration he discusses the status of the Euclidean plane. If we think of the points on the plane, the question arises as to whether these are *parts* of the plane or mere *limits* of the plane. Putnam's point is that this question only makes sense from within the context of some particular theory: 'My view is that God himself, if he consented to answer the question, "Do points really exist or are they mere limits?", would say "I don't know"; not because His omniscience is limited, but because there is a limit to how far questions make sense' (Putnam, 1987: 19). That is to say, the question of 'the way things are in themselves' drops out as being one which is not so much false as unintelligible. Questions only make sense *within* a particular theory; within a theory, questions such as whether we are referring to parts of the Euclidean plane or limits of the plane can be given definite content. At the same time, Putnam argues that his internalist position in no way entails giving up on our responsibility to answer to the world. In affirming that there are definite answers to ontological and epistemic questions, he is clear that internalism remains a form of realism because it continues to insist on our responsibilities to the external world. Internal realism thus traces a path between two equally unattractive extremes. On the one hand it avoids the presupposition of a perspective outside of human practice, but, on the other, it is not committed to the suggestion that our current beliefs and practices constitute the last word. Once we have decided upon a theory, there are objective answers to questions, answers which are true or false independently of what any of us might think.

Putnam came to express doubts about elements of his account of internal realism. He continues to insist on the supremacy of the agent point of view, denying the intelligibility of the God's-eye view and maintaining that no single description of the world is dictated by reality itself, but he now thinks that internal realism fails to do justice to these pragmatist ideas. He argues that this is because internal realism preserves a mistaken assumption – one that it shares with metaphysical realism – namely, its 'allegiance to the traditional conception of our sensations as an "interface" between us and the world' (Putnam, 1998: 45). That is, it presupposes a picture which is now hopefully familiar to us, that of a dualism between the individual mind and the external world.

For this reason Putnam now thinks of internal realism as an unsuccessful attempt to move beyond the externalism of metaphysical realism. Happily, he finds elements of a more successful attempt to do so in the work of William James. To explain it, let's consider the following long sentence from his paper 'Pragmatism and Realism':

> It was only after I began to teach courses on the philosophy of William James and to focus on his *Radical Empiricism* that I gradually began to see that the endless pattern of recoil that we see in modern philosophy, from extravagant versions of realism to equally extravagant versions of antirealism and back again, can never be brought to rest unless we challenge the picture of the mind, and particularly the picture of perception, that makes it seem impossible to take our ordinary talk of perceiving and thinking about objects seriously unless one reinterprets it in terms of a representational theory of the mind – and, when one sees how that theory fails to provide the desired 'foundation' for our ordinary talk (since it is just as much a mystery, in the end, how the supposed 'mental representations' can refer to objects as it is how our ordinary talk can do so) makes it seem that Rortian nihilism must be the only option remaining (although that too, I would argue, is only the illusion of an option, a *fata morgana* that disappears the moment one tries to embrace it). (Putnam, 1998: 49)

Putnam claims that James was prescient in identifying the reason why discussions in twentieth-century philosophy have proved so intractable. Realists and anti-realists alike presuppose a picture in which the mind contains mental representations of the external world: 'First, in perception we receive "impressions," which are immaterial, totally different – separated by a metaphysical gulf in fact – from all the material objects we normally claim to perceive. And second, from the character of our internal mental impressions we infer how things are in the external physical world' (Putnam, 1998: 39–40).

This representationalist theory of perception holds that sensations stand between us and objects in the external world, a picture which inevitably leads to the question of how far our mental representations accurately mirror that world. In so doing it invites scepticism, for if our beliefs stem from internal mental impressions, we have no way to make a comparison between those impressions and the world itself: 'our sensations are as much an impassible barrier between ourselves and the objects we perceive as a mode of access to them' (Putnam, 1998: 37–8).

Putnam's diagnosis of the problems with representationalism is very similar to that offered by both James and Rorty. But he departs from Rorty at least in insisting on the importance of our answerability to the world. Rorty thinks that realism presupposes representationalism, and that the former stands upon and falls with the latter. Putnam disagrees. He thinks Rorty's position an overreaction, one which amounts to nihilism. He takes James to show how representationalism rests on a false picture of the mind and the way in which it perceives the world. With his help, we can move beyond current debates about metaphysical realism but, at the same time, remain realist in seeing that we do not have to go all the way with Rorty and give up on our responsibilities to the world.

How might we do so? Putnam finds in James a defence of what he calls 'direct realism'. Direct realism is characterized by 'the radical rejection of the subject-object split' (Putnam, 1998: 39). It holds that our senses provide us with immediate knowledge of the external world without positing epistemic intermediaries such as sense data existing between us and that world. Putnam explains: 'What I understand by the term "direct realism" here is not a particular metaphysical theory, but rather our implicit and everyday conviction that in experience we are immediately aware of such common objects as trees and buildings, not to mention other people' (Putnam, 1998: 37). Direct realism (or, as Putnam preferred in his Dewey Lectures, 'natural realism') is, he thinks, doubly desirable from a pragmatist point of view. It returns the world to us, enabling us to retain contact with everyday objects and events. And, in so doing, it means that we can set aside the obsolete 'problems of philosophers' that have occupied twentieth-century philosophy.

The entanglement of fact and value

For Putnam, the classical pragmatists should be understood to be presenting a non-metaphysical form of realism. A second thesis which he takes over from them, one which he argues has taken on increasing significance since they wrote, is the denial of a fundamental dichotomy between fact and value.

The dichotomy between fact and value was central to the logical positivists early in the twentieth century. For the positivists, science is the domain of fact because it is empirically verifiable, whereas areas such as ethics are unverifiable and thus merely expressions of preference. In mounting his critique of positivism, Putnam makes common cause with Quine while pushing his argument further. Quine showed that the distinction between analytic statements and synthetic statements cannot categorically be drawn, and that the positivists' understanding of verification is problematic in assuming that individual statements are verifiable when taken in isolation. Putnam agrees with Quine on this, but is also concerned by the way in which the positivists rendered all metaphysical, ethical and aesthetic judgements 'cognitively meaningless'. He suggests that the fact/value dichotomy might properly be seen as 'the last dogma of empiricism' (Putnam, 2002a: 145).

Putnam's thesis, expressed in the title of a recent book, is *The Collapse of the Fact/Value Dichotomy*. Or, more positively, his claim is that facts and values are inextricably entangled. He argues that this entanglement is most evident in the case of epistemic concepts such as 'coherence' and 'simplicity', concepts which he claims cannot be separated into factual and evaluative components. Epistemic notions are not simply descriptive but inescapably normative, framed within a particular context of evaluation: 'judgements of "coherence," "plausibility," "reasonableness," "simplicity," and of what Dirac famously called the beauty of a hypothesis, are all normative judgements in Charles Peirce's sense, judgements of "what ought to be" in the case of reasoning' (Putnam, 2002a: 31).

For many, Putnam's claim that normative considerations bear upon matters such as what is taken to be 'coherent' or 'simple' will sound uncontroversial. It becomes more controversial though when we move from consideration of the coherence or simplicity of individual hypotheses to his suggestion that there is no dichotomy between facts and values *at all*. All epistemic terms, including those employed by the natural sciences, are, he argues, inescapably bound up with normative considerations. In saying this, Putnam might appear to be moving from the trivial to the obviously false; after all, a sentence such as 'The Earth revolves around the Sun' is straightforwardly a statement of fact. Putnam does not deny this. He is opposed not to the drawing of a distinction between facts and values – for particular reasons we may wish to distinguish between them. But doing so depends upon context. For example, the phrase 'would do practically anything for money' might, depending on whether it is used to refer to a business partner or to a friend, be either a factual or an evaluative term (Putnam, 1981: 139). That is to say, statements might express either a factual claim or an evaluative one, but they do so as part of an overall theory of the world. The fact/value dichotomy is, Putnam writes, 'at the very least hopelessly fuzzy because factual statements themselves, and the practices of scientific inquiry upon which we rely to decide what is and what is not a fact, presuppose values' (Putnam, 1981: 128).

Putnam stresses that epistemic terms take on sense only within a particular, normative, theory of the world. He seeks further to soften up the fact/value dichotomy by showing that *moral* terms too cannot be analysed into their descriptive and prescriptive components. He discusses this with reference to Iris Murdoch's argument in her book *The Sovereignty of Good* (1970). There, Murdoch draws a distinction between two different kinds of ethical concept. These are abstract ethical concepts, such as 'good' and 'right', and less abstract concepts such as 'cruel' and 'chaste'. Putnam allows that a categorical dichotomy between fact and value seems easy enough to draw in the case of abstract ethical concepts such as right and good, but points out that things become harder in the case of less abstract concepts. For instance, when we use a thick ethical term such as *cruel*, we are both describing a person's behaviour as a matter of fact *and* passing judgement upon them.

In addition to his efforts to question the fact/value dichotomy by showing that epistemic and moral notions alike combine factual and evaluative considerations, the most significant objection that Putnam levels against the positivism which gives rise to it is that it is untrue to lived experience; in our own lives, we think morality more than an expression of subjective preference. By way of illustration, Putnam takes up the example of his teachers Carnap and Reichenbach. Both philosophers influenced him significantly, particularly in his early work in the philosophy of science. And, more importantly, both were thoroughly decent and principled men who had been steadfast opponents of Nazism when other German philosophers had made their peace with the Hitler regime: 'I am sure that both had deep convictions about right and wrong – convictions that they would have laid down their lives [for] rather than betray' (Putnam, 1990: 145). The problem, however, is that neither was able to account for such convictions within the scope of his philosophy.

Few contemporary philosophers identify with the manner in which the positivists drew the fact/value dichotomy; Putnam claims that many are happy to depart from Carnap by accepting that ethical sentences can be true or false. Yet he thinks a variant of the fact/value dichotomy remains in the belief that the truth of ethical sentences is merely perspectival, relative to some particular point of view. This is the position of Bernard Williams, who posits the existence of what he calls 'the absolute conception of the world', the world that exists anyway, apart from the description given of it by human beings. Unlike the positivists, Williams allows that moral evaluations can be true – but they are not part of the absolute conception of the world and are thus not *absolutely* true. Rather, their truth is a function of one's entitlement to assert them within a particular language game. Williams accepts that this leads to relativism in ethics, which he terms 'the truth in relativism'.

Putnam takes Williams' position to exemplify a dominant trend in contemporary philosophy, one which he thinks is importantly flawed. He argues that the very idea of an absolute description of reality is one which cannot be made sense of; as indicated above, the idea of the God's-eye view is, he thinks, not mistaken but incoherent, for there is no understanding of the world lying beyond the particular descriptions we give of it. The question though is why philosophers such as Williams are so keen either to ascribe statements to the absolute conception of the world or to relegate them to the merely relative. In Putnam's diagnosis, this is because they retain a conviction that some version of metaphysical realism must be correct if we are to account for the success of the natural sciences, with the metaphysical realist holding that sentences are true according to how far they correctly represent objects in the world. But this explanation comes at a cost. For if we tie that success to metaphysical realism, we immediately call into question areas such as ethics and aesthetics which cannot obviously be represented. He suggests that:

> Today we tend to be too realistic about physics and too subjectivistic about ethics, and these are connected tendencies. It is *because* we are too realistic about physics, because we see physics (or some hypothetical future physics) as the One True Theory, and not simply as a rationally acceptable description suited for certain problems and purposes, that we tend to be subjectivistic about descriptions we cannot 'reduce' to physics. Becoming less realistic about physics and becoming less subjectivistic about ethics are likewise connected. (Putnam, 1981: 143)

In saying this, Putnam in no way intends to denigrate the importance or the success of physics. Physics has had spectacular success in explaining the world around us but, as a pragmatist, Putnam is clear that it is a tool well-suited to some purposes but not to others. There is no God's-eye view which physics somehow manages to approximate or represent more accurately than ethics, and to think otherwise, as Williams does, betrays 'a hangover from prescientific metaphysics' (Putnam, 1990: 173) – a metaphysics which the classical pragmatists overcame, notably in viewing the world from a Darwinian perspective. In our own lives we allow that ethical claims are more than merely subjective expressions of preference. By loosening the attractions of metaphysical realism, Putnam hopes that pragmatism will encourage us to accommodate this fact within our philosophical thinking.

Between scientism and relativism

A theme which has emerged in Putnam's writings and which forms the background to the discussion of his work thus far in this chapter is that the classical pragmatists offer a way beyond the stalemate in which he thinks much contemporary philosophy is caught. On the one hand, some philosophers are committed to a form of what he calls 'scientism', the view that 'science, and only science, describes the world as it is in itself, independent of perspective' (Putnam, 1992: x). According to scientism, ethical discourse must be reducible to the language of the natural sciences or else can be dismissed as merely emotive or rhetorical. On the other hand, those Putnam thinks of as relativists refuse to allow science this elevated position by mistakenly holding that humans are not answerable to the world at all. The common error of those attracted both to scientism and to relativism is that they do not allow for the normative dimension of our lives.

Putnam takes much contemporary philosophy to be committed to a form either of scientism or relativism. Unfortunately, this extends even to some of those who identify with pragmatism, and two philosophers who, he thinks, exemplify these mistakes are Quine and Rorty respectively. He is concerned that Quine loses sight of the normative element of our non-scientific practices by retaining the fact/value dichotomy. *Within* science, Quine is a pragmatist in the tradition of James because he thinks 'that the scientific method is not an algorithm, but an informal matter of "trade-offs" between such desiderata as preservation of past doctrine, predictive efficacy, and simplicity' (Putnam, 1994: 154). However, he continues to believe in a dualism between fact and value: 'the dualism of science, or rather science as formalized in the notation of symbolic logic, and everything that Quine regards as of only "heuristic" value, including intentional idioms and value idioms' (Putnam, 1994: 153). In this, Quine is more faithful to the logical positivists than to the classical pragmatists in thinking that those areas of life which are not the domain of science are in some sense second-rate.

Putnam's criticisms of Quine's continued attachment to logical positivism are similar to those that have been levelled by Rorty – for them both, pragmatism means giving up the idea that natural science is epistemically privileged. However, Putnam thinks the problems he identifies in Quine are repeated in important ways by Rorty, who is said similarly to miss the normative dimension of language. Putnam points out that sentences can be true or false, right or wrong, and that is because they answer to the world which exists independently of us. To be sure, the world to which we are answerable is not the world of the metaphysical realist but the more modest, though normatively important, world of everyday items such as mountains and chairs, but is real for all that. While Rorty does not privilege natural science, Putnam criticizes him for seeking undesirably to level down all areas of inquiry so that in ethics, politics *and* science, 'justification is just to be counted as a justification by some bunch of people' (Putnam, 2000: 84).

We must be clear about the nature of Putnam's concern. Rorty is said to be unable to allow for the possibility of a middle way between metaphysical realism and a relativism according to which what is justified is no more than whatever people happen to *think* justified. He argues that Rorty would deny a proposition that he himself holds, namely: 'Whether a statement is warranted or not is independent of whether the majority of one's cultural peers would *say* it is warranted or unwarranted' (Putnam, 1990: 21). Putnam thinks that, although standards of warrant are historically contingent, they are not simply whatever a particular community happens to settle upon. Pragmatism allows for a '*situated* resolution of political and ethical problems and conflicts...that claims concerning evaluations of – and proposals for the resolution of – problematical situations can be more and less *warranted* without being *absolute*' (Putnam, 2004: 129). That is to say, Putnam recognizes the situatedness of standards of warrant, but thinks that pragmatism provides a way of identifying intersubjectively agreed standards of warrant within overarching conditions of good inquiry in a way which avoids the kind of relativism about justification to which he thinks Rorty committed.

In situating himself in relation to Quine and Rorty, Putnam seeks to avoid scientism on the one hand and relativism on the other. The former concern leads to the dichotomy of fact and value and shows how far Quine remains a positivist. But quite how far apart Putnam is from Rorty is harder to specify. To say that Rorty denies *any* notion of responsiveness to the world is to miss what is entailed by his view of inquiry as seeking to secure solidarity. As we have seen, Rorty does not deny the causal impact of the world upon us and the necessity of attempting to cope with it. The point rather is that we are not answerable to the world itself; we are answerable to our fellow human beings, in the light of our shared causal relations with the world.

In chapter 1 we saw that Peirce sought to distance his position from that of James, whereas for his part James tended to focus on their similarities. A similar tendency marks the difference between Putnam and Rorty. On several occasions, Rorty expresses surprise that Putnam should think their positions so different, suggesting that it stems from what he regards as Putnam's anxieties about relativism. This is probably correct. If we recall Putnam's comment about his teachers Carnap and Reichenbach, his view is that philosophy must be part of a substantive moral vision and he fears that theirs is inadequate in not allowing for condemnation of the evil of Nazism. This is a failing he thinks Rorty shares: 'a fascist could well agree with Rorty at a very abstract level – Mussolini, let us recall, supported pragmatism, claiming that it sanctions unthinking activism' (Putnam, 1990: 24–5). However, at a less abstract level a response is available to Rorty. Although justification is a matter of seeking solidarity, this leaves open the possibility of offering alternative interpretations and seeking to justify *them*. Rorty points out that 'many (praiseworthy and blameworthy) social movements and intellectual revolutions get started by people making *un*warranted assertions', assertions that were not justified by the standards and norms of the time (Rorty, 1998: 50). In such cases, the point of such movements was to change those standards. In other words, Rorty thinks his position allows us to block a relativism in which anything goes by maintaining that what goes has to be justified to a community (in the light of the causal input of the world).

Rorty seeks to downplay the differences between Putnam and himself. And indeed, Putnam seems in some respects to be rather closer to Rorty's position than he allows for. We can see this most vividly in his understanding of objectivity. For the metaphysical realist, objectivity stems from correspondence to a world existing independently of us. In giving up this idea as incoherent, Putnam argues that we can nevertheless retain a notion of objectivity if we come to see that the fact that we are shaped by particular historical circumstances in no way precludes the possibility that our knowledge-claims aspire to objectivity:

> This may mean giving up a certain metaphysical picture of objectivity, but it does not mean giving up the idea that there are what Dewey called 'objective resolutions of problematical situations' – objective resolutions to problems which are *situated* in a place, at a time, as opposed to an 'absolute' answer to 'perspective-independent' questions. And that is objectivity enough. (Putnam, 1990: 178)

This understanding of objectivity is not spelt out as fully as one might wish, but it indicates something similar to Rorty and Davidson, for whom objectivity is a matter of being bound by intersubjective standards. This does not mean uncritically accepting those standards, for example by adhering to tradition or religious authorities. It means rather starting from where we are, and in so doing working out better and worse approaches to pressing questions in relation with our conversational peers. That is to say, objectivity is the result of reflecting upon our particular epistemic situation, with disagreements about values amounting to *'rational disagreements calling for a decision as to where the better reasons lie'* (Putnam, 2002a: 121). This is what is missed by someone like Bernard Williams, who fails to allow for any alternative to his absolute conception of the world and what Putnam describes as his scepticism about ethics.

> The third possibility [between scientism and scepticism] is to accept the position we are fated to occupy in any case, the position of beings who cannot have a view of the world that does not reflect our interests and values, but who are, for all that, committed to regarding some views of the world – and, for that matter, some interests and values – as better than others. (Putnam, 1990: 178)

In explaining how we might differentiate better and worse views of the world, Putnam approaches Rorty's call to shift questions of epistemology and metaphysics over to questions of 'cultural politics'. What matters for them both is that people have freedom with which to put their ideas forward; in particular, that they can speak freely about whatever it is they take to be true (one of the freedoms denied of course by the Nazis). And in speaking freely about what they believe to be true, they produce such beliefs for public consumption and critique and thus enter into a dialogue of inquiry as to the justification of those beliefs. As we shall now see, the importance of this freedom lies at the heart of Putnam's view of the role of pragmatism in continuing the project of the European Enlightenment.

Pragmatism as a third Enlightenment

Reflecting on the classical pragmatists, Putnam writes that what interests him most in the writings of Peirce, James and Dewey is the connection they each saw between pragmatism and freedom. This connection centres on their opposition to authoritarianism, be it religious, political or philosophical:

> We live in an 'open society,' a society in which the freedom to think for oneself about values, goals, and mores is one that most of us have come to cherish. Arguments for 'moral realism' can, and sometimes unfortunately do, sound like arguments against the open society; and while I do wish to undermine moral skepticism, I have no intention of defending either authoritarianism or moral apriorism. It is precisely for this reason that in recent years I have found myself turning to the writings of the American pragmatists. (Putnam, 1994: 152)

According to Putnam, the classical pragmatists showed that the way to counter authoritarianism is by attending to freedom in all areas of human life by attempting to secure 'reflective transcendence' (Putnam, 2004: 96). Reflective transcendence is a matter of reflecting on received conventions and authorities and asking why they should be accepted, and revising them should reason to do so emerge.

It was noted in chapter 1 that James excitedly expressed the hope that pragmatism might come to be seen as a movement comparable in importance to the Protestant Reformation. Putnam makes a similar suggestion, writing that, correctly understood, the pragmatists' objections to authoritarianism might contribute to a third Enlightenment. His hope is that pragmatism will complete the transition, begun in ancient Greek thought and developed in the European Enlightenment, from an uncritical reliance on traditional forms of authority through to a truly free society.

Putnam writes that reflective transcendence was a central theme of the European Enlightenment in the eighteenth century, but it finds its origins in what he describes as the earlier, Greek, enlightenment. This enlightenment refused to allow moral questions to be decided by appeals to the authority of religious texts or myths. The two enlightenments also shared an emphasis on science, albeit for the European Enlightenment it was the new science (specifically, Newtonian physics) rather than Euclidean geometry, as it had been for Plato. The aim of securing reflective transcendence and the esteem accorded to the natural sciences combined in the European Enlightenment in its break from tradition and unvindicated sources of authority.

Putnam goes on to identify a radically new theme which was introduced by the European Enlightenment. Although the ancient Greeks were hostile to revealed authority, many were equally hostile to democracy; Plato, for instance, advocated the rule of the philosopher-kings, those uniquely capable of identifying the Form of the Good. In contrast, thinkers of the European Enlightenment spoke of the importance of the social contract which, in all its forms, holds that the legitimacy of government stems from the consent of the governed.

Yet, just as the European Enlightenment built upon the earlier Greek enlightenment with something approaching a democratization of political and moral legitimacy, Putnam argues that it too needs to be supplemented. In different ways, the ancient Greeks and the philosophers of the European Enlightenment placed reason at the centre of their concerns. Both opposed the authority of the clergy by emphasizing reason (in the hands of the few for the ancients, the many for the moderns) as a faculty through which humans might arrive at immutable truths. This fed into two related and, in Putnam's view, equally mistaken assumptions: that the truths to which philosophers lay claim are knowable *a priori* (that is, without empirical investigation), and that they are accessible to the individual in isolation from society.

By setting its face against these two views, the central departure of pragmatism, as Putnam sees it, is that it emphasizes the importance of community. Enlightenment thinkers tended to understand the individual as existing prior to society. Correspondingly, they viewed freedom as a matter of non-interference, seeking to protect individuals from the threats posed to them via a social contract; Putnam echoes Dewey's criticisms of the individualism of the classical liberals when he remarks that the Enlightenment 'derived sociability as well as morality from an idealized image of the law of contracts, from *property law*' (Putnam, 2004: 103). This presumption blinded them to the intrinsic interrelation between individuals and their society. Individuality is a social creation which can only be achieved within a community, one that provides a range of meaningful choice. This difference in understanding of the individual's place in their community leads to a difference in the philosophical task of the enlightenments. The European Enlightenment sought to justify the existence of society and of our contracting away our supposedly natural freedoms, but pragmatists are not concerned with this question, which, for them, simply does not arise. The task is rather to show how individual freedom might be rendered consistent with communal life. In other words, the issue of justifying the existence of community drops out, to be replaced with the need to 'justify the claim that morally decent communities should be *democratically* organized' (Putnam, 2004: 104).

For Putnam, pragmatism offers the response that democracy is justified because it provides the means to achieve reflective transcendence by conjoining epistemic and political commitments. In a paper entitled 'A Reconsideration of Deweyan Democracy', he presents what he calls an 'epistemic justification of democracy'. According to Putnam, democracy is justified because it is the means by which political and social questions are best addressed, allowing every member of society to play a part in solving them: 'Democracy is not just one form of social life among other workable forms of social life; it is the precondition for the full application of intelligence to the solution of social problems' (Putnam, 1992: 180). One might object that nowhere do Dewey's writings contain anything that is referred to as an epistemic justification of democracy; as we've seen, Dewey was suspicious of the claims of modern epistemology, which he satirized with the label 'the epistemology industry' (see Westbrook, 2005: 179). However, the term is appropriate in the sense in which Putnam intends, in which democracy is seen as a method of inquiry in which social intelligence is applied to political questions. Putnam is conscious that he is taking up and filling out Dewey's thought that there are better and worse ways for inquiry to be conducted. He takes himself to be following Dewey in arguing that experience tells us that the results of inquiry are likely to be superior when all members of a community are able to express their views and examine alternatives.

5

Between Europe and America: Jürgen Habermas and Richard J. Bernstein

Jürgen Habermas

Louis Menand identifies the trauma of the American Civil War as one of the defining influences on the thinking and temperament of the classical pragmatists. The work of Jürgen Habermas (b. 1929) should be understood as emerging from the context of a twentieth-century tragedy, that of Nazism and the Holocaust. Habermas compares to Dewey in terms of his influence beyond academic philosophy. Today he is Germany's foremost public intellectual, frequently commenting on social and political issues and participating in political life. Habermas has not always associated himself with pragmatism, but from his earliest writings he evidences an interest in approaches to questions of truth and knowledge which, he has come to see, were anticipated by Peirce and Dewey.

From subject-centred to communicative rationality

The context of Habermas' writing is not that of American pragmatism but rather the German Frankfurt School. The School was based in the Institute for Social Research, and comprised not only philosophers but also sociologists, psychologists and historians. The theme uniting its members was the concern that, explicitly or implicitly, different academic disciplines were subscribing to the positivist view that the purpose of inquiry is to investigate a world of mind-independent facts. Frankfurt School thinkers such as Horkheimer and

Adorno held that inquiry does not stand outside of history but grows out of particular circumstances. They were critical of the idea of the disinterested inquirer, arguing that reason always incorporates historically contingent interests and presuppositions. The task therefore is for inquiry to become self-reflective in examining the circumstances of its emergence and the beliefs to which they give rise in order to demonstrate how they may tacitly legitimize particular social structures. Horkheimer's and Adorno's 'critical theory' stood apart from the prevailing positivism of the day, seeing even natural science as growing out of historical processes.

Habermas has become known as belonging to the second generation of Frankfurt School theorists. He shares the emphasis Horkheimer and Adorno placed upon practice and their hostility to positivism, but distances himself from the pessimism that marked especially their later work. He agrees with them that the advent of modernity was not without cost, among which he includes emotivism, relativism and scientism, all of which connected to the priority placed by the Enlightenment on 'instrumental reason'. Instrumental reason is a matter of calculating the most efficient means to secure a given end, without regard to the value of that end. In doing so, it is said to reduce all relationships to one of domination, in which one person seeks his or her ends by using others as the means to do so. Habermas argues, however, that reason need not take this form. The root-and-branch pessimism of works such as Horkheimer and Adorno's *Dialectic of the Enlightenment* (1947) is, in Habermas' view, philosophically mistaken, and a recurrent theme in his work is the need to separate the positive from the negative elements of modernity by identifying what he thinks of as the emancipatory role for reason.

This concern is central to Habermas' first book, *The Structural Transformation of the Public Sphere* (1962). There he examines how the notion of the public emerged in modern democratic societies. The social and political conditions of freedom of expression and of association that emerged in the eighteenth century led to the creation of what Habermas calls the 'public sphere'. Located in no particular institution, the public sphere consisted of the loose connection of venues within which citizens met and discussed matters of common interest on a footing of equality, being free of economic and political interests. As it grew, the public was able to exert an influence on government by offering a test of its legitimacy. In so doing, it itself became the source of legitimacy to which governments had to be responsive.

The Structural Transformation of the Public Sphere provides a description of the emergence of the public sphere, but also offers a critique. For while, in principle, the public sphere manifested the Enlightenment ideals of freedom and equality, in practice participation in it was limited to propertied males. The result was that the good identified in the public sphere was not in any sense the common good, but rather reflected the interests of that small section of the population who were able to participate. The distorting influence of power and wealth blurred the distinction between the 'general interest' and what Habermas calls the '*appearance* of the general interest' (Habermas, 1992: 88, emphasis added).

In his earliest work Habermas subscribed to the Marxist view that legitimacy cannot be identified with what is *taken* as legitimate. In this, he is indebted to Adorno's understanding of ideology as a form of what Marx called 'false consciousness'. Ideologies are described by Marx as widely held beliefs which do not reflect people's genuine interests but serve instead to legitimate the interests of a certain section of society by presenting them as being in the interests of all. In work in the 1970s, however, Habermas gave up on the idea of the distinction between true and false understandings of both individual and collective interests. To be able to make that distinction would require a standpoint outside of culture and history from which we might specify precisely what genuine human interests are. Habermas came to think that no such Archimedean point is available. Instead, he came increasingly to focus on the inevitable situation of human life, and to theorize from this basis.

For pragmatists, the most important element of Habermas' early writings is his turn away from what he calls the 'philosophy of the subject' or the 'philosophy of consciousness'. The philosophy of consciousness, which can be traced back to Descartes, distinguishes sharply between subject and object. Habermas writes: 'Still caught up in the tradition of Platonism, the philosophy of consciousness privileged the internal over the external, the private over the public, the immediacy of subjective experience over discursive mediation' (Habermas, 2003: 2). The philosophy of consciousness expresses itself in several distinctions, some of which we have already examined. In terms of social theory, it takes individuals to possess beliefs and interests prior to their entry into society. Reasoning is viewed as a matter of individuals calculating instrumentally from their particular situation, with the consequence that decisions stem from these prior calculations of interest. The philosophy of the subject is thus complicit in the instrumental reason which Horkheimer and Adorno criticized. Habermas thinks there is more to be said, however. What is needed is to move from the philosophy of the subject to the intersubjective structure of what he calls 'communicative rationality'.

Transcendental pragmatism

In *Knowledge and Human Interests* (1968), Habermas identifies pragmatism as offering an alternative to the philosophy of the subject. Since then, his relationship with pragmatism has become more and more marked. In his comments in a collection of essays published in 2002 entitled *Habermas and Pragmatism* (Adoulafia et al., 2002), Habermas explains what he takes to be pragmatism's strengths and weaknesses. He writes with approval of what he calls the pragmatist 'combination of fallibilism with anti-skepticism, and a naturalist approach to the human mind and its culture that refuses to yield to any kind of scientism' (Habermas, 2002: 228). Like the pragmatists, Habermas presents an account of knowledge as generated and legitimated through social interaction. His claim is that society is structured around collective understandings and meanings, which form the background in which what he calls 'validity claims' are raised: 'Epistemic authority passes over from the knowing subject, which supplies from within herself the standards for the objectivity of experience, to the justificatory practices of a linguistic community' (Habermas, 2000: 39).

By taking seriously the resources offered by social practices, Habermas shares much with the classical pragmatists. However, he differs from them in one important respect. Writing of the weaknesses of pragmatism, he laments that 'the anti-Platonic distrust in an ideological misuse of abstract ideas is misunderstood as the denial of the transcending force and unconditional meaning of claims to truth' (Habermas, 2002: 228). In his work, Habermas claims that we can transcend our particular social-historical location not simply by being fallibilist and open to alternative possibilities, for there is a universal perspective available to us. His key move is to locate the universal *within* the local and particular by holding that our own practices contain universal presuppositions. Habermas describes his position as 'transcendental pragmatism'. It is transcendental in the Kantian sense of seeking to identify the presuppositions of thought and action, but, crucially, these conditions are said to be immanent within our own practices; as he writes, transcendental philosophy 'aims to discover the deep-seated structures of the background of the lifeworld. These structures are embodied in the practices and activities of subjects capable of speech and action' (Habermas, 2003: 11).

Habermas' claim is that, whether or not we are aware of it, the presuppositions of our assertions take us beyond the particular context in which we make them:

> Inasmuch as communicative agents reciprocally raise validity claims with their speech acts, they are relying on the potential of assailable grounds. Hence, a moment of *unconditionality* is built into *factual* processes of mutual understanding – the validity laid claim to is distinguished from the social currency of a de facto established practice and yet serves it as the foundation of an existing consensus. (Habermas, 1987: 322–3)

In other words, when one makes an assertion, even though one addresses a particular audience, that assertion implicitly points beyond its reception by that audience and lays claim to universality.

With this in mind, let's return to the issue that animated Habermas' early writings: of how to guard against false consciousness and the kind of relativism which takes it that claims are validated by nothing more than agreement. Habermas seeks to avoid these things by recourse to a distinction between 'instrumental' and 'communicative' rationality. Instrumental reason is based upon the philosophy of the subject, in which people use one another in order to secure their ends. Habermas shares the concerns of Horkheimer and Adorno about the role of such reasoning in modern society, but departs from them in thinking that their criticisms do not apply to communicative reason. In the case of communicative reason,

> Whoever enters into discussion with the serious intention of becoming convinced of something through dialogue with others has to presume performatively that the participants allow their 'yes' or 'no' to be determined solely by the force of the better argument. However, with this they assume – normally in a counterfactual way – a speech situation that satisfies improbable conditions: openness to the public, inclusiveness, equal rights to participation, immunization against external or inherent compulsion, as well as the participants' orientation toward reaching understanding (that is, the sincere expression of utterances). (Habermas, 2000: 46)

Although 'improbable', these conditions are said by Habermas to be implicit in our practices. Horkheimer and Adorno did not allow for the distinction between communicative and instrumental reason, but Habermas argues that if it is made it provides for an emancipatory role for reason. By participating in a communicative setting in which one is able to express oneself free from domination or the threat of domination from others, one is thereby able to argue for what one really thinks, and have one's views examined by others similarly situated.

If Habermas is correct, instrumental and communicative rationality are not different alternatives, for instrumental reason itself relies upon a background of already existing understandings. Participants in discourse are, simply by virtue of being participants, compelled to endorse certain norms, for example listening to each other and responding to the objections they may have. That is to say, they do not *decide* whether or not to endorse these norms but are *required* to do so by the structure of communication. This is a very strong claim, and it raises the question of what is to be said to those who do not think themselves committed to such norms. What if one asserts that one is quite consciously seeking only to address a specific audience? Habermas claims that the person who says this is guilty of what he calls 'performative self-contradiction' (Habermas, 2000: 39). A performative self-contradiction arises when one makes a statement which contradicts the assumptions that make that statement possible. For instance, the statement 'everything is relative' is a performative self-contradiction, because a universal claim is made which contradicts the assertion that there is no such thing. Habermas takes this to show that one's assertions, even those which purport to be quite parochial in character, necessarily lay claim to universality.

The orientation towards unconditional truth

Habermas outlines the idea of communicative rationality most fully in his two-volume *The Theory of Communicative Action* (1981). For our purposes, the key point concerns the aim of communication, which is said to be to raise and justify validity claims. Habermas proposes that there are three types of validity claim: truth, normative rightness and sincerity (Habermas, 1986: 137). These three types of claim are said to be raised in different 'worlds': the objective world, the intersubjective (or social) world, and the subjective (internal) world respectively. In the objective world individuals make claims to the truth. In the intersubjective world they make claims for rightness. And in the subjective world they are committed to expressing themselves with sincerity. These three types of validity are said to be different, and for any given claim one will be prominent and the others left implicit.

If we turn first to truth, for a time Habermas adopted an essentially Peircean position in which truth is identified with that which will be identified at the end of inquiry; or, as he preferred to put it, under ideal conditions. He reasoned that, since truth is not relative, and since justification points in favour of truth, justification must itself be non-contextual but seek universality: 'there has to be an internal relation between truth and justification. How, otherwise, would it be possible to explain that a justification of "*p*," successful according to our standards, points in favor of the truth of "*p*" [?]' (Habermas, 2000: 40). However, he subsequently gave up on this position, thinking it mistaken to view truth in epistemic terms as assertibility under ideal conditions. Simply enough, it is impossible to tell when those conditions have been met, for one can never finally be sure that all sources of domination have been rooted out. A point that Habermas continues to insist on, though, is that truth is tied to the world which exists independently of us:

> Reaching understanding cannot function unless the participants refer to a single objective world, thereby stabilizing the intersubjectively shared public space with which everything that is merely subjective can be contrasted. This supposition of an objective world that is independent of our descriptions fulfills a functional requirement of our processes of cooperation and communication. Without this supposition, everyday practices, which rest on the (in a certain sense) Platonic distinction between believing and knowing unreservedly, would come apart at the seams. (Habermas, 2000: 41).

We can perhaps get a better grip on what Habermas seeks from the concept of truth if we consider the position he thinks it important to avoid. This is what he calls 'contextualism', a position he attributes to James and Rorty. Contextualists are said to be unable to make sense of our practices of justification because they see truth as no more than that in which it is good for us and our community to believe. Contextualism is guilty of 'performative self-contradiction', for we do not think that truth is merely what we *take* to be truth; if we make an assertion, we do not simply seek to secure the agreement of our peers but think that assertion to be correct irrespective of what those peers make of it. In other words, when I raise a truth-claim and seek to justify it to my discursive partners, I also take myself to be committed to something which exists independently of what they may believe or agree upon:

> There is a *practical* necessity to rely intuitively on what is unconditionally held-to-be-true. This mode of unconditionally holding-to-be-true is reflected on the discursive level in the connotations of truth claims that point beyond the given context of justification and require the supposition of ideal justificatory conditions – with a resulting decentering of the justification community. For this reason, the process

of justification can be guided by a notion of truth that *transcends justification* although it is *always already operatively effective in the realm of action.* (Habermas, 2000: 49)

As we have seen, Rorty conceives of justification as always justi-fication to a particular *ethnos* – his ideal ethnos is a liberal one. Habermas' view in contrast is that the ideal ethnos is not a com-munity marked by such *substantive* characteristics but rather by *procedural* ones; its members agree not on *values* but rather on the *principles* by which conflicts between values might be settled. These procedural conditions include notions of freedom and inclusivity, and characterize what he once called the 'ideal speech situation'. Habermas came to give up reference to the ideal speech situation: since we can never know whether or not our speech conditions are ideal, the idea has no pragmatic import. Nevertheless, he continues to insist that the exercise of reason commits us all to certain norms, such as openness and preparedness to engage in dialogue with each other. As participants in communication, we aim beyond mere jus-tification to the members of our social practice and adopt what he calls '[t]he orientation toward unconditional truth' (Habermas, 2000: 48).

Habermas connects justification and truth, but for many pragma-tists there is no inference from the one to the other. Rorty maintains that there is a difference between justification and truth; a belief, no matter how well supported by reasons and evidence, may yet turn out to be untrue. Cheryl Misak makes a similar objection, directed at the notion of transcendentalism. As she remarks, 'we need to note how odd it is for one with pragmatist leanings to look to transcen-dentalism to overcome challenges of justification. The quest for nec-essary truths stands in tension with pragmatism itself' (Misak, 2000: 45). Habermas thinks that there are universal preconditions for knowledge and understanding, but Misak takes this to conflict directly with pragmatism. The notions of unconditional truth and of transcendentalism are an overreaction to the classical pragmatists' sense of contingency and are flatly incompatible with Peirce's injunc-tion to remind ourselves continually of our fallibility.

Theoretical philosophy and practical philosophy

Habermas distinguishes between 'theoretical philosophy', which aims to explicate truth, and 'practical philosophy', which concerns moral-ity. Truth is tied in to the idea of an objective world existing inde-pendent of our descriptions. He argues that there is no such world in the case of morality; morality seeks intersubjective validity, with moral norms a matter of securing agreement.

To understand why Habermas insists on a distinction between theoretical and practical philosophy, we need to turn to his under-standing of modernity. In *The Philosophical Discourse of Modernity* (1987), he claims that modernity gave rise to a problem, one concern-ing the consequences of the recognition that we can no longer justify our beliefs and practices by reference to traditional sources of author-ity. As he writes, 'Modernity can and will no longer borrow the criteria by which it takes its orientation from the models supplied by another epoch; *it has to create its normativity out of itself*' (Haber-mas, 1987: 7). Moral frameworks such as those of Judeo-Christianity were for centuries taken to be the fixed background against which people lived their lives, but this is no longer the case. Freed from traditional sources of authority, modern societies must create their own standards, but, in so doing, they raise the questions of whether, and how, such standards can be justified.

A second issue raised by modernity is that of pluralism. Modern societies are not structured around shared traditions but are multi-faceted and peopled by citizens with a wide diversity of values. Relat-edly, the members of modern societies no longer see themselves as defined primarily by their social roles. Together these claims find their philosophical expression in classical liberalism, in which individuals (as distinct from people defined by their social roles) are seen as the bearers of natural rights which they can claim from their government and community.

Habermas' account of modernity as having presented a challenge to traditional monotheism and as opening the way to a plurality of sources of normative authority shares many of the ideas we have encountered in the work of Dewey and of Rorty. Unlike either of these pragmatists, however, Habermas suggests that we can retain the Christian ideas of universality in the form of universally valid moral norms. And, importantly, he does so while seeking to respect plural-ism. In works from the 1990s, notably *Between Facts and Norms* (1992), he addresses this characteristic of modern life by distinguish-ing between 'moral' and 'ethical' discourses. Under the idea of 'ethics' Habermas considers several issues, but the most important is that ethics is personal, concerning what is good and bad for individuals and the communities to which they belong. In contrast, 'morality' is held to be universal.

Unlike much post-Kantian philosophy, Habermas thinks that Kant was correct to argue for the universal validity of moral norms.

Kant held that the absence of a law-giver or *telos* did not preclude the universal validity of such norms; rather, universality is preserved in norms that we give to ourselves as autonomous agents. Habermas thinks Kant mistaken in arguing that such norms could be provided through the philosophy of the subject, in which rationality is viewed as a relationship between the individual and the world. We can, however, keep faith with Kant, and with the Enlightenment, by thinking of moral norms as validated through intersubjective communication.

Once again, however, Habermas is not satisfied with the assimilation of intersubjectivity with whatever a particular community happens to agree upon. He writes: 'Using Wittgenstein's concept of a language game, a convincing case can be made to the effect that important components of a culture's practical wisdom congeal in its evaluative vocabulary and in the rules for how to use normative sentences. To that extent, I agree with Putnam. But this does not tell us in what sense this evaluative wisdom or knowledge enjoys the status of *objectivity*' (Habermas, 2003: 226). Something more is needed if we are to avoid moral relativism. This Habermas addresses in his account of 'discourse ethics'. The task for discourse ethics is not to provide answers to questions about the nature of the good life, but is rather to identify principles by which citizens might answer these questions for themselves. Habermas argues that the principles are those which are produced through a procedure which is itself acceptable to the people who will be bound by the principles it generates, and it is the task of producing such a procedure that he hopes to perform in his account of discourse ethics. According to discourse ethics: 'Those moral judgements that *merit* universal recognition are "right", and that means that in a rational discourse under approximately ideal conditions they could be agreed to by anyone concerned' (Habermas, 2003: 229). Or, put negatively, a norm is invalid if it is reasonably rejectable by those people adversely affected by it. This argument leaves open some important questions; for instance, 'anyone concerned' could be interpreted narrowly or very broadly (perhaps even including future generations). What is clear enough, though, is that discourse ethics preserves Kantian universalism, albeit a universalism secured through discourse. While there is no single good in life, there is, Habermas argues, a universal means of judging the conflicts that arise between different views of the good.

Habermas' moral and ethical writings have generated a considerable amount of discussion and criticism, but for pragmatists the principal concern has centred on the firmness of the distinction he draws between ethics and morality, and the priority afforded to the latter. This has been thought by some to beg the question. Many ethical conceptions, for example those of monotheistic religion, make universalistic claims, and these will lead to different views of what constitutes an appropriate procedure for deciding moral norms. The point has been pressed by Putnam, who, as we saw in chapter 4, argues that all areas of human life are lived in the context of particular understandings, something which upsets the distinction that Habermas draws between universally valid norms and culturally specific values (Putnam, 2002a: 128–9). Putnam here develops a point which had been made earlier by Dewey, for whom democracy took a substantive form from which ethical considerations cannot be separated. Procedures such as democratic discussion and argumentation presuppose, Dewey argued, a specific ethos. In other words, the very principles of discursive inquiry that Habermas identifies as transcending specific cultural contexts are themselves culturally and, more significantly, normatively situated.

From discourse ethics to deliberative politics

Habermas has come to believe that the importance he placed on universal moral norms did not offer an adequate account of the complex ways in which modern societies are actually structured. Missing from his account is an understanding of the role of legal and political institutions. This absence was remedied in his book *Between Facts and Norms*. Recalling *The Structural Transformation of the Public Sphere*, the later book locates civil society alongside more formal institutions of politics, discussing the role of legislative bodies and political parties as well as societal institutions more generally.

An important part of the discussion in *Between Facts and Norms* concerns the nature of the law. In more traditional societies, laws reflected the particular (for Europeans, typically Christian) values held by the large majority of the members of society. Today, however, there is no such shared source of common value, and the law is required to address the important task of helping citizens to get along without presupposing such values. For this reason, it is especially important to find a way of establishing the legitimacy of the law. Habermas argues that this can only be done through democratic procedures. A democracy provides the means for citizens to participate in making laws which they can see as reflecting their own wills, and thus their status as autonomous agents.

In his account of democracy, Habermas seeks to bring together two political traditions that are often thought opposed, those of liberalism and republicanism. Liberalism emphasizes the importance of the individual, guaranteeing their freedom by providing a protected sphere of rights. Republicanism, in contrast, focuses on the idea of popular sovereignty and the collective will. Habermas seeks to overcome the apparent conflict between liberalism and republicanism by showing how, properly understood, the two are mutually dependent. Individual freedoms are, of course, important, but these are only guaranteed within a political community. Like Dewey before him, Habermas maintains that rights are not pre-political but rather constituted within political society. Political participation is therefore not merely an instrument to secure individual freedoms, as the classical liberals tended to believe, but is rather an essential ingredient of that freedom. At the same time, he distinguishes himself from republicans in denying that political communities embody a pre-political collective will; in modern pluralist societies, this would illegitimately privilege one such conception. In his work, Habermas seeks to accommodate liberalism and republicanism without giving undue priority to one or the other: 'The system of rights can be reduced neither to a moral reading of human rights nor to an ethical reading of popular sovereignty, because the private autonomy of citizens must neither be set above, nor made subordinate to, their political autonomy' (Habermas, 1996: 104).

The reconciliation of the classical liberal concern with individual freedom and the importance placed by republicans on political participation is struck within a *deliberative* form of democracy, which Habermas calls 'the discursive theory of politics'. This politics embodies the form of justification which is central to his account of moral validity, in which legitimacy stems from agreement under free and open communicative conditions. Deliberative democracy differs from the form of liberal democracy familiar to us in focusing on the mechanisms within which beliefs are expressed. It holds that, prior to voting, citizens should hold their views open through a process of deliberation, with the result that their views might be revised in the light of exposure to other citizens.

It should be noted that this *deliberative* form of democracy differs from the *participatory* democracy advocated by Dewey. Habermas is not so much concerned with the actual process by which citizens might participate as he is with the need for political outcomes to be reached on the basis of an informed citizenry, a citizenry which has had the opportunity to present and collectively examine the views of all. In other words, the focus of politics should not be on the problems associated with *representation* but rather on *legitimation*. The aim of deliberative democracy can be said to follow directly from Habermas' account of communicative rationality, in which the political will ought to be created in a way that ensures that it is considered and informed, and encompasses the views of all citizens, rather than as is the case with current forms of representative democracy which merely aggregate the preferences that citizens happen to have at any given time.

In line with his recognition of the pluralism of ethical beliefs, Habermas argues that the law is local and filled out with social understandings, and subject to the kind of argument about interest that necessitates compromise. Furthermore, politics cannot assume agreement on any particular value or way of life. What then might unite the citizens of modern societies? He proposes what he calls 'constitutional patriotism', according to which modern democratic societies are framed around a shared commitment to a constitution. Citizens need not share a substantive ethical framework but only a commitment to social and political institutions:

> Once one gives up the philosophy of the subject, one needs neither to concentrate sovereignty concretely in the people nor to banish it in anonymous constitutional structures and powers. The 'self' of the self-organizing legal community disappears in the subjectless forms of communication that regulate the flow of discursive opinion-and-will-formation in such a way that their fallible results enjoy the presumption of being reasonable. This is not to denounce the intuition connected with the idea of popular sovereignty but to interpret it intersubjectively. (Habermas, 1996: 301)

The discourse in such a society is 'subjectless' not because it presupposes that participants adopt a neutral perspective (however that might be achieved) but rather because the process of deliberative discourse itself neutralizes the subject-centred contributions of the participants. This enables modern societies to avoid conflict between individual and collective autonomy because, properly understood, they are interrelated.

Habermas hopes that the discursive theory of politics will come to play a central part in a larger social system (the public sphere). For instance, his view of a plurality of publics being filtered through deliberation into laws feeds into his work on the European Union (see, for example, Habermas, 2001). In that work, he addresses the concern that the European Union will never be able to command legitimacy because it is peopled by citizens with a wide variety of values and histories by arguing for a European constitution, one which might claim legitimacy on the basis of agreement not on values but on procedures.

Richard J. Bernstein

Pragmatism has been a central interest for Richard J. Bernstein (b. 1932) throughout his intellectual life. His doctoral thesis, published as his book *John Dewey* (Bernstein, 1966), sets out an understanding of Dewey which, though it stands as an excellent account of its subject's philosophy, also serves notice of Bernstein's own philosophical interests. In his work, he has engaged with alternative philosophical traditions, notably deconstruction and critical theory as well as the social sciences more generally, in order to develop a post-positivist account of inquiry. In the course of these studies, Bernstein argues that themes from both analytic and Continental philosophy were in many instances anticipated by the classical pragmatists, and that the most interesting developments in recent philosophy are those which have taken up their ideas and moved them forward.

Escape from Cartesian Anxiety

In his book *Praxis and Action*, published in 1971, Bernstein signals his desire to take pragmatism seriously by examining it together with traditions then more central to philosophical discussion: Marxism, existentialism, and analytic philosophy. In so doing, he proposes that pragmatism is not simply a philosophy worthy of consideration alongside these more influential alternatives but, in an important sense, it has anticipated and (often implicitly) informed them. In numerous books and essays, the most recent of which is *The Pragmatic Turn* (2010), Bernstein argues that the important conclusions in twentieth-century philosophy can be understood as 'variations on pragmatic themes' (Bernstein, 2006a: 4).

Bernstein joins Peirce, Dewey, Rorty and others in thinking that pragmatism is animated by a reaction to 'the spirit of Cartesianism'. Descartes is the father of modern philosophy but, as Bernstein remarks, 'If we are to judge by philosophy during the past hundred years, this title can best be understood in a Freudian sense. It is a common characteristic of many contemporary philosophers that they have sought to overthrow and dethrone the father' (Bernstein, 1971: 5). They have sought to do so because they have grown suspicious of Descartes' assumptions and aspirations; Bernstein sees both analytic and Continental philosophy as united in the view that philosophy should not take up Descartes' quest to provide an indubitable foundation for knowledge. And he argues that they have done so by developing themes first identified by pragmatists in the late nineteenth and early twentieth centuries.

Throughout his work, Bernstein examines how pragmatism has responded to the presumptions and challenges of Cartesianism. He is interested less in the details of Descartes' philosophy than in the psychological motivations which he takes to lie behind it. Descartes' work led to an unease about the possibility of knowledge, which Bernstein calls 'Cartesian Anxiety'. This is the fear that, without a foundation for knowledge outside of any particular human perspective, we are left adrift in a morass of relativism and nihilism; as Bernstein puts it, '*Either* there is some support for our being, a fixed foundation for our knowledge, *or* we cannot escape the forces of darkness that envelop us with madness, with intellectual and moral chaos' (Bernstein, 1983: 18).

According to Bernstein, it is to Descartes that is owed the continued oscillation between objectivism and relativism that marks so much modern philosophy. In *Beyond Objectivism and Relativism* (1983), objectivism is closely related to foundationalism, to the hope that knowledge might be grounded on some indubitable basis. Bernstein acknowledges that his use of the term 'objectivism' is broader than the more usual sense in which it is associated with metaphysical realism, the idea that reality has a determinate nature independent of us. For him, though, this is but one element of objectivism. His interest is the larger foundationalist attempt to identify an ahistorical framework for all current and future knowledge. On this understanding, Kant is as much an objectivist as the rationalists and empiricists he criticizes, because he undertook to find the necessary conditions for knowledge. In turn, relativism is diagnosed as an overreaction to the idea that objective foundations are not available; seeing that objectivism so construed is not possible, the relativist recoils by claiming that notions of rationality, truth and the good are relative to particular societal or cultural frameworks.

For Bernstein, one of the strengths of the classical pragmatists was to have seen that the psychological fears of Cartesian Anxiety were the product of a historically contingent, and thus optional, vocabulary. Throughout their work, they showed that humans are able to make sense of their beliefs, values and commitments without needing back-up from the fixed foundations offered by religion or philosophy, while at the same time resisting nihilism and relativism:

One of the major themes in philosophy during the past hundred years – from Peirce through Sellars and Quine to Rorty – has been that it is a mistake to think we can (or need to) give strong foundational justification in any area in human inquiry. But this doesn't mean that we can't distinguish better from worse reasons when we are evaluating a scientific hypothesis or the interpretation of a poem – even if what are to count as 'good reasons' are themselves historically conditioned and contestable. (Bernstein, 1991: 277)

The question is then: how might we distinguish between better and worse reasons? Dewey suggested that philosophy must attend to what he called the 'precious values embedded in social traditions' (Dewey, MW 12: 94). Bernstein too thinks that those traditions and values provide the resources which might enable us to distinguish between reasons. They do so through our coming to appreciate and yet critically engage with the plurality of belief that constitutes our traditions.

Pluralism was as we have seen important for James. However, the term 'pluralism' has different connotations, and Bernstein spends some time distinguishing desirable forms from those he thinks best set aside (Bernstein, 1991: 335–6). What he calls 'fragmenting pluralism' is the pluralism in which different groups are pushed apart and no communication takes place between them. A second form, 'flabby pluralism', is the superficial acceptance of other ideas without any serious attempt to understand them. A third is 'polemical pluralism', a matter of affecting to respect diversity until one is in a position to set it aside in order to install one's own perspective as the single truth. Finally, 'defensive pluralism' demands the freedom to act as one desires without being held responsible or accountable to others.

In their different ways, each of these understandings of pluralism fails to be open to alternatives. They all confine one's interest to a specific group out of the belief that there is nothing of value to be learnt from others. In contrast to them all, Bernstein argues for what he calls 'engaged fallibilistic pluralism' which enjoins us to seek to understand each other and, in the process of so doing, criticize our own views as well as those we encounter. 'It demands that we make a serious effort to really understand what is other and different from us. It requires that we engage in the *critique* of our own views as well as those of the people we encounter' (Bernstein, 2005: 35). An engaged fallibilistic pluralism requires the cultivation of specific habits of inquiry, among which Bernstein speaks of two in particular: those of openness and fairness and a willingness to change our minds, and those of imagination. We should not see ourselves as bound by tradition but be encouraged to be open to new alternatives. It is, he writes, only by the cultivation of these two habits 'that one can advance our knowledge and reconstruct...human experience so that it becomes funded with meaning, freer, and esthetically coherent' (Bernstein, 1971: 315).

A fusion of philosophical horizons

Bernstein's thesis is that pragmatist themes have been central to the most interesting developments in both analytic and Continental traditions during the twentieth century. In his work, he has engaged with major figures from those traditions, focusing attention on areas of agreement between them. For our purposes, let's consider three to whom he has repeatedly returned: Rorty, Gadamer and Habermas.

The importance of Rorty for Bernstein is perhaps the most obvious. Bernstein and Rorty were contemporaries, attending the University of Chicago together as undergraduates and later Yale as graduate students. Bernstein later acted as one of the readers for *Philosophy and the Mirror of Nature* for Princeton University Press, and later still dedicated his book *The Pragmatic Turn* to Rorty and his wife, the philosopher Mary Varney Rorty. However, Bernstein has an ambivalent relationship to Rorty's work. On the one hand, he regards Rorty as a major philosopher who successfully demonstrates how we might give up entirely on the idea of foundations standing apart from culture and history, combining fallibilism with a commitment to an engaged and pluralistic public life: 'The content of Rorty's pragmatism...is the defense of the Socratic virtues, "the willingness to talk, to listen to other people, to weigh the consequences of our actions upon other people"' (Bernstein, 1983: 203). On the other hand, he thinks that Rorty does not follow through adequately on his commitment to those virtues. This is because Rorty suffers from a form of Cartesian Anxiety, a refusal to allow for the existence of a middle ground between an appeal to current practice and an untenable foundationalism. He is said to be so anxious to avoid ahistorical foundations that he lurches into an embrace of what is local and ethnocentric, without paying sufficient attention to how we might distinguish better and worse forms of ethnocentrism; on Bernstein's interpretation of Rorty, 'the *only* alternatives open to us are *either* appealing to what is local and ethnocentric *or* appealing to fixed permanent ahistorical foundations' (Bernstein, 1987: 550).

The cause of Rorty's own Cartesian Anxiety is diagnosed by Bernstein as stemming from a failure to distinguish between two different senses of 'rational justification' (Bernstein, 1990: 54). Rorty is correct to see that there is no way to justify a belief to every possible audience. But, crucially, this is not to say that one cannot give better and worse reasons for our beliefs, reasons that may be unpersuasive to some and yet remain good or valid. We can, in other words, identify and distinguish between the quality of our reasons even if the criteria for making that distinction are themselves historically contingent. By conflating these two senses of rational justification and maintaining that *all* attempts at justification are fruitless, Rorty's position has the consequence of precluding public deliberation on matters of social concern. Bernstein thinks this conflation of two different senses of rational justification is especially marked in Rorty's political writings: 'Rorty's politics seems to be one in which there is *no* public space – the space in which human beings come together to *debate* and *argue* with each other. This is what Dewey (one of Rorty's heroes) called the "eclipse of the public." For public debate presupposes what Rorty seems to want to eliminate – that we can be locked in *argument* with each other' (Bernstein, 1990: 64). However, if we accept the distinction that Bernstein makes between two senses of rationality and argumentation, there is no reason for Rorty (or anyone else) to deny the importance of argument about matters of public concern, and rational debate about how best to address them.

In an attempt to advance beyond the situation in which he takes Rorty to leave us, Bernstein turns, in works such as *Beyond Objectivism and Relativism* (1983) and *Philosophical Profiles: Essays in a Pragmatic Mode* (1986), to other philosophical traditions, finding in them not only greater commonality with analytic philosophy than might be expected, but also ways in which their writings develop ideas found in classical pragmatism.

One writer to whom Bernstein has often turned is Hans-Georg Gadamer. Gadamer's hermeneutics places a strong emphasis on local forms of understanding. Rather than dismissing these as unimportant or (as is the case with Habermas) thinking them a poor second to universal standards, he embraces them as being vital if we are to have any understanding of ourselves and our world at all. For Bernstein, the importance of Gadamer's work lies in the fact that he does not try to dismiss historically informed traditions but instead shows (more successfully than Rorty) how they do not commit us to a relativism in which we are trapped like prisoners within a particular worldview. Rather than seeking to escape from our circumstances by the attempt to find the God's-eye view, we seek what Gadamer calls a 'fusion of horizons' whereby our understandings are enlarged and enriched through encounter with others (Bernstein, 1983: 143).

Bernstein suggests that, in arguing in this way, Gadamer has developed a theme found in Dewey: namely, an opposition to the idea that experts might take the place of open democratic dialogue. For Gadamer, the view that they might do so stems from the positivist belief that science is value-free and, if correctly applied, capable of solving social problems. This misses the historical dimension of scientific thought and encourages the view that citizens can legitimately be excluded from public discussion. What is needed is a much broader conversation in which differing points of view are considered, something which Bernstein takes to be central to Gadamer, at least in his later writings. The idea is 'that the quintessence of our being is to *be dialogical*. This is not just the "mode of being" of the "few", but is a real potential of every person – a potential that ought to be actualized' (Bernstein, 1986: 65).

Despite agreeing with so much in Gadamer, Bernstein also fears that he tends not to recognize how our understandings might be distorted. Gadamer writes of the dangers posed to dialogue by modern forms of technology, but Bernstein thinks he needs to go further. Recalling his case for 'engaged fallibilistic pluralism', he writes: 'Tradition itself is not a seamless whole, and what is most characteristic of *our* hermeneutical situation is that there are *conflicting* traditions making claims upon us' (Bernstein, 1986: 68). Bernstein writes that it is here that Habermas' work is most useful. Bernstein suggests that Gadamer's writings point implicitly to Habermasian themes, to the idea that our particular situation contains principles of communication that enable us to move beyond our current horizons of understanding. This is evidenced (as Davidson also argues) by the fact that we can always come, in principle, to understand societies and languages which initially appear very different to our own.

Bernstein was instrumental in bringing Habermas to the attention of American audiences. He arranged for Habermas to lecture at Haverford, then Bernstein's own university, in the 1960s. And in his work, Bernstein has sympathetically examined the implications of Habermas' work for social science in *The Restructuring of Social and Political Theory* (1976) and for analytic philosophy in *Beyond Objectivism and Relativism*. But this is not to say that he uncritically endorses Habermas' project. In various commentaries, he has suggested that Habermas speaks with two voices, the transcendental and the pragmatic. His work evidences an unresolved tension between his pragmatist acceptance of the inescapably practical nature of all forms of inquiry and his transcendentalism, which seeks to identify a universally valid set of commitments (Bernstein, 1976: 220–3; Bernstein, 1986: 72). Bernstein is not unsympathetic to the latter. But although he agrees with Habermas about the importance of seeking to move beyond one's hermeneutic situation, one cannot do so by recourse to transcendental arguments of the kind Habermas himself employs. In particular, Bernstein challenges his assumption that universal validity is built into the very idea of discussion. He also questions his claim that different domains of inquiry are animated by different cognitive interests, arguing (along with Dewey) that there is continuity between *all* forms of rational inquiry. Inquiry, be it scientific, moral or political, involves the same methods and is understood with reference to human interaction with the world. If we jettison these aspects of Habermas, Bernstein argues that we find ourselves in something like the condition that Gadamer identifies. According to Bernstein, Gadamer's account of our hermeneutic situation enables us to 'get a clearer grasp of what Habermas is actually *doing* (as distinguished from what he sometimes says he is doing)' (Bernstein, 1986: 78).

Bernstein moves back and forth between different philosophers, reading them against each other in an attempt not merely at criticisms but to show how they lend mutual support and indeed strengthen each other's arguments. His work is animated in large part by the belief that philosophy will benefit enormously from this kind of interplay between analytic and Continental philosophy. Although these have become divergent traditions, with members of each often ignoring the other, Bernstein is concerned to tease out and highlight shared interests and conclusions. To be sure, he does not suggest that the writers he admires are all saying the same thing; his point, rather, is to draw attention to unacknowledged areas of commonality. With Gadamer, he sees traditions as storehouses of knowledge to be drawn upon, but with Habermas he thinks it important to identify critical standards by which traditions can be robustly examined. And he agrees with the emphasis that Rorty places on moral imagination as an important source of social hope and means for reform. By interweaving the ideas and insights of members of different philosophical traditions, Bernstein argues for the transformation of ourselves and of our societies. This is achieved not by reference to an objective perspective, but through pluralist and self-reflective conversation. This proposal is pragmatist in holding that, through dialogue, we can reach a situated but non-relativist consensus. Bernstein speaks of 'a dialogical model of rationality that stresses the practical, *communal* character of this rationality in which there is choice, deliberation, interpretation, judicious weighing and application of "universal criteria," and even rational disagreement about which criteria are relevant and most important' (Bernstein, 1983: 172).

Democracy as the task still before us

Bernstein's attempt to map a pathway beyond objectivism and relativism is motivated not solely out of an interest in narrowly philosophical questions but by what he thinks the practical importance of so doing; as he writes, 'the movement beyond objectivism and relativism is not just a perplexing theoretical quandary but a practical task that can orientate and give direction to our collective *praxis*' (Bernstein, 1983: xv). By reading a diversity of thinkers as fellow participants in a democratic conversation, Bernstein places centrestage the Deweyan view that philosophy should attend to the problems of men and women. The philosophers he discusses are presented as engaging with the problems of their times, the most important of which is how to improve the quality of democracy. In this, he is clear that he is following Dewey, whom he thinks correct in maintaining that the most important task for philosophy is to justify and strengthen democracy: 'Democracy was never simply one topic among others for Dewey. All of his thinking – whether concerning education, experience, aesthetics, philosophy, politics, or inquiry – sprang from and led back to reflections on democracy' (Bernstein, 2006b: 191).

One of the clearest differences between Bernstein and Rorty lies in their views on the legacy of Dewey's political writings. Rorty is sympathetic to the liberalism of writers such as Mill and Berlin, and like many contemporary liberals speaks readily of the compatibility of liberalism and democracy. He thus largely ignores work such as Dewey's *The Public and Its Problems*. Bernstein, in contrast, joins with Dewey in his criticisms of liberalism, and thinks its deficiencies might be addressed in a radical form of democracy. In his political writings, Dewey is taken by Bernstein both to have anticipated later writers and in some ways to have seen beyond them; Habermas, for instance, insists upon a distinction between questions of justice and questions of ethics and the good life, but Bernstein claims that Dewey was correct to argue that one cannot firmly draw a line between them (Bernstein, 2010: 195–6). Though important, just democratic procedures are but a part of a broader ethical concern, that of securing 'growth'. Bernstein highlights Dewey's insistence on democracy as an ethical and moral ideal. Ethically, it is only through participation in different forms of life that individuals can grow. Morally, Bernstein underscores the connection Dewey made between democracy and experimental science as a means of communication and discussion of the ends of life. He shares Dewey's belief that this requires a democratic community, one which affords the opportunity for individuals freely to put forward their ideas and to examine with care responses and challenges that are put to them.

Bernstein is not uncritical of Dewey. He regrets that Dewey's call for a 'reconstruction of philosophy' has failed to materialize, and indeed that philosophers today seem more obsessed than ever with the problems of philosophers rather than the problems of men (Bernstein, 1986: 270). The fault for this cannot in itself be said to be Dewey's, and yet Bernstein thinks he can be criticized for providing little in the way of guidance about how we might address the problems he identified. These problems include the breakdown of local communities and the way in which corporate interests distort social life, things which certainly animated Dewey but which he did not adequately address. Bernstein thinks he can in particular be said to have lacked sensitivity to the differences in relations of power within modern society, and how this impacts upon democracy: 'If Dewey is to be faulted, it is because, at times in his reliance on metaphors of harmony and organic unity, Dewey underestimates the conflict, dissonance, and asymmetrical power relationships that disrupt "the harmonious whole"' (Bernstein, 1998: 149).

And yet even here, Dewey's work is said to contain elements at least of a part of a solution to such problems. Bernstein interprets him as saying that it is because of different relations of power within society that citizens need to develop habits of behaviour by which they might examine and address the problems which stem from them. These habits must be understood as every bit as important as the more formal rights that liberals tend to emphasize. Bernstein notes that Dewey (who on this point can be read as anticipating an objection to some contemporary forms of deliberative democracy) was worried by overly rationalistic accounts of democratic life. For this reason he preferred to speak of *organized intelligence* rather than *reason*, because the latter implies a special faculty, belief in which led to the proposal made by Dewey's student Walter Lippmann of rule by experts. Dewey, as we have seen, rejected this proposal, thinking that the speciality of experts is ill-suited to addressing the collective problems of modern life. Those problems can only be adequately addressed by the people who are affected by them, and their doing so requires active involvement in public life to a far greater degree than was typical in Dewey's day – or indeed, in our own.

The pragmatic mentality

In his recent work, Bernstein has turned his attention to a topic that is clearly central to the twentieth century, that of evil. In his book *Radical Evil: A Philosophical Interrogation* (2002), he investigates what philosophers such as Kant and Hegel, as well as twentieth-century writers such as Freud and Arendt, have contributed towards our understanding of evil. He cautions that the many different manifestations of evil defy complete comprehension. But it is precisely the fact that evil escapes our understanding that opens the door for the term to be used and abused. This concern animates Bernstein's shorter, somewhat polemical book, *The Abuse of Evil* (2005). That work is a political intervention which examines the way in which politicians in the United States, with the support of the Religious Right, have invoked the language of evil in a way which Bernstein thinks harms public discussion.

In *The Abuse of Evil*, Bernstein argues that pragmatism might have a direct bearing on public discussion. In contrast to Rorty, whose contributions to public discourse were not obviously informed by pragmatism, Bernstein seeks to draw a direct connection between the two. Recall that James described philosophy as being marked by different temperaments, the tough and tender-minded. Bernstein speaks of different *mentalities*, by which he means mindsets which frame how we understand and act in the world. These mentalities concern not the familiar differences between the secular and the religious, but the ones between those who are attracted to absolutes and those who are open to fallibilism: 'What we are confronting today is *not* a clash of civilizations, but a *clash of mentalities*. And the outcome of this clash has significant *practical* consequences for how we live our everyday lives – for our morality, politics, and religion' (Bernstein, 2005: 17). Those mentalities divide according to one's attachment to certainty. Those attached to certainty in morality, politics and religion are said to be dangerous because they seek to circumvent democratic deliberation. Bernstein suggests that their confidence in the truth of their convictions leads them to absolutes and away from the kind of discourse he thinks required to establish and justify moral and political norms.

Bernstein writes not against moral and religious certitude. We can quite legitimately be convinced that our moral or religious beliefs are absolutely true. The danger lies in moving from one's personal *certitude* to objective *certainty*, to the thought that the strength of one's convictions justifies seeking to impose them on those who do not share them. Bernstein relates this to his earlier analysis of Cartesian Anxiety:

> I believe that those today who claim religious or moral certainty for dividing the world into the forces of good and the forces of evil are shaped by this Cartesian Anxiety. For they are *claiming* the type of certainty for their moral and political convictions that Descartes claimed for his indubitable foundation. They also make use of the grand Either/Or when they attack their opponents. For they claim that the only alternative to solid foundations and moral certainties is to be lost in the quagmire of relativistic opinions. (Bernstein, 2005: 28)

Their doing so cuts across the divide between the religious and the secular, for theists and atheists are equally prone to these mentalities. Bernstein considers the dangers of religious fundamentalism, in which believers are utterly convinced of the rightness of their cause and use that confidence to justify whatever actions they think necessary to advance it. He also makes the point in terms of the Bush administration's reaction to the events of 9/11. Bush distinguished sharply between the forces of good and evil, something which, while the actions of the terrorists were indeed evil, has, Bernstein claims, led to a simplistic approach to morality, religion and politics. Talking in these terms, for example in Bush's phrase 'the axis of evil', 'may be highly successful in playing on people's fears and anxieties, but it blocks serious deliberation and diplomacy. It is used to "justify" risky military interventions and to *trump* serious consideration of alternatives in responding to real dangers' (Bernstein, 2005: 83).

Bernstein's purpose in writing *The Abuse of Evil* is to address the challenge levelled by those attracted to absolutist thinking who maintain that the only alternative to their position is a relativism which removes the capacity for one to be committed to one's beliefs. He presents adifferent alternative, his *engaged fallibilistic pluralism*, as a suitable response to absolutism. He draws on the criticisms that Peirce, Dewey and Sellars have made of the notion of incorrigibility: 'if we mean by "certainty" something that is incorrigible – something that can never be questioned, modified, or corrected, then the pragmatists are telling us that there is no such thing!' (Bernstein, 2005: 66). Fallibilism, as we have seen, is important for pragmatism, and not just as a philosophical position. Bernstein thinks that it serves as a counter to the unwarranted certainty that we find in the world, bringing with it nuance, an awareness of different sides of an issue, and a preparedness to engage with other people. Pragmatic fallibilism also lends support to democratic institutions, to the ideas that no one has the last word on questions of public importance, and that the solutions to those problems are always temporary and open to revision. This is impeccably Deweyan, but is appropriately brought to bear by Bernstein on the problems of men and women in the twenty-first century.

6

The Return of Peirce:
Susan Haack and Cheryl Misak

Susan Haack

Recent work in pragmatism has seen a resurgence of interest in the work of Peirce. This chapter examines the work of two contemporary pragmatists who take their principal inspiration from his work. Susan Haack (b. 1945) sets out to defend a Peircean understanding of both truth and scientific inquiry against those whom she thinks insufficiently attentive to their importance. In her book *Evidence and Inquiry* (1993), Haack applies pragmatist insights to contemporary discussion in epistemology. Two questions stand out for her: identifying good standards of evidence for belief; and identifying good standards of inquiry. In addressing them, she has increasingly come to emphasize the ways in which her work belongs to the pragmatist tradition: the original subtitle of *Evidence and Inquiry* is *Towards Reconstruction in Epistemology*, but for 2009's second edition this is revised as *A Pragmatist Reconstruction of Epistemology*.

A reconstruction of epistemology

Haack begins *Evidence and Inquiry* by arguing that questions such as what makes for good evidence, the relationship between the evidence for belief and that belief being true, and the nature and purpose of inquiry, are important and worth investigating. In addressing them she presents hers as a voice of moderation among what she takes to be the misplaced extremes of austere scientism on the one hand and of relativism on the other. Her targets include philosophers impressed by developments in cognitive science who claim that beliefs can be reduced to psychological states, as well as strains in Continental philosophy which dismiss questions of epistemology as misconceived. Those who have attacked the worthiness of epistemological questions have been encouraged to do so because of problems with traditional approaches. Haack has some sympathy, agreeing that those approaches have been unsatisfactory. However, she thinks it important to defend the task of identifying good standards of evidence and inquiry against those she describes as 'enthusiasts of the latest developments in cognitive science or neuro-physiology, through radical self-styled neo-pragmatists, to followers of the latest Paris fashions' (Haack, 1993: 1). In her work, she does so by offering a *reconstruction* of epistemology.

The project of reconstructing epistemology falls into two parts. The first, the 'project of explication', concerns what counts as good or sound evidence for belief. The second, the 'project of ratification', concerns the relationship between well-supported belief and the reasons for thinking those beliefs true.

Turning first to the project of explication, Haack shares the naturalism of the classical pragmatists, believing that epistemology must connect to human cognitive capacities. However, she strongly resists any form of reductive naturalism, and one way of understanding her position is to see how she distinguishes it from Quine's naturalized epistemology (see chapter 3). Examining Quine's arguments, Haack finds that he runs together three very different ideas. These are: (i) that epistemology is not a purely *a priori* discipline but depends upon the nature of human cognition; (ii) that questions in epistemology should be turned over to sciences of cognition, in particular psychology; and (iii) that epistemological questions are illegitimate and should be replaced by scientific questions about human learning processes (Haack, 2003: ch. 6). Haack is firmly in agreement with (i), maintaining with both Quine and the classical pragmatists that epistemology is a discipline which must recognize and theorize on the basis of an understanding of what natural science tells us about ourselves. She argues, however, that this in no way commits her to (ii) or (iii). The question of what constitutes better or worse evidence is legitimate, and not one that can adequately be addressed by psychology or the natural sciences.

The question for epistemology is: what makes for good evidence? In addressing it, Haack turns to the two classical theories, foundationalism and coherentism. Foundationalism makes two claims. First, that justification depends upon epistemically basic beliefs which do not require justification by reference to other beliefs; and second, that these basic beliefs in turn serve as the basis upon which to justify further non-basic beliefs. There are a variety of foundationalisms; Haack distinguishes those philosophers who take basic beliefs to be empirical from those who think them non-empirical, for example truths of logic or mathematics. She limits her discussion to empirical foundationalism but presents her arguments as applying to all forms. That argument focuses upon foundationalism's one-directional understanding of knowledge, according to which basic beliefs justify non-basic beliefs, but basic beliefs never receive justification of any kind from non-basic beliefs. Foundationalism, that is, assumes a firm distinction between basic beliefs and derived beliefs, but in Haack's view this is problematic. This is because inquiry does not have this deductive character but is rather a matter of mutual support among beliefs.

But the alternative, coherentism, fares no better. For coherentists, there are no epistemically basic beliefs, and justification is rather a matter of securing coherence through the mutual support among beliefs. The problem though is that coherence can be achieved fairly easily; Haack cites C. I. Lewis' objection that it can mean nothing more secure than two drunken soldiers supporting one another by leaning back to back. That is to say, coherentism squeezes out any relationship between justification and truth: for the coherentist, 'it could not be supposed that a belief's being justified could be an indication of its truth, of its correctly representing how the world is' (Haack, 1993: 27). This is because coherentism does not allow for the role that experience plays in justifying beliefs.

Haack develops this last point through a critique of Davidson. For Davidson (and Rorty) justification is exclusively a relation between beliefs. Davidson distinguishes firmly between reasons and causes, holding that although beliefs may be *caused* by sensations, a causal explanation does not show how those beliefs might be *justified*. For Haack, in contrast, to be plausible any theory of justification must acknowledge and provide for the role played by experience: 'some of a person's belief-states are prompted, at least partly, by his experiences, his sensory interactions with the world; so sets of sentences which are the contents of such states are a better choice than sets of sentences, *simpliciter*, because this anchoring is, as it were, built in' (Haack, 1993: 71). In other words, experience and reasons are both elements in justification, and an adequate theory of justification must show how they work together.

In order to account for the role of experience, an adequate theory of justification must be what Haack calls a 'double-aspect theory', one which is partly causal and partly evaluative. More technically, it must make room for both belief-states (which she labels 'S-beliefs') and belief-contents ('C-beliefs'). Belief-states are causal – a person's belief-state *about* p will include experiential input. Belief-contents, in contrast, are logical – a person's belief *that* p will be constituted by a set of propositions inferentially related to other propositions. Haack argues that how justified a person is in their belief *that* p depends upon the content of their beliefs *about* p, and the content of those beliefs is dependent upon causal or sensory input.

Haack calls her own double-aspect theory 'foundherentism'. As its name indicates, foundherentism combines elements of the two standard accounts, foundationalism and coherentism, both of which she thinks have important things to say but neither of which is in itself adequate. Foundherentism accepts with some forms of foundationalism that experience plays a role in justifying belief, but it agrees with coherentism that there is no privileged class of epistemically basic beliefs. In turn, foundherentism takes up the coherentist belief that justification is not (as foundationalism has it) one-directional and sees it rather as a matter of mutual support among beliefs. Yet it is superior in seeing justification not merely as a matter of mutual support among beliefs but in acknowledging that belief requires evidential support.

For Haack then, the correct way to understand justified belief is as a matter of a train of reasoning stemming not from a single indubitable source but from mutually supporting and well-evidenced beliefs. This idea is captured in an analogy she draws with a crossword puzzle:

> How reasonable one's confidence is that a certain entry in a crossword puzzle is correct depends on: how much support is given to this entry by the clue and any intersecting entries that have already been filled in; how reasonable, independently of the entry in question, one's confidence is that those other already filled-in entries are correct; and how many of the intersecting entries have been filled in. (Haack, 1993: 82)

Inquiry viewed in this way recalls Peirce's analogy to a rope, the strength of which is the result of the combination of many different strands. But foundherentism fleshes out this analogy by making it clear that the quality of evidence (the strength of the rope) rests on two factors: how well a belief is supported by evidence and how well individual beliefs cohere with other beliefs.

The project of ratifying truth

Foundherentism integrates what Haack takes to be the best insights of foundationalism and coherentism, constituting what she thinks is the most satisfactory theory of epistemic justification. The second project in *Evidence and Inquiry*, the project of ratification, is to explain the relationship between well-justified beliefs and the likelihood that such beliefs are true.

Here, Haack sounds a note of scepticism. She notes the difficulties confronted by attempts to offer a substantive definition of truth. She considers Aristotle's understanding that 'to say of what is, that it is, or of what is not, that it is not, is true' (Haack, 1998: 21). This account of truth is, she thinks, accurate as far as it goes but is unhelpfully vague. She also takes Peirce's understanding to be inadequate. Peirce defined truth 'as the Final Representation, the Ultimate Opinion that would be agreed upon were inquiry to continue long enough' (cited in Haack, 1998: 22). Haack agrees with his definition of truth as that which is independent of what anyone thinks, yet thinks this view mistaken in entailing that those questions which inquiry could not answer, even if pursued with sufficient rigour, are meaningless. This issue, which Peirce labelled the problem of buried secrets, holds that there are some truths which may forever be inaccessible to us – for example, whether or not Churchill sneezed fifty-six times in 1942 (Haack, 1998: 26). Haack points out that our inability to determine the truth of that question does not render it meaningless, for clearly it is either true or false.

Haack takes Aristotle and Peirce to exemplify a more general failure of philosophy to have provided a fully worked-out definition of truth. She argues, however, that there is no reason to set aside the importance of truth, for doing so mistakenly denies the role that truth plays in our lives. One of the commitments we undertake when we justify a belief is to think that belief true, and it is integral to her definition of belief that the belief-holder both asserts its truth and is willing to defend it as true against challenge. As she remarks, '*to believe that p is to accept p as true.* (This...is not a sophisticated remark about truth but a truism about belief.)' (Haack, 1993: 192).

If there is a connection between well-justified belief and truth, the question then is why foundherentist criteria should be thought to be truth-indicative. Haack's argument in answer to this question is a modest one. Like the classical pragmatists, she is a fallibilist, thinking it not open to the epistemologist to claim that justification *will* result in truth. This is a claim that she accepts for her own foundherentism; she is careful to say that she will not claim that foundherentism will lead to the assurance that a belief is true. Rather, she proposes that 'if any truth-indication is possible for us, the foundherentist criteria are the best truth-indication we can have' (Haack, 1993: 222).

The argument to support the contention that foundherentist criteria are the best truth-indication available to us is largely negative. One important source of the suggestion that there is no connection between well-justified belief and the thought that such beliefs are true is that different people and societies have different understandings of what constitutes well-justified belief. It is sometimes said that epistemic standards vary across cultures and communities, evidenced by the apparent fact that people in different times and places have counted different things as evidence – consider, for instance, the authority granted to different religious texts in different times and places. This Haack denies. Such apparent differences are not a matter of different 'standards of evidence'. Rather, different 'background beliefs' lead them to differ over what to *accept as* evidence. Differences in background beliefs lead inquirers to place greater or lesser emphasis upon certain features and to interpret evidence differently. This does not, however, point to different standards of evidence, which Haack takes to be fixed between different cultures and communities of inquiry. In the case of the history of science, she points out that 'in appraising the security of a belief, pre-scientific as well as scientific people, and converts to the new paradigm as well as defenders of the old, may be assessing its fit to their experience and to their other beliefs' (Haack, 1993: 207). All inquirers, no matter what their background beliefs, seek to ground their beliefs in experience and ensure that they are mutually supporting – just as foundherentism says they will. Once again, this is not to say that foundherentism will result in true beliefs, but it is to say that foundherentism is the best available means of doing so.

The method of science as genuine inquiry

We saw in chapter 1 that Peirce sought to demonstrate that well-justified belief is intimately connected to the means by which beliefs are arrived at. After distinguishing four methods of inquiry he argued that only the 'method of science' is capable of fixing belief. Haack sees the same connection between well-justified belief and inquiry, and joins Peirce in examining what constitutes better and worse forms of inquiry.

It is important for Haack's account of different methods of inquiry to examine the *motives* of inquirers. She does so by contrasting the importance placed by the classical pragmatists on integrity in inquiry with more recent writers who dispute and undertake to unmask that ideal. The 'genuine inquirer' is a diligent investigator who is motivated by no preconceived ends or aspiration to shore up some particular assumption. Rather, he or she seeks the truth, allowing themselves to be directed wherever the evidence leads: if 'you really want the truth...you will want the best evidence possible; which means you will care what (competent) others think, because that is an important way to extend your evidential reach and sharpen your judgement of evidence' (Haack, 1998: 20).

Genuine inquiry contrasts with what Haack calls 'pseudo-inquiry', according to which 'what the "inquirer" wants is not to discover the truth of some question but *to make a case for some proposition determined in advance*' (Haack, 1998: 8). There are two forms of pseudo-inquiry. The first is what Peirce called 'sham reasoning', which is a matter of making a claim for a proposition to which one is already committed. Such an inquirer is not interested in confronting or assessing evidence which might conflict with their preconceived ideas but rather casts around for whatever seems to support them. By way of example, Haack cites those who seek to combine evolutionary theory with the literal truth of the Bible. While claiming to be scientific, these inquirers do not hold the attitude which is central to science, namely a preparedness to give up beliefs in the face of inadequate or conflicting evidence. Their concern is not disinterestedly to examine the claims of evolution and of the Bible but to show that the former must cohere with the latter.

The second form of pseudo-inquiry is perhaps even more pernicious. This is 'fake reasoning', which is not to care about the truth of the proposition one is advancing. The fake reasoner is concerned with style and with the fame that arguing in a certain manner will bring, and is indifferent to the truth of what it is they assert. While different from Peirce's notion of sham reasoning, Haack claims that the fake reasoner's concern with style over substance is what Peirce had in mind when he expressed exasperation about those 'studying in a literary spirit'. Fake reasoning has the consequence of undermining inquiry and would, if taken seriously, mean that it could only be undertaken cynically. Among fake reasoners she numbers, as we will examine below, Rorty: 'Rortyesque dilettantism, leaving room only for "conversation," fake reasoning, can do justice neither to science nor to literature' (Haack, 1998: 65).

Haack accepts that the distinction between genuine and pseudo-inquiry is not a firm one. All of us more or less genuinely seek the answer to some questions, are more or less driven by the right motives, and are open to be tempted by the attractions of fake

reasoning. However, this does not mean the difference is unimportant. Haack argues that the value of genuine inquiry is that it is
required if progress is to be made in inquiry: 'there is instrumental
value in intellectual integrity, because in the long run and on the
whole it advances inquiry, and successful inquiry is, by and large,
instrumentally valuable' (Haack, 1998: 13). Against this, it might be
objected that some findings reached by the genuine inquirer will not
in fact advance inquiry. They might yield boring or unimportant
results or, more significantly, they could lead to disaster and thus
prevent further inquiry (think of discoveries which led to the development of chemical and nuclear weapons). Haack's response is to argue
that, although unwelcome results may sometimes be uncovered, in
general it is best to pursue our inquiries wherever they may lead, and
to recognize that intellectual integrity is the virtue required to do so.

Having identified the epistemic significance of well-conducted
inquiry, Haack examines the means by which such inquiry might be
conducted. Here again she turns to Peirce, supporting what he called
the method of science, which she describes as entailing 'the attitude
of disinterested truth-seeking' (Haack, 1998: 49). We have seen that
both Peirce and Dewey advocated the method of science, but more
recently pragmatists have adopted a more cautious approach to
natural science, in no way wishing to downplay its many achieve-
ments but avoiding the suggestion that natural science is epistemically
privileged. Haack, too, is keen to avoid what she regards as an overly
reverential attitude towards natural science. The methods employed
by natural scientists are important for genuine inquiry, but they are
not those of science alone but characterize well-conducted inquiry in
general. Haack shares Peirce's 'insistence that philosophy should
become scientific', but specifies that she means this in the sense that
'there is an attitude of mind and a method of inquiry manifested, not
invariably or exclusively, but primarily, by natural scientists, which
all inquirers can and should adopt' (Haack, 1998: 49).

In locating her view of natural science, Haack positions herself
between what she takes to be two unwarranted extremes. Those she
calls the 'Old Deferentialists' believe that natural science possesses
special epistemic authority because there is something uniquely rational and objective about it as a method of inquiry. However, Old
Deferentialists have been unsuccessful in identifying exactly what that
method might be. And, from this failure, they have lent support to
those she dubs the 'New Cynics'. New Cynics draw two conclusions:
that there are no objective standards in inquiry, and that natural
science enjoys no epistemic privilege. Science is thus to be treated
with suspicion, its claims to knowledge treated as mere expressions

of power. Haack dismisses both points. Natural science is, she agrees, not epistemically privileged, yet it is distinctive in its wholehearted commitment to testing hypotheses critically, to experimentation, and to systematic analysis of evidence. Those who assert that science is a 'social construction' exploit the ambiguities afforded by this term to make claims which she thinks importantly wrong. They falsely infer from the fact that scientific knowledge is the product of negotiation between different scientists to the conclusion that its findings are nothing more than a matter of agreement. Against this, Haack argues that 'the processes through which scientific knowledge is achieved are not *merely* a matter of social negotiation; they are processes of seeking out, checking, and assessing the weight of *evidence*' (Haack, 1998: 112). Haack claims that science is not reducible to a matter of what is agreed by scientists, because *agreement* is not the same thing as *warrant*; as she writes, 'not everything that has thus far survived those processes [of social negotiation] is knowledge; what survives those processes is what *counts* as knowledge, what is *accepted* as knowledge – but not all of it is, necessarily, knowledge. Some may, despite surviving those processes, not be warranted; some may turn out to be false' (Haack, 1998: 112).

Vulgar pragmatism?

The nature of the relationship between well-justified belief and the truth of such beliefs lies behind many of the disagreements in recent discussion of pragmatism. As we have seen, Habermas at one point proposed a notion of truth as idealized justification and, although he gave up on that idea, he continues to argue that inquiry has to aim at more than agreement between participants in social practices. For this reason, it is worth spending a little time examining the difference between Haack, who insists as fully as anyone on the relationship between well-justified belief and truth, and Rorty, who emphatically does not. Because of what she takes to be Rorty's refusal to see some such connection, she criticizes him for distorting the insights of prag-matism and of the classical pragmatists to such a degree that he is no longer entitled to lay claim to belong to the same tradition; this prompts her to refer to him as a 'vulgar pragmatist'.

In *Evidence and Inquiry*, the issue between Haack and Rorty is said to revolve around foundationalism. If foundationalism means the theory of justification in which certain beliefs are basic, that is, justified without reference to other beliefs, then she and Rorty are in agreement. However, she identifies two further ideas which have been labelled as foundationalist and which she faults Rorty for running together. One is *foundationalism*, which conceives of epistemology as an *a priori* discipline, with criteria of justification requiring *a priori* demonstration. The second is FOUNDATIONALISM, the thesis that criteria of justification are in need of objective grounding and are satisfactory only if they are truth-indicative. Having thus distinguished between three forms of foundationalism, Haack argues that it is possible to affirm one whilst rejecting the other two. This tripartite classification is important for her reconstructed epistemology, because the project of ratification concerns solely FOUNDATIONALISM. Once it is clearly seen that the real issue for epistemology is FOUNDATIONALISM, Rorty can be seen to have failed to show why *this* form of foundationalism is untenable, and any success that he can claim for his arguments against it stems from his having confused it with the other, indefensible, versions.

By claiming that criteria of justification are in need of objective grounding and are satisfactory only if they are truth-indicative, Haack opposes what she refers to as Rorty's 'conversationalism'. Conversationalism is comprised of two elements, 'contextualism' and 'conventionalism'. Contextualism's answer to the project of explication (that of identifying what constitutes good evidence for belief) is to say that epistemic standards are entirely a matter of whether a belief satisfies the epistemic standards of the community to which the person seeking justification addresses herself. In turn, conventionalism answers the project of ratification (explicating the relationship between well-supported belief and the reason for thinking that belief true) by maintaining that epistemic standards themselves are entirely conventional and that there is no sense in asking whether those standards are truth-indicative. Haack claims that conversationalism so construed is at once relativist and cynical. It is relativist because justification is seen solely as a matter of whatever a particular epistemic community happens to agree on, and ignores the possibility of appealing to the truth-indicativeness of justification. And it is cynical because:

> one cannot coherently engage fully – non-cynically – in a practice *of justifying beliefs* that one regards as wholly conventional. *For to believe that p is to accept p as true.* (This...is not a sophisticated remark about truth but a truism about belief.) And, since to believe that p is to accept p as true, for one who denies that it even makes sense to suppose that there is any connection between a belief's being justified according to our practices, and its being true, it is impossible to see why a belief's being justified, conforming to those practices, should be thought to have any bearing on whether one should hold it. (Haack, 1993: 192)

Haack claims that it is only if one is committed to the truth of one's belief that one can be said to have a good reason to hold that belief. Without regard for the truth, one becomes a cynic because one holds that belief for some other (necessarily) insincere reason.

In a response to Haack, Rorty discusses her interpretation of his work in a way which helps us to appreciate further the differences – and similarities – between them. In terms of the project of explication, Rorty is clear that, if justification is a matter of assessing evidence in the light of one's experience and other beliefs, then he is in agreement with her. However, for him this is not to say very much. His view of Haack's claim that standards of evidence do not vary between cultures, for instance between ancient and modern scientific communities of inquiry, is not that it is mistaken but that it is trivial. He writes: 'how *else* would you assess a belief than by assessing its fit to experience and other beliefs? How could we *help* doing that?' (Rorty, 1995: 151).

In terms of the project of ratification, the question is whether one can say that, because humans always adopt the same standards of evidence, those standards are truth-indicative. Rorty agrees with Haack that to believe that p is to accept p as true (Rorty, 1995: 148). Yet this says nothing about whether success in justifying p indicates that p is *actually* true. This is because, as we have seen, for him there is no test for truth other than justification. The most we can do is seek to justify our beliefs, but even the most justified of beliefs may not be true. Because of what Rorty regards as the impossibility of moving beyond justification to truth, he joins Davidson in thinking that the goal of seeking truth drops out of view. Haack differs in thinking it important to keep clear that truth is the goal of inquiry, yet beyond affirming the need to care about truth, and the suggestion that foundherentism is truth-apt, she does not indicate how we can know which of our beliefs are true. Given this, it is not clear exactly what separates her from Rorty in terms of the project of ratification.

The exchange between Haack and Rorty was somewhat acrimonious and evidenced a degree of mutual misunderstanding which masks a greater degree of agreement than either realized. Sometimes Haack provides an especially uncharitable reading of Rorty. For instance, she complains that, by '[d]ropping any connection of justification and evidence, he assumes that to justify a belief is to defend it to some audience or other' (Haack, 1998: 20). This is accurate as far as it goes, but it neglects Rorty's Sellarsian insistence on the difference between the space of reasons and the space of causes. There is no way to justify a belief by dropping reference to an audience and appealing directly to evidence, but recognizing that in order to justify a belief one must justify it to an audience in no way means giving up on evidence – it is difficult to see how one would justify a claim to an audience unless one was able to produce some evidence to support it.

Rorty denies that there is anything cynical in thinking that there is no way to appeal beyond social practice to the truth. In a comment in the second edition of *Evidence and Inquiry*, Haack suggests that 'Rorty might see the cynicism if he imagined himself a juror in a capital case, voting "guilty" on grounds he took to be purely conventional, unrelated to the truth of the matter' (Haack, 2009: 21). But this misses what is meant by 'purely conventional'. The convention of voting on a jury is that of forming a judgement of innocence or guilt based on the evidence and the arguments presented by the prosecution and defence, and there is no reason why this need be cynical, or to think Rorty would deny it. Haack takes a dismissive view of conventions, seemingly associating them with the whims of whatever individuals or communities happen to think. Rorty takes conventions more seriously. Conventions, in the case of the law as in all areas of life, are summations of detailed historical practices and understandings. In the case of science, as Haack notes these will include testing hypotheses through experiment; in the case of historical research, they entail consulting archives and the work of earlier authorities. Moreover, such conventions contain the sources of their own correction – if one is found to be inadequate to its task, this inadequacy will itself be the spur to improvement in the form of seeking to find something better suited to purpose.

Despite lamenting 'vulgar pragmatism', Haack and Rorty are closer than either seem to recognize in terms of the projects of explication and of ratification. The difference between them, rather, recalls Peirce's and James' differing interpretations of the pragmatic maxim. For Peirce, the experiential consequences identified by the pragmatic maxim are entirely general, whereas James interpreted consequences in terms of their effects on the life of the individual believer. Haack's focus is similar to that of Peirce; for her, consequences do not include an individual's psychological needs but that which would be experienced by any genuine inquirer. She explains this point in a discussion of the philosophy of science, where New Cynics are criticized for their failure to distinguish between *warrant* and *acceptance* (Haack, 1998: 108). As we saw above, Haack thinks warrant a *normative* notion, in which justification is a matter of the strength of the evidence supporting a belief or proposition. In contrast, acceptance is *descriptive*, an account of how far a proposition is taken to be justified by a community. Ideally, warrant and acceptance would be correlated – that is, those beliefs which are accepted will be those which are warranted. But it is, Haack claims, a mistake to think that they will always be correlated, or that warrant can be reduced to acceptance. Rorty, in contrast, is sympathetic to James' dictum that 'the trail of the human serpent is over everything'. To distinguish between the strength of evidence and the ability to justify it to others is to make a difference that makes no difference, for the task of securing agreement with one's conversational peers and that of getting things right resolve to the same thing. The former can only be secured in the light of the reasons supporting the latter, and the only test of the latter is our ability to justify our claims to each other.

Cheryl Misak

In her work, Cheryl Misak (b. 1961) has drawn heavily but not uncritically on Peirce. Her doctoral dissertation, which was supervised by Susan Haack (together with David Wiggins) and subsequently published as *Truth and the End of Inquiry: A Peircean Account of Truth* (1991; second edition, 2004), highlights that her interest in pragmatism concerns primarily the work of Peirce, but she reworks his ideas, notably his theory of truth, in the light of objections that have been put to it. In so doing, she shows that the gap between Peircean pragmatists and others is not as large as is sometimes thought. She has also sought to apply Peirce's insights beyond epistemology into questions of morality and politics in a way he did not, and of which he would possibly not have approved. This is central to her argument for a deliberative form of democracy which, although it makes approving reference to Dewey, is worked up from the avowedly anti-democratic Peirce's theory of inquiry.

Misak's Peirce

Misak opens her book *Truth and the End of Inquiry* by suggesting that 'Pragmatists of all stripes...might have profited by paying more attention to Peirce himself' (Misak, 2004a: 1). She then proceeds to show what might be gained from so doing. Yet her task is not simply reconstructive. Peirce's writings were produced over a period of some forty years and, as indicated in chapter 1, he revisited his position during this time, not least due to the spur provided by writers such as James. Misak is not concerned simply to offer an exegesis of

Peirce's writings, but to develop her own position out of it: 'The cognitivist position I articulate...is presented very much on Peirce's behalf – as one which he ought to have held, not as one that he actually held' (Misak, 2004a: 169).

Misak takes Peirce's most important insight to have been to identify clearly the relationship between knowing the meaning of a hypothesis and knowing what experiential consequences would follow, were that hypothesis true. This relationship invites difficulty, however. For it tends either to define 'consequences' too harshly and thereby rules out some hypotheses which it ought not, or it defines them too liberally and fails to rule out illegitimate hypotheses. For example, Peirce held that the question of the existence of free will is a legitimate one, but on some interpretations of his pragmatic maxim it is ruled out as a meaningless topic of inquiry. In his writings, Peirce offers slightly different formulations of the pragmatic maxim, in part to address this issue, but Misak argues that none is wholly successful. He sometimes presents the pragmatic maxim in such a way as to rule out hypotheses concerning metaphysics, but this contradicts his more general intentions in which metaphysical propositions such as the existence of free will are seen as legitimate. At other times, his attempts to allow for some legitimate non-empirical hypotheses were overly permissive, leaving him, as Misak sees it, 'with a criterion so weak that every hypothesis meets the standard. And he certainly wanted something stronger than that' (Misak, 2004a: 4).

In her work, Misak has sought to make good on this desire for something stronger. Peirce's lack of success in providing a wholly persuasive account of the pragmatic maxim reveals something which, when identified, benefits pragmatism. This is to see that the consequences of belief are different in different areas of inquiry: 'Peirce's indecision about what sorts of consequences count as practical reflects an important feature of language: different sorts of hypotheses have different sorts of content. They thus require different sorts of practical consequences' (Misak, 2004a: 26). In natural science, a practical consequence is something that can be verified by the framing and testing of hypotheses. Misak argues that it is, however, a mistake to conclude (as the logical positivists did) that statements can only be meaningful if they are open to being tested *in this way*. Statements of morality can, she argues, properly be seen as meaningful, even though they are not open to scientific testing.

The distinction between different types of statement sets the stage for Misak's discussion of truth. It is important for her interpretation of Peirce that he not be seen as offering a *definition* of truth; Peirce himself observed that the task of providing definitions, in the sense of identifying necessary and sufficient conditions, is problematic. Instead of seeking to provide a definition, Misak suggests that we ought to focus upon the *consequences* of holding a true belief: 'Whenever we can, we ought to formulate hypotheses the truth or falsity of which would have experimental effects' (Misak, 2004a: 34). However, experimental effects should not be thought limited to those identified by natural science. Inquiry aims at truth, but those truths are not necessarily narrowly scientific truths:

> For 'truth' here is just a catch-all for the particular local aims of inquiry – empirical adequacy, predictive power, coherence with other beliefs, simplicity, elegance, explanatory power, getting a reliable guide to action, fruitfulness for other research, greater understanding of others, increased maturity, and the like. There is nothing over and above the fulfilment of those ends, nothing metaphysical, to which we aspire. (Misak, 2007b: 70).

Truth is an important concept, but it must be understood in the context of our lives and not as something metaphysical which stands apart from them. And, in thinking of truth in this way, Misak argues that we will see that truth denotes a variety of aims, aims which connect to the various goals we pursue in different areas of inquiry.

Truth and its role in inquiry

The pragmatic account of truth that Misak develops from Peirce contains two conditionals: (i) that, if inquiry is pursued as far as it might be, then the resulting belief will be true (which Misak calls the 'I-T conditional'); and (ii) that, if a belief is true, then it will be confirmed if inquiry is pursued sufficiently far (the 'T-I conditional').

In terms of the I-T conditional, the question is why we should think that inquiry will lead to truth. This question is particularly acute for Peirce, who, as Misak notes, held that 'the sole aim of inquiry' is to settle belief (Misak, 2004a: 46). The often-raised objection to this claim is that it seems that if, for instance, a totalitarian regime settled belief through the use of coercion, Peirce would have to accept that it thereby settled the truth of the matter. And, as Misak points out, it is not open to him to respond to this objection by invoking an independent standard of rationality in order to judge the beliefs which have been settled upon, because his naturalistic account of inquiry precludes such a notion (Misak, 2004a: 56). Misak's own approach is to see Peirce's understanding of truth in the light of his essay 'The Fixation of Belief'. As we have seen, Peirce claimed that inquiry is provoked by doubt, and that doubt cannot genuinely be dispelled by any method of inquiry other than the scientific. The difference between the scientific method and the others turns on sensitivity to evidence and experience; the method of authority, for instance, does not address the evidence available but simply seeks to enforce a predetermined belief. Only those who employ the method of science address evidence in order to form a belief. And, as Misak remarks, 'genuine belief, I suggest, must be sensitive to evidence or experience, broadly construed' (Misak, 2004a: 59).

In this way, Misak calls attention to the relationship between inquiry and true belief. We can only be confident that our beliefs are true if they have been settled in such a way as to remove doubt, and the only satisfactory way to do that is through inquiry which is responsive to reasons and evidence. That is to say, the aim of inquiry 'is to get beliefs which are not merely fixed, but which are fixed in such a way that they fit with and respond to the evidence' (Misak, 2004a: 60). In contrast, those methods which presuppose the truth of some belief (the *a priori* method) or which seek to impose it by decree (the method of authority) are ultimately incapable of settling belief because they do not address recalcitrant experience and thus offer no security from doubt.

Misak argues that much in Peirce's account of truth should be taken to be uncontroversial; it is difficult to imagine anyone seriously disputing the claim that in order to fix belief we should attend to evidence through a robust form of inquiry. But what is distinctive in Peirce is the claim that there is *nothing more* to be said about truth other than that it will be the result of properly conducted inquiry. It is here, of course, that Peirce meets with objections. One difficulty is that a hypothesis, however well founded through inquiry, may yet not be true. If we consider this claim in respect to the I-T conditional, according to which inquiry would result in truth if pursued as far as possible, it seems to entail that humans create the truth. But how can this be, given our being subject to contingency and our propensity to error? It seems at odds with the fallibilism that lies at the heart of pragmatism. Misak argues that this objection misunderstands what is intended in the I-T conditional. That conditional holds not that inquirers *determine* the truth; rather, through properly conducted inquiry, they will be led to and *uncover* the truth: 'truth is not a matter of what inquirers happen to think. The objective truth of the matter is that which inquiry *would* determine' (Misak, 2004a: 135).

Misak claims that the Peircean view of truth as that which would be agreed upon in genuine inquiry is all that can be asked by way of truth. The benefit of conceiving of truth in this way is that it connects truth to our actual practices. One objection to the correspondence theory of truth is that it elevates truth beyond its role in our practices. In contrast, attending to the connection between truth and inquiry by examining what is entailed by notions of belief, doubt and experience returns truth to us. And, if we accept that truth must not transcend experience but must be seen in terms of the role it plays in our lives, Misak claims that we are thereby also committed to the T-I conditional such that, if H is true, H would be believed if inquiry were pursued as far as it could be. This condition too is one that has attracted criticism. It led some, for instance Bertrand Russell, to claim that, if the world ended today, today's beliefs would be true because they would be those held at the end of inquiry. Misak responds by again calling attention to the difference between a *definition* of truth and an *account* of truth. Peirce's position is held up not as a definition of truth, but as a regulative assumption of the practice of inquiry.

To make this last point as vividly as possible, in her subsequent book *Truth, Politics, Morality* (2000) Misak revises her view of how best to express Peirce's position. There she distances herself from one interpretation – intimated in the title of her own *Truth and the End of Inquiry* – according to which a true belief is one which would come to be agreed upon at the end of inquiry. The idea of the end of inquiry is problematic and, as we have seen, has been challenged by Rorty. Misak shares this concern but, rather than thinking of it as a reason to give up on Peirce's account of truth, offers an alternative formulation of it. This is to drop reference to the end of inquiry in favour of the view that 'a true belief is one that would withstand doubt, were we to inquire as far as we fruitfully could on the matter' (Misak, 2000: 49). This is a subtle but important difference. It avoids the problem of prematurely ending inquiry through what she thinks of as the doomed task of specifying the conditions that would characterize its end. It also guards against the widespread misinterpretation according to which Peirce is held to be concerned not with truth but with agreement. To be sure, agreement *is* important for Peirce, but what is important is that it is agreement as to the truth of some matter.

Misak's revision of Peirce is not without cost. It means that we must accept that we can never finally be sure of the truth of our beliefs. Bernstein has objected that Misak's reformulation of the Peircean account of truth entails that 'we are never in a position to assert that any of our current beliefs are actually true. If we take her reformulation literally, we cannot even speak about any actual "true beliefs," because any of our current beliefs may be

overturned in the future by "recalcitrant experience and argument"'
(Bernstein, 2010: 115). It seems, though, that here Bernstein forgets
Peirce's injunction to be careful to keep in mind the difference between
fallibilism and scepticism. We must be mindful that our beliefs,
however confident we may be in them, might turn out to be false,
but, if we genuinely attend to the evidence and reasons that are
presented to us, there is no reason not to confidently claim that
they are true. Misak asks: 'What more could we aim for? What is
added by wondering whether the hypothesis is *really* true?' (Misak,
2004a: 166).

The question remains: why hold T-I as a regulative condition of
inquiry? Why think that if a belief is true, it will be confirmed as such
if inquiry is pursued sufficiently far? Misak's reasoning here has
become clearer in writings following *Truth and the End of Inquiry*.
She has come to argue that the T-I conditional reflects our (usually
implicit) practices and norms of inquiry. It explains why disagreement
matters to us: we think that those who reach different conclusions
are in error, as distinct from simply expressing an alternative point
of view. We take ourselves to be engaging with them over the issue
of the rightness or wrongness of our assertions, something we cannot
make sense of if we deny that our inquiries aim at truth. Drawing on
an argument advanced by Huw Price (discussed in chapter 7), Misak
writes: 'In order to really *engage* others in conversation or dialogue,
we have to see their disagreement as implying a mistake on someone's
part. Otherwise, we are merely talking past each other' (Misak,
2004b: 16). In other words, truth is a norm of inquiry, one which we
call upon in order to make sense of our practices. Rorty's claim that
we can do no more than seek to justify ourselves to a particular
epistemic community is said to be inconsistent with what we take
ourselves to be doing when we inquire, for our own practices demonstrate that it is insufficient to say that what is sought in inquiry is
solely agreement with a community of inquiry. Furthermore, Misak
argues that aiming at truth is not merely a contingency which might
be set aside: 'Trying to give up the concept of truth is not something
we can do, for it would require too radical a change in our practices
of communication and engagement with others' (Misak, 2004b: 19).
As we will now see, she takes the role of truth to be central in all of
our practices, including those of morality and politics.

Truth in politics and morality

Misak's Peircean account of truth has the advantage of permitting us
to be cognitivists without relying on representationalism. Rather than

seeing truth as a relation between beliefs and the world, truth is a matter of the capacity of belief forever to withstand challenge. This understanding of truth is thoroughly pragmatist in seeing that, in order to grasp a concept, we must examine its role in our practices. In contrast to the logical positivists who required that a hypothesis be open to verification by empirical evidence, Misak's position allows that matters of logic and (some) questions of metaphysics can be considered meaningful. In works such as *Truth, Politics, Morality*, she extends her account of truth and inquiry directly into political and moral questions. Among pragmatists, typically it is Deweyans who focus on the political implications of pragmatism, but Misak shows how Peirce might also be useful in this regard.

Truth, Politics, Morality is a less overtly Peircean work than *Truth and the End of Inquiry*. In part, this perhaps indicates Misak's growing confidence in offering her own position rather than drawing on Peirce in order to support her claims. But it also reflects Peirce's limited interest in those questions. In the first edition of *Truth and the End of Inquiry*, Misak argues that Peirce was a non-cognitivist in ethics, holding that ethical questions are not truth-apt but are rather simply a matter of social convention. Thus, in a work seeking to defend cognitivism in moral and political matters, it is unsurprising that she should not draw upon Peirce.

But although references to Peirce are fewer in *Truth, Politics, Morality*, his influence remains. The role of truth and inquiry in moral and political questions is developed directly from that offered in *Truth and the End of Inquiry*. Specifically, Misak argues that Peirce's writings contain elements of a more attractive and normatively substantive account of democracy than that of the avowedly democratic Dewey. How does the argument go? Following Peirce, she observes that if we believe something, we believe it to be true. She also points out that we may be mistaken in what we think true. This is a point that we all recognize and take to be important; we do not like to think that our beliefs are held on insufficient reason, for example as the result of coercion or indoctrination. Rather, as Misak writes, 'In order to believe *p* I have to be convinced that I have good reason to believe it' (Misak, 2004b: 13). The only way to assure ourselves of the truth of our beliefs is by being prepared to attempt to justify them by offering reasons for, and responding to objections put to, them. Misak's conclusion is that this epistemic argument justifies democracy in political life. For, to ensure as far as possible that our beliefs are supported by good reasons, we ought to engage in a process of inquiry whereby we accept that those beliefs are open to challenge, something which holds for moral and political questions just as much as scientific ones. She argues that this requires a *deliberative* form of democracy: 'In the moral and political realm, this requires that everyone be given the chance to contribute to debate' (Misak, 2000: 6).

In developing her thesis, Misak has come to argue that, contrary to her initial thoughts, this view is in fact one shared by Peirce. In a new fifth chapter written for the second edition of *Truth and the End of Inquiry*, she argues that Peirce should be taken to be just as committed to truth in ethics as in science: 'what Peirce calls "science" is extremely broad. Any inquiry which aims at getting a belief which would forever stand up to experience and argument abides by the method of science' (Misak, 2004a: 176).

In focusing on the role that truth plays in political questions, Misak runs up against the currently dominant approach in political theory. Many political theorists, most notably John Rawls, have argued that truth is too controversial a matter for politics to concern itself with. Better, it is said, for politics to be agnostic on the issue of the truth of the beliefs of citizens and to focus instead on seeking to provide a fair constitutional settlement in which citizens who differ on what they take to be true can come together freely and fairly. The appeal of avoiding controversy about truth in political matters is one which Misak acknowledges, but she argues that it is nevertheless both impossible and undesirable to seek to do so. It is impossible because it misses the role that truth plays in our lives. We take ourselves to have true beliefs and are concerned to establish that we are justified in thinking that they are true, and so, insofar as political theorists do not address this, they fail to do justice to lived experience. And it is undesirable, because the failure or refusal to explore the role of truth in such questions has deleterious consequences. In particular, giving up on truth deprives us of the means to justify democracy in the face of those who wish to denigrate its importance. Rawls' argument presupposes certain values – notably justice and the reasonableness of democracy – and yet he nowhere provides a *justification* for these values. Rather, he takes them to be the result of particular historical contingencies. Misak thinks this is inadequate: 'The problem is that, even if Rawls' social ontology were right, even if such ideas were so deeply entrenched that they were shared by everyone, nothing about that fact warrants the thought that that is what we ought to aim at' (Misak, 2000: 26).

This problem is said not to be limited to Rawls but to be endemic among contemporary liberals. For instance, Rorty is criticized not just for his failure to offer a non-question-begging justification of democracy but for *celebrating* the contingency of all justification. Misak sees the failure of liberals such as Rorty and Rawls to attempt to offer such a justification to be not merely a narrowly philosophical matter but one that has profound consequences for society. Without such a justification there is nothing that can be said to stem the instances of intolerance that we face today: 'the response to pluralism and to the absence of a universal basis of adjudication has too often been intolerance, an intolerance which has sometimes culminated in genocide' (Misak, 2000: 11–12).

The stakes then are very high. By offering a justification of a deliberative form of democracy, Misak joins with those political theorists who see deliberation between citizens as a means to address many of the problems of modern society. Deliberative democrats argue that encouraging deliberation between citizens will increase the sense of identification and solidarity between them, leading to the transformation of their preferences and greater legitimacy for political decisions. However, Misak's position is different to many in that its primary focus is on questions not of *legitimacy* but rather of *epistemology*. She argues that Peircean deliberative democracy entails a set of epistemic norms and principles which are central to inquiry itself, norms and principles which preclude (for instance) majority tyranny: 'Once it is acknowledged that we have beliefs, then we can say that *qua believers*, we must abide by certain principles' (Misak, 2000: 46). These include the principle that one must listen carefully to the reasons of one's fellow citizens, consider them, and either provide reasons against them or revise one's own beliefs in order to meet their challenge. Not doing so, for example by dismissing reasons because of the ethnicity of the person offering them, means that we have adopted a poor means to assure ourselves of the truth of our beliefs. In short, the epistemic commitments of believers require the acceptance of an engagement with principles of inquiry. The result of such a conception is a deliberative democracy with the resources to block the epistemological tyranny of the majority.

Misak criticizes political theorists such as Rawls for setting aside truth in questions of politics. How though does she address the issue that leads Rawls and others to do so, namely the pluralism of views of the good life that characterize modern society? Misak of course acknowledges the empirical fact of pluralism. Like Rawls and James, she thinks this situation unlikely to change, and thus distances her pragmatist position from those deliberative democrats who assume that deliberation will lead to convergence upon a single best answer. Her deliberately modest claim is that, in some cases, agreement might be available, and that the best means to achieve this will be through the kind of free and open deliberation she identifies: 'The pragmatist agrees that it is likely that we will not all come to think that one particular thing is the right thing to do in a given situation. But that does not prevent us from aiming at the truth or from aiming at agreement' (Misak, 2000: 144).

A moderate version of pragmatism

In *Truth and the End of Inquiry* Misak offers a reconstruction of Peirce's understanding of truth and its relation to inquiry. In *Truth, Politics, Morality*, she develops a Peircean account of deliberative democracy. In both cases, truth is at the centre of her concerns. And, in focusing on truth, she strives to navigate between two opposed views. Truth is not something which transcends all contexts, but equally it is not relative to any such context. Misak describes hers as a 'moderate version of pragmatism' (Misak, 2004a: 33). In developing it, she seeks to distinguish it from two equally problematic extremes, the transcendental pragmatism of Habermas on the one hand and the ethnocentrism of Rorty on the other.

Habermas, as we have seen, claims to offer a transcendental argument for democratic procedures. Democracy is said to be presupposed in social life, because anyone who makes an assertion assumes principles of inquiry that are unavoidable and which can only be provided for within a democratic framework. This is demonstrated, he claims, by the fact that anyone denying them would be guilty of a 'performative self-contradiction': the very act of denying those principles relies upon principles that are being denied. Misak argues that this claim is too strong. For it is a simple fact that anti-democrats (she cites Carl Schmitt) are able to communicate without presupposing the conditions which Habermas claims unavoidable: 'it is just not the case that being alive or being an identifiable individual or being sane requires the adoption of the democratic principles' (Misak, 2000: 42). In speaking as he does, Habermas lacks plausibility, to the cost, Misak claims, of his justification of democracy.

It might be thought, however, that Misak's position is not so very far from that of Habermas. For them both, the very fact that we have beliefs commits us to seek to justify them through the democratic process. This leads to the striking conclusion that we are all necessarily committed to democratic procedures: 'any opponent is committed to having her beliefs governed by reasons, so any opponent is committed, whether he acknowledges it or not, to debate and deliberation' (Misak, 2000: 106). Misak anticipates and rejects the suggestion that her argument brings her into line with that of Habermas. The claim that one holds beliefs and is therefore committed to justifying them is for her a 'thin' requirement. Her pragmatist account of belief and inquiry gives up transcendentalism and instead calls attention to our actual practices and the commitments that they place upon us. The fact that we hold beliefs means that we commit ourselves to reason-giving and exchanging, and it is this which justifies democracy. It does not, however, mean that we are in a position to say that critics of democracy such as Schmitt are guilty of performative self-contradiction. At most, it provides us with reasons which can satisfy *ourselves* that these others are mistaken (Misak, 2000: 6).

Thus far, Misak concurs with the objections levelled at Habermas' transcendental pragmatism by Rorty. However, she is equally critical of Rorty, thinking him mistaken in his view of truth. Rorty, as we have seen, argues that truth is not a goal of inquiry, and for Misak the problem is that this seems to rule out the possibility of judging the worth of different practices and beliefs. Rorty argues for the superiority of liberal democracy over, for instance, fascism, but for Misak he has deprived himself of the means by which he might do so. She remarks: 'how, we will want to ask, can he [Rorty] assert that democracy, liberalism, and unforced agreement are best, if what is best is simply what is taken by some group to be best?' (Misak, 2000: 13). As Misak understands him, for Rorty our reasons are 'merely historically conditioned reasons, no different in status or worth from the neo-Nazi's reasons based on inequality and hatred of those who are foreign' (Misak, 2000: 16).

Misak in effect diagnoses in Rorty the same mistake as that identified by Bernstein, namely that he recoils from an untenable foundationalism to the view that there is nothing more to justification and inquiry than what a community happens to agree on. She insists that this is not entailed by pragmatism: 'The best kind of pragmatist replaces the old dichotomy between neutral standards and no-standards-at-all with a substantive, low profile, conception of truth and objectivity, a conception which nonetheless can guide us in inquiry' (Misak, 2000: 14). Rorty denies that this intermediate position exists, but it is one that Misak hopes to have identified in her moderate form of pragmatism which allows that inquiry pursues the truth. For, if we drop the correspondence theory of truth, we can see that inquiry aims at truth in the modest but important sense of aiming at beliefs which would forever resist being defeated.

As pragmatists, Misak and Rorty share a commitment to linking philosophical concepts to the contingencies of practice, and give up on the idea that there are transcendental principles underlying those practices. The difference between them concerns the remaining role of truth. And even here, there is reason for thinking that the difference is not too great. As we saw in chapter 4, Rorty does not abandon the concept of truth. It is not a *goal* of inquiry because it is impossible for us to know that we have reached it, yet he insists upon the cautionary use of truth in order to contrast it with justification. This small but important role for truth is, he thinks, all there is to be said. Further claims on behalf of the truth, even the moderate role ascribed to it by Misak, are, he thinks, without pragmatic significance, since there is no behavioural difference that can be identified between those who aim at justification and those who claim to be seeking the truth. He writes that: 'the burden is on Peirceans to explain what actions are motivated by a desire for indefeasibility that are not motivated by a desire for justification' (Rorty, 2010a: 45). For her part, Misak has come to think that the differences between Rortyan pragmatists and Peirceans such as herself may not be as great as she once thought (Misak, 2010: 28). She is, for instance, as clear as Rorty that we can never finally be sure that we have reached the truth: 'We might in fact believe all sorts of truths, but we cannot know when we are in such a position, precisely because we cannot know when we have a belief which would for ever satisfy our aims' (Misak, 2007b: 83). That is the lesson of Peirce's fallibilism, but it is equally the moral of Rorty's cautionary view of truth.

7

Rationalist Pragmatism and Pragmatic Naturalism: Robert B. Brandom and Huw Price

Robert B. Brandom

Robert B. Brandom (b. 1950) is one of the most important philosophers writing today to identify with pragmatism. The most direct influence on his writings is Sellars, but also evident are shades of Rorty, who supervised his doctoral dissertation and from whom he derives his somewhat contentious understanding of the classical pragmatists. Brandom argues that the classical pragmatists were inattentive to the normative dimension of human life, the dimension which distinguishes us from non-human animals. In consequence, although he describes himself as a pragmatist, he qualifies this with an adverb that would have troubled James and Rorty: his is a *rationalist* pragmatism. This pragmatism operates at two levels. As a methodological approach to philosophy, Brandom's pragmatism focuses on the primacy of the practical, a point which he shares with the classical figures. But his more specific concern, in the philosophy of language, is to present an account of 'normative pragmatics', in which individuals are treated as being committed to and responsible for their assertions by the fellow members of their social practices. It is here where Brandom thinks his position departs markedly from the classical pragmatists. The principal figures in his philosophical world are not James and Dewey but Kant and Hegel, who, he argues, show us how to account for the normative dimension of human practice without giving in to the problems that Peirce identified in Cartesianism.

A *rationalist pragmatism*

As we have seen throughout this book, pragmatists of all stripes place human behaviour at the heart of philosophy. In his work, Brandom distinguishes between a narrow and broader understanding of pragmatism. He writes that, narrowly, pragmatism can be thought of 'as a philosophical school centered on evaluating beliefs by their tendency to promote success at the satisfaction of wants' (Brandom, 2002b: 40). This he associates with the classical figures. But there is a broader and, to Brandom, much more interesting and important sense. In this sense, pragmatism is 'a movement centered on the primacy of the practical, initiated already by Kant, whose twentieth-century avatars include not only Peirce, James and Dewey, but also the early Heidegger, the later Wittgenstein and such figures as Quine, Sellars, Davidson and Rorty' (Brandom, 2002b: 40).

The classical pragmatists understood concepts in terms of their function in our practices, rather than seeing them as representing items in the world. And they understood normative concepts such as right or wrong and true or false as assessments made within those practices. The emphasis upon the primacy of the practical has the advantage of being consistent with what our best science tells us about ourselves. Human agency is understood in terms of habitual responses, which are in turn evolutionary adaptations to our environment.

According to Brandom, this understanding is so significant that it is worthy of being regarded, as both Rorty and Putnam have argued, as constituting a further enlightenment (Brandom, 2004). However, this understanding needs to be supplemented. For the classical pragmatists joined in with the European Enlightenment assumption that human behaviour might be understood reductively in terms of causal processes alone. Recalling an objection levelled by Sellars, Brandom claims that the classical pragmatists failed to see the distinctively *normative* dimension of our practices: 'For they focus exclusively on *instrumental* norms: assessments of performances as better or worse, correct or incorrect, insofar as they contribute to the agent's success in securing some end or achieving some goal' (Brandom, 2002b: 50). The attractiveness of this picture seems clear enough. Consider, for example, something as apparently simple as an animal scratching itself. Here, the notion of 'felt satisfaction' can be called upon to explain the animal's behaviour – it knows that it itches, knows that scratching will relieve the itch, and knows when the itch has been relieved (it stops scratching). On this basis we can attribute beliefs and desires to the animal – we can attribute to it the desire not to itch because it scratches, and we can attribute the belief that scratching is the way to relieve the itch. Brandom argues that, for all its apparent plausibility, this train of reasoning is mistaken, and that for a familiar reason. The mistake is a form of the Myth of the Given. The notion of 'felt satisfaction' runs together two different things: a non-conceptual sense in which one can discriminate between satisfaction and dissatisfaction; and the sense that being either satisfied or dissatisfied counts as knowledge, for which reasons or evidence might be offered: 'Felt satisfaction of a desire, in playing both these roles, is a paradigm of givenness in the sense Sellars insists is a myth' (Brandom, 2002b: 52).

Brandom thinks of the classical pragmatists as having failed to take the full measure of the normative dimension of human life; specifically, they did not take account of the difference between *nature* and *culture*. A recurring theme in Brandom's work is his attention to similarities and differences between humans and non-human animals, differences that he thinks the classical pragmatists tended to overlook in their exclusive focus on the instrumental task of pursuing ends. He thinks that the key difference is that we, and we alone, are rational, and that the task for philosophy is to explain what, precisely, this means.

Brandom explains what he means by rationality by introducing a distinction between *sentience* and *sapience*. All animals are sentient in the sense that they respond to the world around them. Humans differ in that we are also sapient, seeing ourselves as responsible for our commitments and actions. In his favourite illustration of the difference between sentience and sapience, Brandom compares the ability of a competent English-speaker to report the colour red with a parrot trained to squawk whenever it encounters red objects. Drawing on Sellars, Brandom argues that knowledge is a matter of standing in the 'space of reasons'. Our understanding of the concept 'red' is a matter of placing it within a web of inferential relations, so that when couched in propositions it can both serve as a reason for other beliefs and itself, if questioned, stand in need of reasons. In order to be taken as making a claim when asserting 'That's red', a person must also be taken to be committed to what that claim entails. The parrot does not know that 'That's red' commits it to 'That's scarlet' and precludes it from uttering 'That's green' – any more than a piece of iron can be said to know that it is raining when it responds by rusting. Brandom concludes: 'What is the difference that makes the difference here?...I think the answer is that *you*, but *not* they, can use your response as the premise of *inferences*. For *you*, but *not* for them, your response is situated in a network of connections to other sentences, connections that underwrite inferential *moves* to it and from it' (Brandom, 2009: 170).

What exactly does it mean to be responsible for one's assertions and the inferences which follow from them? Brandom claims that to be responsible is to be prepared to give *reasons* for one's actions. It is to undertake commitments and in so doing to acknowledge and respond to the reasons and sanctions of the members of one's linguistic practice:

> To be a rational being in this sense is to be subject to a distinctive kind of normative appraisal: assessment of the *reasons* for what one does – in the sense of 'doing' that is marked off by its liability to just that sort of appraisal. Rational beings are ones that *ought* to have reasons for what they do, and *ought* to act as they have reason to. They are subjects of rational obligations, prohibitions, and permissions. (Brandom, 2009: 2–3)

We are rational because, once we have undertaken commitments, we become open to appraisals about the correctness of the behaviour that follows from having so committed ourselves.

Brandom distinguishes his version of rationalism from what he describes as two irrationalist alternatives. The first is the Nietzschean idea that the game of giving and asking for reasons is nothing more than a form of power, according to which power is not a matter of violence or the threat of violence but the more subtle and pernicious form in which the language in which people understand themselves is itself manipulated and controlled. The second form of irrationalism is the Romantic view that the practice of exchanging reasons is merely one game among others, such as artistic expression, which philosophers have wrongly taken to be privileged. For Brandom, both positions are equally mistaken. There is more to reason than manipulation (something which, he points out, even Foucault eventually went some way to conceding). And the game of giving and asking for reasons cannot be seen simply as one practice among others, because it is the practice that institutes the meanings which are presupposed by all those others. Brandom writes: 'I am here disagreeing with Wittgenstein, when he claims that language has no downtown. On my view, it does, and that downtown (the region around which all the rest of discourse is arrayed as dependent suburbs) is the practices of giving and asking for reasons' (Brandom, 2009: 120).

We might object to Brandom's interpretation of the classical pragmatists. Putnam, for instance, argues that, were he to attend to the details of their work, he would see that none was committed to the instrumentalism of which he indicts them (Putnam, 2002b). He points out that the classical pragmatists allowed for normativity, and that they did not identify truth with success in satisfying wants. Putnam is correct in saying that the classical pragmatists were more sensitive to the normative dimension of human life than Brandom allows, but equally, as Brandom points out, they certainly did say things that support his interpretation (Brandom, 1994: 285–91). But, leaving aside exegetical matters, what is important for him is that pragmatism contains the resources to overcome what he takes to be the problems with an instrumental understanding of human behaviour. Combining the insights of the classical pragmatists with those of Kant and Hegel yields what Brandom calls 'a *rationalist* pragmatism'. This form of rationalism gives 'pride of place to practices of giving and asking for reasons, understanding them as conferring conceptual content on performances, expressions, and states suitably caught up in those practices' (Brandom, 2000b: 11).

A pragmatist conception of norms

Brandom's understanding of pragmatism encompasses a loose family of thinkers and ideas. The idea that is of especial interest to him, and which he thinks was also of concern to these other philosophers, is the relation between pragmatics and semantics. Representationalist philosophers hold that semantics is prior to pragmatics: semantic notions, notably truth and reference, account for the use of other terms, such as inference. Brandom objects to representationalism that it does not in fact succeed in accounting for these terms. This is because it attempts to explain the relationship between words and the objects they purport to represent in isolation from the role those words play in our actual practices. Representationalist semantics:

> envisage[s] an explanatory strategy that starts with an understanding of representation and on that basis explains the practical proprieties that govern language use and rational action. It is not clear, however, that a suitable notion of representation can be made available in advance of thinking about the correct use of linguistic expressions and the role of intentional states in making behavior intelligible. (Brandom, 1994: 69)

Brandom's pragmatism, in contrast, holds that semantics must answer to pragmatics – the meaning of linguistic terms must be explained in terms of their use, of the role they play in our practices.

Brandom's project of semantic pragmatism is outlined most fully in his 1994 book *Making It Explicit*. Rorty proposes that this book can 'usefully be seen as an attempt to usher analytic philosophy from its Kantian to its Hegelian stage' (Rorty, 1997b: 8–9). By this, he means that the key to Brandom's project is, as we will see, that the meaning of concepts is constituted within social practices.

The first task of *Making It Explicit* is to provide an account of what Brandom calls 'normative pragmatics', in which the most important activity for humans as rational beings is said to be that we undertake commitments. For Kant, rationality is a matter of following rules. But, as Wittgenstein showed, this invites a regress, for we need rules specifying how *those* rules are to be applied, and so on. There is, however, a way to arrest this regress, which is to see rules and norms as operating *within* particular practices. This is Brandom's suggestion. Normative statuses of commitment and responsibility are *social* statuses, instituted and sustained by human communities and presupposing a background of implicit understandings (and supplying the rules about rules which Wittgenstein sought). His is 'a *pragmatist* conception of norms – a notion of primitive correctnesses of performance *implicit* in *practice* that precede and are presupposed by their *explicit* formulation in *rules* and *principles*' (Brandom, 1994: 21).

Social practices provide two things. First, they specify the *content* of norms in terms of practice, thus avoiding the regress threatened by Kant. Second, they provide an account of how one might correctly or incorrectly follow a norm by viewing individuals as being responsible to the fellow members of a social practice. Once one has bound oneself, responsibility is not exhausted by one's attitude towards those responsibilities. For in binding oneself, one enters into relations of *commitment* and of *entitlement*. Notions of commitment and entitlement are, moreover, *normative*: one acknowledges the responsibilities which follow from them.

Brandom captures the relation of responsibility in the notion of 'deontic scorekeeping'. Members of a practice keep score of each other's commitments and entitlements, acknowledging valid moves and issuing sanctions in the case of invalid ones: 'We sapients are discursive scorekeepers. We keep track of our own and each other's propositionally contentful deontic statuses. Doing that requires being able to move back and forth across the different perspectives occupied by those who undertake commitments and those who attribute them' (Brandom, 1994: 591). Deontic scorekeeping institutes a difference between what we may think ourselves committed and entitled to, and what our fellow participants in a linguistic community *take us* to be committed and entitled to. Once one has committed oneself to a belief, one is committed to the inferential consequences of that belief, whether or not one recognizes them. In Brandom's terms, there is a difference between beliefs *de dicto* and beliefs *de re* – that is, between one's subjective attitudes and one's objective commitments: 'If I claim that the coin is copper, I have said something that, whether I know it or not, is *correct* only if the coin would melt at 1084°C and would *not* melt at 1083°C. If you promise to drive me to the airport at three tomorrow, it is not up to you what would count as fulfilling that promise' (Brandom, 2009: 145).

Normative pragmatics holds that the meaning of linguistic terms is a matter of their use, with one's entitlement (or lack of entitlement) to make a particular claim being acknowledged (or not) by scorekeepers in a social practice. But what is it exactly that constitutes such a practice? Brandom's claim is that the distinctive aspect of *linguistic* practice is that sentences contain propositional content. Building on this account of normative pragmatics, the second element of his project in *Making It Explicit* is to outline an 'inferential semantics', according to which the meaning of a proposition is a matter of its inferential relations to other propositions.

To explain inferential semantics, let's turn again to Sellars' rejection of the Myth of the Given, the idea that sensory stimulation provides knowledge independently of conceptual understanding. Brandom agrees with Sellars in rejecting the given. He locates the given in the context of what he calls 'Enlightenment epistemology', which he claims 'was always the home for two somewhat uneasily coexisting conceptions of the conceptual' (Brandom, 2000b: 46). The first conception is that the content of concepts is given by representations. Representationalism attempts to explain how words represent items in the world, with the meaning of words seen as the function of those words in representing those items. Representationalism contrasts with a second way in which concepts are given content, which is through inference. Inferentialism holds that the meaning of words is a function of their role in a web of commitments and entitlements: 'States and acts acquire content by being caught up in inferences, as premises and conclusions' (Brandom, 2000b: 46). Inferentialism turns from word–world relations to relations between beliefs, with representations of items in the world seen as the *product* of legitimate inferences.

The centrepiece of inferential semantics is the idea of *material inference*. A correct inference is governed by the norms of social practices, as these are characterized in the game of giving and asking for reasons. Relations of commitment and entitlement give rise to inferences, and these in turn produce meaning. This relation is distinguished from *logical inference*, according to which inferences are valid or invalid by reference to a logical structure held to be independent of any particular practice. Brandom argues that we can render norms in the form of logical rules, but this is to make explicit prior, implicit, material inferences. In other words, the claim to having made a logical inference presupposes an already existing material inference, so that the rule 'If p then q' derives not from some objective logical mechanism underlying the structure of reality, but from the fact that this principle has been applied effectively thus far within our social practices.

Here Brandom develops a point that was raised by the classical pragmatists. They saw that the ability to wield concepts presupposes a background of implicit belief and understanding, and opposed the intellectualism of which James in particular had complained, according to which the ability to make an assertion presupposes that one has already grasped some set of principles. Brandom argues that intellectualism gets things the wrong way around. Principles are themselves worked up (in his term, 'made explicit') from a background context of practical knowledge. Inferential semantics addresses the deficiencies of representationalism by focusing on the role that words play in our practices, with those practices providing the meaning of our claims by specifying the circumstances in which we are entitled to make them.

The account of inferential semantics provides a role for semantic notions of truth and reference. These are, however, derived from the prior notion of inferentialism rather than, as representationalists see it, coming first as a primitive notion. To explain, the representationalist thinks that the meaning of concepts is given by the conditions under which they are made true; the idea is that there is a single set of conditions which are sufficient for a concept to be applied. In contrast, inferential semantics sees conceptual content as given not by truth but by inference. Representationalism says that facts render statements true; inferentialism says that the inferences allowing us to generate those facts confer truth. That is to say, truth shifts to the process of determination, not the identification of some state of affairs as being the way it is. Brandom writes:

> The talk of 'knowledge' here is very different from that involved in knowledge of truth conditions. For it is a kind of knowing *how* rather than knowing *that*: knowing how to *do* something, namely distinguish in practice between good inference and bad inference in which the sentence appears as a premise or conclusion, rather than knowing *that* the truth conditions are such-and-such. (Brandom, 2009: 169)

Brandom wishes to rework rather than give up the concept of representation by revising the order of explanation that has traditionally been given for it. On this point, he takes himself to differ from Rorty, who, as we have seen, characterizes pragmatism as anti-representationalism. For Brandom, this is mistakenly to move from giving up on the idea of privileged representations (in particular, transparent meanings and the given) to giving up on on the idea that we might represent objects in the world at all. He thinks that the account of pragmatism that he develops allows for a notion of representation. But, importantly, it is representation that is viewed as a consequence of inferentialism, not the basis from which inferences can be made: 'The *representational* dimension of propositional contents reflects the *social* structure of their *inferential* articulation in the game of giving and asking for reasons' (Brandom, 2000b: 183).

For his part, Rorty seeks to minimize the difference between Brandom and himself on this point. He writes that the inferential account of representationalism is very different from the traditional view, for it is simply to say that our words are about some thing, a view with which he has no difficulty. He writes:

> By the time Brandom has finished deflating it, 'represents' has become interchangeable with 'is about': all assertions are about something, and in that deflated sense they all represent something. So there is no room in Brandom's thinking for the metaphysical claim that some assertions seem to represent but do not, or that they are *really* about something different from what they initially appear to be about. (Rorty, 2010b: 290)

This has the double advantage, as Rorty sees it, both of allowing that our statements about, say, politics and morality are just as real as those about physical particles, and of ruling out *metaphysical* questions about the accuracy of those representations.

The structural conditions of objectivity

Representationalism accords with our sense that our words describe items or events in the world. The problem with representationalism, as pragmatists have long pointed out, is that the relationship between word and world remains unspecified; no clear account can be given of that relationship because there is no way (as Wittgenstein put it) to stand between language and its object in order for us to see how the one represents the other. Inferentialism asks us to turn from word–world relations to relations between beliefs and assertions, with representations the *product* of legitimate inferences in the game of giving and asking for reasons. However, inferentialism too presents a problem. For in focusing on the relationship between beliefs, what happens to the world? Brandom acknowledges that he shares with Rorty wariness about the very idea of our being responsible to 'how things already in any case are' (Brandom, 2000c: 370). There is no perspective outside of social practices by which our commitments and entitlements may be tracked; there is 'no bird's-eye view above the fray of competing claims from which those that deserve to prevail can be identified, nor from which even necessary and sufficient conditions for such deserts can be formulated' (Brandom, 1994: 601). Even principles that purport to stand apart from controversies about particular claims are themselves implicated in those controversies, and so an appeal to them to settle the controversy will simply beg the question of their authority: 'The status of any such principles as probative is always itself at issue in the same way as the status of any particular factual claim' (Brandom, 1994: 601). On what basis then can we judge our practices? Are we, for instance, able to say that one practice is more successful than another in enabling us to address the problems that we confront as we move about in the world?

Brandom is well aware of the objection that his view amounts to a form of relativism. He replies by challenging the assumption that relativism can only be avoided by identifying a perspective outside of social practice. He recognizes that we respond to the physical world and are constrained by it, but the important point is that these constraints must be seen as standing *inside* our social practices. We acknowledge an independent objective reality, but this results from our social processes of interaction and scorekeeping rather than from something that exists prior to that acknowledgement:

> It is wrong to think of facts and the objects they involve as constraining linguistic practice from the outside – not because they do not constrain it but because of the mistaken picture of facts and objects as outside it. What determinate practices a community has depends on what the facts are and on what objects they are actually practically involved with, to begin with, through perception and action. The way the world is, constrains proprieties of inferential, doxastic, and practical commitment in a straightforward way from *within* those practices. (Brandom, 1994: 332)

Kant held that there are no commitments in the world prior to our committing ourselves, and Hegel added to this the idea that those commitments are upheld within social practices. Brandom's claim is that, once we have committed ourselves in our social practices, those commitments are (causally) responsive to the external world.

The game of giving and asking for reasons, in which participants keep track of each other's commitments, is held by Brandom to be sufficient to provide for an account of objectivity; that is, it is sufficient to account for the difference between what is the case and what anyone *thinks* is the case. Recognizing this difference is a structural requirement for all communities if they are to function successfully: 'the distinction between claims or applications of concepts that are objectively correct and that are merely taken to be correct is a structural feature of each scorekeeping perspective' (Brandom, 1994: 595). A helpful illustration is provided by Jeffrey Stout. Stout points out that, in the case of sandlot baseball and street soccer, there are no umpires or referees. Rather, the players themselves keep track of the runs and goals scored, and of the behaviour of the opposing team. This process of mutual checking and responsibility is, Stout claims, sufficient to provide for objectivity:

> For the same reasons that baseball can be played on the sandlots and soccer can be played in the streets, ethical discourse can retain an objective dimension without there being a single authority on questions of truth and falsity. In ethics, as in most other forms of objective discourse, we are all keeping track of our interlocutors' attitudes, as well as our own. (Stout, 2004: 272)

In ethics – as, for Brandom, in most domains of human life – we all keep score of each other.

Brandom explains the structural account of objectivity by drawing a distinction between 'I-thou' and 'I-we' accounts of social practices. *I-we* construals find objectivity in whatever a community takes to be objective. This, Brandom is clear, is inadequate precisely because it cannot allow for the community itself to be in error, and it is *this* formulation which, he thinks, leads to relativism. *I-thou* relations constitute a different way of understanding objectivity by preserving the difference between correct and incorrect application of concepts, where correctness or incorrectness is determined by developed social practices undertaken in the light of the causal impact of the world. On this account, it might be the case that the entire community is mistaken about any particular belief. The difference between these two accounts of social practice reflects their *symmetry*. *I-we* relations are asymmetric, for the *we* is the privileged perspective to which individual members of a linguistic community must defer. In contrast, the crucial feature of *I-thou* relationships is the symmetry of relations between individuals assessing each other's actions.

Brandom joins pragmatists such as Putnam and Rorty in focusing on the structural (as they would say, political) conditions within which individuals hold each other to question. *I-thou* scorekeeping is a process forever open, one in which anyone can raise a new claim in the game of giving and asking for reasons:

> In exploring the inferential significance of novel claims, we are not simply tracing out paths already determined in advance. For the inferential norms that govern the use of concepts are not handed down to us on tablets from above; they are not guaranteed in advance to be complete or coherent with each other. They are at best constraints that aim us in a direction when assessing novel claims. They neither determine the resultant vector of their interaction, nor are they themselves immune from alteration as a result of the collision of competing claims or inferential commitments that have never before been confronted with one another. (Brandom, 2000a: 176)

The importance of the space to make novel moves that our social practices make available to us is, as we will now see, developed by Brandom in his discussion of different understandings of freedom.

Expressive freedom and normative constraint

It is central to Brandom's argument that, as sapients, the only commitments we have are those which we undertake and impose upon ourselves. But, once we have done so, we are held responsible by each other for what follows from those commitments. This account of rational constraint is important for Brandom's understanding of freedom.

At first sight, freedom and constraint might appear antithetical, for one seems free precisely insofar as one is *not* subject to constraint. Brandom, however, sees them as intrinsically interlinked. On the one hand, being subject to norms constrains us insofar as some things, for instance some uses of words, are precluded by those norms. But on the other, norms enable us to say and do things that we would otherwise not have the ability and resources to do. Put differently, we lose some of our *negative freedom* (from constraint by norms) but gain *positive freedom*, or, as Brandom calls it, 'expressive freedom' (the freedom to do certain things):

> This is a kind of positive freedom, freedom *to* do something rather than freedom *from* some constraint. For it is not as if the beliefs, desires, and intentions one comes to be able to express when one acquires a suitable language have been there all the time, hidden

somehow 'inside' the individual and kept from overt expression by some sort of constraint. Without a suitable language there are some beliefs, desires, and intentions that one simply cannot have. (Brandom, 1979: 194)

By having access to expressive freedom, we are *positively* free because we are able to formulate ends otherwise unavailable to us, thus creating new opportunities to be self-determining sapient creatures.

Brandom develops this understanding of expressive freedom with reference to different accounts of sapience. On one view, sapience is a matter of pursuing goals with the aim of satisfying desires. This Brandom describes as the Humean view, and he also attributes it to the classical pragmatists. As we have seen, according to him the classical pragmatists understood sapience exclusively in instrumental terms, according to which it is a matter of deploying means–end rationality as the means to satisfy ends. Kant adds to this understanding an account of sapience as a normative achievement, in which it is viewed as the ability to undertake commitments and to acknowledge the ensuing responsibilities. To this Kantian position, Hegel adds a third account of sapience, in which humans are conceived of as creatures possessing expressive freedom: 'self-creating beings, who can change what we are *in* ourselves by changing what we are *for* ourselves, by identifying with new descriptions of ourselves, by adopting new vocabularies' (Brandom, 2009: 155).

By conceiving of freedom as positive and expressive, Brandom takes himself to depart from both classical and more recent pragmatists. Returning to his claim that Peirce and Dewey were instrumentalists, he argues that this is evident in their view that belief, concepts and language are tools which enable us to secure ends. This problem recurs in different ways in both Rorty and Habermas: Rorty thinks of language as a tool to help us pursue our various ends; Habermas as one by which we might achieve intersubjective agreement on norms. In one sense of course, there is nothing wrong with these ideas: just as tools are used for different purposes, language enables us to undertake different projects. But Brandom takes these positions to be equally mistaken, because they both preserve the idea of interests existing prior to language. He objects to the idea of language as a tool that enables us to pursue *antecedent ends*, because it means conceiving of an end as something that can be grasped independently of the means by which it might be reached: 'The very intelligibility of the ends depends on our linguistic capacities. They are precisely *not* goals that we can make sense of *first*, so that later, language can be brought into the picture playing the role of a possible tool for achieving them' (Brandom, 2002b: 57). For Brandom, ends are themselves expressed in linguistic practice and cannot be conceived of as something apart from that practice.

Brandom takes up the question of how this account of freedom as constraint by norms carries over into political questions. He notes that Hegel, and following him Marx and T. H. Green, rejected the Enlightenment assumption that constraints on negative liberty were justified only to the extent that they made possible greater human freedom and the satisfaction of an individual's wants. On this view, an individual's preferences are treated as something fixed and existing prior to their entry into society, with collective life justified solely in terms of how far it facilitates the satisfaction of these pre-social wants. Brandom claims that Hegel rejected this picture, but at the same time was aware of the anti-individualist consequences of so doing. Seeking a path between them, he argued that constraints upon individual freedom are justified only insofar as they make possible a form of expressive freedom:

> On the Hegelian conception of us, then, one of the great goods for us is the availability of an inexhaustible supply of new vocabularies in which to express, develop, constitute, and transform ourselves and our institutions, and for understanding the process by which we do that. This is the great positive, expressive freedom that makes us what we are. (Brandom, 2009: 150)

How though are the trade-offs between different freedoms to be settled? Here, Brandom is clear that there is no *a priori* answer available to us: 'For what we really, essentially are, *in* ourselves, depends on what we are *for* ourselves. It depends on which vocabulary for self-description we adopt, endorse, interpret ourselves in terms of, and so identify with' (Brandom, 2009: 155). Although he does not mention him in this regard, his argument here calls to mind Dewey, who emphasized the dialectic between individual and community and who, in his notion of 'growth', refused to specify too fully which direction the good or edifying life might take us. What Brandom calls expressive freedom permits novel forms of expression which, by definition, escape current forms of categorization.

Huw Price

For Huw Price (b. 1953), interest in pragmatism arises principally from his interpretation of the work of philosophers such as Hume and Wittgenstein rather than the classical pragmatists, although his position is worked out through detailed engagement with Rorty and

Brandom. He presents pragmatism as combining two positions. The first is a linguistic focus: pragmatists are not concerned with *material* questions about objects and their properties but rather *linguistic* ones about the role of concepts such as truth and goodness in our lives. In examining them, pragmatism is said to offer not *metaphysical analyses* of such concepts but rather *anthropological explanations* of their use. The second element of Price's pragmatism is anti-representationalism, a position which he derives in part from Rorty, but with whom he ultimately differs. In his work Price is also concerned to defend an account of truth which plays a normative role in our inquiries over and above that of securing solidarity with our peers. The resulting position is a form of pragmatism which Price locates between those of Rorty and Brandom.

Linguistic priority without representationalism

Price presents pragmatism as a metaphysically quietist philosophy. The term 'metaphysical quietism' requires some care. It must be distinguished from 'anti-metaphysics', for it does not take a stand on metaphysical questions but suggests instead that we set them aside. Consider, for instance, those who argue that moral or aesthetic values are useful fictions, albeit ones which people happily use in their everyday lives. This is a metaphysical view, taking a stand on ontological questions of what *really exists*. Price argues that, for the pragmatist in contrast, such questions drop out of consideration. Pragmatism affirms the existence of the objects of our experience – beliefs, values, causes – but refuses to ask the metaphysical question of whether these things really exist, downplaying it in favour of other, practical, questions. In a paper co-authored with David Macarthur, Price writes: 'The pragmatist we have in mind wants to dismiss or demote such metaphysical puzzles in favour of more practical questions, about the roles and functions of the matters in question in human life' (Macarthur and Price, 2007: 94).

How does Price propose addressing these more practical questions? He argues that we should view them in *linguistic* terms – for example, by offering an explanation of the distinctive character of evaluative concepts such as good and evil:

> Pragmatism...begins with *linguistic* explananda rather than *material* explananda; with phenomena concerning the *use* of certain terms and concepts, rather than with things or properties of a non-linguistic nature. It begins with linguistic behaviour, and asks broadly anthropological questions: How are we to understand the roles and functions

of the behaviour in question, in the lives of the creatures concerned? What is its practical significance? Whence its genealogy? (Macarthur and Price, 2007: 95)

The priority afforded to language is itself not exclusive to pragmatists. Some recent work in metaphysics also takes a linguistic approach to philosophical questions, for example in examining semantic terms such as truth and reference. Typically, however, metaphysicians ask the question of what it is that *makes* sentences true. They focus on 'truth-makers': starting with statements taken to be true, they ask of them what makes those statements true. This leads back to representationalism, and to the task of accounting for the relationship between the world and the languages which seek to represent it. In doing so it raises the familiar problems – of scepticism, of the external world and of other minds – that pragmatists from Peirce to Putnam have argued that we should set aside. Price shares their concern, thinking that representationalism encourages us to shift our gaze from useful questions about the utility of different languages and vocabularies to metaphysical questions. For him, the result of the combination of a linguistic starting-point coupled with a rejection of semantic or representationalist presuppositions is a form of pragmatism. For pragmatists, the task is that of explaining the use of linguistic terms. Once this has been achieved, there is no remaining task of explaining the relationship between the use of those terms and the world.

Like Rorty and other pragmatists, Price has to confront the question of why we would want to give up on representationalism. After all, representationalism seems to provide an intuitively useful account of the relationship of language to the world. Price's particular complaint is that representationalism gives rise to so-called 'placement problems', problems of how to locate, or place, certain objects and events (notably moral values) in the world. He diagnoses 'placement problems' as resulting from the often implicit coupling of representationalism with a second presumption, that of naturalism. Naturalism places constraints on the kinds of sentence that are capable of expressing truths, for the only items in the world that it seems to recognize are those identified by natural science: 'In this form, these 'placement problems' stem from a presupposition about the ontological scope of science – roughly, the naturalist assumption that all there is, is the world as studied by science' (Macarthur and Price, 2007: 94). The difficulty is that of placing items such as truth or goodness or beauty which, whatever else they may be, are not obviously permitted a role by our best science. This issue is one which has concerned a variety of pragmatists – for instance, it animated James' belief that philosophy must provide room for religious belief. Price shares this concern but points out that the items which it seems impossible to accommodate in the language of natural science include not only moral concepts, but also those which scientists themselves utilize and would not wish to be without, for instance those of probability, causation and necessity.

We saw in chapter 1 that James was sceptical of naturalism. In contrast, most contemporary philosophers are happy to endorse a naturalistic understanding of the world, accepting that human beings are a part of the natural world and that philosophy must understand them as such. Price's argument, however, is that both presume a problematic (and optional) conception of naturalism, which he calls 'object naturalism'. Object naturalism is a metaphysical doctrine which holds that what exists is what is explained by natural science. He contrasts object naturalism with an alternative, termed 'subject naturalism'. As Michael Williams points out, subject naturalism is not a *metaphysical* doctrine but a *methodological* one (Williams, 2009: xv). It asks us to begin with what science tells us about ourselves, and holds that philosophy must recognize and work on a basis consistent with this: 'Science tells us that we are natural creatures, and if the claims and ambitions of philosophy conflict with this view, then philosophy needs to give way' (Price, 2004: 73). Price argues that subject naturalism provides a way of reconciling the demands placed on philosophy by scientific knowledge without opting for a reductive 'scientism' in which the only things that count are the objects of scientific inquiry.

Price identifies two reasons why subject naturalism, so understood, supports the suggestion that philosophy should give up on representationalism. The first – familiar from Dewey – is that representationalism takes humans to be passive observers of the world rather than, as subject naturalism sees them, active participants whose activities bring shape to that world. Second, representationalism ignores the different functions of the various vocabularies that we employ in our dealings with the world. For the subject naturalist, different vocabularies serve different purposes, but there is no purpose which is metaphysically privileged. Here, Price raises the issue of pluralism, a topic which pragmatists since James have acknowledged as important in our lives.

In his work, Price identifies two different dimensions along which pluralism obtains (Price, 2011: 36). 'Horizontal pluralism' maintains that different views may be equally valid because there is a plausible range of different viewpoints within a particular domain of inquiry. This is for instance the pluralism that Quine had in mind in his doctrine of ontological relativity, which holds that different scientific theories might equally explain the data at hand. Price distinguishes this form of pluralism from what he calls 'vertical pluralism', which holds that there is an irreducible plurality of *kinds* of discourse. Vertical pluralism allows for both the autonomy and the legitimacy of these different discourses. It provides for autonomy in the sense that different domains of inquiry are not reducible to one another; it holds for instance that the vocabulary of morality cannot be reduced to that of physics. And it holds that each of these separate domains is legitimate; it doesn't require that moral values be explicable in the terms of physical science in order for morality to constitute a legitimate domain of inquiry. Price is a vertical pluralist, and thinks that this form of pluralism challenges representationalism: 'One of the reasons that the representationalist model is a bad theory, the pragmatist wants to say, is that it does not pay enough attention to these factors. It is blind to the "located" character of various bits of language – to their dependence on various contingent features of the circumstances of the natural creatures who use them' (Price, 2011: 12).

What, though, of the claim that natural science seems to offer the best explanation of the world? For Price, we can account for the privilege accorded to natural science in anti-representationalist and subject naturalist terms. For the purposes of predicting and controlling the physical environment, the natural sciences enjoy privilege over others. However, this privilege is not metaphysical but pragmatic, because it is to say no more than that the language of natural science is best suited to a particular task. As Price remarks, 'Science is only one of the games we play with language. Each game privileges its own ontology, no doubt, but the privilege is merely perspectival. Science is privileged "by its own lights," but to mistake this for an absolute ontological priority would be to mistake science for metaphysics, or first philosophy' (Price, 2011: 31). Put otherwise, while science is best suited to manipulation of the physical world, it is poorly suited to the understanding of the normative, or emotional, or metaphorical. It is this vertical pluralism that Price thinks representationalism cannot allow for, but that is nevertheless perfectly consistent with subject naturalism.

Pragmatism as global expressivism

Price argues that pragmatism is committed to quietism, but notes that quietism comes in different forms. Pragmatism is a form of *metaphysical* quietism, by which is meant that it rejects metaphysical questions about what really exists. But it is not committed to a different kind of quietism, which Price labels 'use-explanatory quietism'. Pragmatists 'take some relevant theoretical matters very seriously indeed: in particular, some broadly anthropological issues about the roles and genealogy of various aspects of human linguistic behaviour. . . . What distinguishes pragmatism is its commitment to addressing them without the resources of a representationalist model of language' (Macarthur and Price, 2007: 101).

In a letter written in 1905, Dewey wrote that pragmatism would 'give the *coup de grace* to *representationalism*' (Price, 2010a: 269; from a letter quoted in Menand, 2001: 361). Dewey wrote, however, more in hope than in expectation, and representationalism continued to flourish in twentieth-century philosophy. Price argues that, a century later, representationalism is at last being overcome, and from *within* the tradition of analytic philosophy. Acknowledging his debts to Wittgenstein, Dewey and Rorty, Price claims that challenging representationalism need not be seen as a radical measure undertaken by those outside analytic philosophy. Rather, what he calls the 'non-Representationalist utopia' turns out to be very similar to current positions within analytic philosophy (Price, 2008: 3).

It is, in particular, a position very close to one which has come to be known as *expressivism*, which Price traces back to the work of David Hume. Humean expressivism makes a point which, as we saw in the previous section, Price thinks central to pragmatism: 'In place of metaphysical questions about the nature of value, or modality, say, it [expressivism] offers us questions about the role and genealogy of evaluative and modal vocabularies – and these are questions about human behavior, broadly construed, rather than questions about some seemingly puzzling part of the metaphysical realm' (Price, 2010a: 280). Some would consider statements about morality to be meaningless because they fail to describe some object or event in the world. However, this understanding assumes that the point of language is to describe the world, but, if the expressivist is correct, there are some uses, such as expressing an emotional attitude, that are not descriptive but still perfectly real. One influential version of expressivism is the *quasi-realism* of philosophers such as Simon Blackburn and Allan Gibbard. Quasi-realism holds that we are entitled to regard our commitments as being true, but we cannot necessarily see them as true because they represent some item in the world. Quasi-realism asks about the use and practical significance of vocabularies, holding that the function of some of our statements is not, as might be thought, to describe things. In this way, the quasi-realist and the Humean expressivist capture what Price regards as an important insight. This is that, at least within certain domains, the metaphysical understanding of placement problems rests upon a mistaken account of language. Once this is recognized, he argues that there is no need to deny that statements about morality are meaningful. The expressivist

> agrees full voice with the everyday folk, and argues that the attempt to raise further issues – Are there *really* any such facts? – rests on a mistake about language. Once we see that moral claims are not genuinely descriptive, the expressivist assures us, we see that such metaphysical issues rest on a category mistake. See things properly and you see that they simply don't arise. (Price, 2008: 6)

Price raises expressivism and quasi-realism for two reasons. First, he is keen to show that the anti-representationalist position which he defends is not as iconoclastic as Dewey and Rorty sometimes present it as being but takes a central place in contemporary philosophical discussion. These pragmatists are not alone in maintaining that the idea that some statements represent items in the world is a mistaken and misleading account of the relationship between our beliefs and the world, nor in accepting the (subject) naturalist point that languages have different functions and are used by natural creatures to cope with different parts of their environments.

Second, Price raises quasi-realism in order to situate his own position. For he wants to go beyond quasi-realism in one important respect. Quasi-realists are *local* expressivists – they think that some claims *are* genuinely descriptive in the sense assumed by representationalism. The local expressivist asks whether or not some particular area of language, for instance moral or aesthetic language, is entitled to be thought of as genuinely descriptive. The problem with local expressivism, as Price sees it, is that it tends to focus attention on what he regards as the wrong questions. It assumes what Rorty has called the 'Bifurcation Thesis': that there is a bright line between descriptive and non-descriptive uses of language. Price claims that we should dispense with the idea that representation is *ever* a useful way of understanding the relation between language and the world. He argues: 'The right thing to do, as theorists, is . . . to stop talking about representation altogether, to abandon the project of theorizing about word–world relations in these terms' (Price, 2011: 10). Rather than adopting a local expressivism in certain cases, Price proposes a *global* expressivism or, as he thinks it, pragmatism.

What does Price's global expressivism look like? To explain it, he draws on Brandom's inferentialism. In answer to the question of what gives content to assertions, Brandom, as we have seen, argues that it is not a matter of their representing (or failing to represent) some item in the world. Rather, that content is given in the game of giving and asking for reasons. Price takes Brandom's inferentialism to be entailed by global expressivism, according to which the *use* of linguistic expressions is what gives rise to the *content* of those expressions (and not the other way around, as the representationalist picture has it).

Global expressivism entails what Price calls a 'two-level picture of assertoric language' (Price, 2011: 20). At the higher level, assertoric languages share the fact that they entail making and justifying assertions in the game of giving and asking for reasons. At the second, lower level, different vocabularies serve different purposes. If we give up on the idea that language represents items in the world and instead endorse a form of global expressivism, we will see that there is a (vertical) pluralism about the uses of language, stemming from the different practical stances that we, as agents, adopt. The different circumstances that we confront, and the different tasks we undertake, explain the different tasks that languages are called upon to perform.

By arguing that there is a plurality of vocabularies, there might be thought to be a difference between Price and Brandom. As we have seen, Brandom thinks that language has a 'downtown': the practice of undertaking commitments and of giving and asking for reasons is important for *all* vocabularies. Price, in proposing pluralism about kinds of discourse, might seem to be suggesting something very different. However, he thinks there is no difference that makes a difference on this matter. Vertical pluralism is consistent with a unitary account of language in the sense that different vocabularies are all characterized by relations of inference, which they depend upon to provide their meaning. It is rather at the different, lower, level where pluralism obtains, with different vocabularies serving different, irreducible, functions. Price writes: 'Thus I think we can follow Brandom here – agree that language has a downtown – without sacrificing key pragmatist territory. What we need is the idea that although assertion is indeed a fundamental language game, it is a game with multiple functionally distinct applications – a multifunction tool, in effect' (Price, 2010a: 275).

Like Brandom, Rorty and other pragmatists, Price has to confront the issue of accounting for the world and how it relates to our beliefs *about* the world. Price claims that his account of pragmatism in no way commits him to idealism, the view that objects in the world only exist insofar as we talk about them. He makes the useful distinction between two forms of constraint. One is the familiar idea of constraint by one's environment. Here Price joins with other pragmatists in denying both that there is a single description that the world seeks to impose on us, and that the purpose of language is to represent it accurately. As he remarks, 'there is no useful, external notion, *of a semantic kind* – in other words, no useful, general, notion of relations that words and sentences bear to the external world, that we might usefully identify with truth and reference' (Price, 2011: 21). The second form of constraint is what Price calls 'in-game externality'. This holds that *within* a particular language game, players bind themselves to standards which exist beyond themselves. These constraints are external to and independent of any particular player, but at the same time are internal to that game itself; Price gives the example that, when playing chess, one is bound by rules that are external to the players and yet are internal to chess. The distinction between the two forms of constraint enables Price to guard against the claim that he is proposing idealism, such that, in speaking a particular language, we thereby bring facts into being. This is to conflate two different issues: it is certainly the case that we cannot speak of facts without playing the language game in which they figure but, once we are *inside* that game, we do not create the facts-whatever we may believe, it is a fact that pawns cannot move backwards.

Between Brandom and Rorty

Price's argument draws on Brandom's work on key points. However, Price thinks that Brandom goes too far in trying to make peace with traditional notions of representationalism. Thus, whereas he thinks of Dewey and Rorty as having placed anti-representationalism at the heart of pragmatism, Price suggests that Brandom can be read as constituting a counter-revolutionary tendency. As he puts it, Brandom sometimes appears to be delivering not what Dewey called a *coup de grâce* to representationalism but instead a *coup d'état*, 'to take over the representationalist empire intact, by rebuilding its walls on properly pragmatic foundations' (Price, 2010a: 273). Price thinks this a mistake, one that can be seen as such if we take full account of the lesson of Humean expressivism. We have seen that Sellars took himself to be seeking to move analytic philosophy from its Humean to its Kantian phase by focusing on the importance of the conceptual, and that Rorty suggests that Brandom should be read as attempting to effect a further shift from Kant to Hegel in recognizing that concepts are socially constituted. However, Price thinks there is still a valuable lesson to be learned from Hume:

Hume's expressivism may well be a large step behind Kant in failing to appreciate the importance of the conceptual; and a further large step behind Hegel in failing to see that the conceptual depends on the social. But it is still at the head of the field for its understanding of the way in which what we would now call pragmatism simply turns its back on metaphysics. (Price, 2010a: 284)

This Humean lesson is one he thinks Brandom in particular is in danger of missing in his attempt to re-describe, rather than set aside, metaphysical concepts.

The problem, as Price sees it, is that Brandom does not adequately distinguish between what he (Price) calls 'metaphysical inquiry' and 'philosophical anthropology'. With this distinction in hand, Price seeks to deflate the residual metaphysical side of Brandom and bring him four-square in line with global anti-representationalism. Price points out that Brandom sometimes presents himself as seeking to construe referential relations in terms of inferential ones. This, according to Price, remains a metaphysical position, one which he thinks inconsistent with pragmatism as a metaphysically quietist philosophy. Price writes that, in speaking in these terms, Brandom misrepresents what he is doing. For, despite sometimes claiming to offer a reconstruction of semantic terms, Brandom in fact offers a pragmatist *use-explanatory account* of those terms.

> In the observance…what Brandom actually does is not to "construe referential relations" (as having such-and-such a nature, for example), or to "make sense of reference" (itself), but rather to offer us an account of the use of referential *vocabulary*: he tells us about the use of the *term* "refers," not about the reference *relation* – about *ascriptions* of reference, not about reference itself. (Price, 2010a: 276–7)

Price argues that his interpretation of Brandom as torn between a metaphysical and an anthropological understanding of his project is borne out in Brandom's concerns about naturalism. Brandom is critical of the way the classical pragmatists focused on the continuities between humans and non-human animals, and in particular for ignoring Sellars' insight that the game of giving and asking for reasons is a normative game which takes us out of the realm of nature and into culture. Price, however, thinks that Brandom has no reason for anxiety if we distinguish between object and subject forms of naturalism. As we've seen, object naturalism is a metaphysical doctrine according to which what exists is what is explained by natural science, and as such contrasts with subject naturalism as a methodological principle which tells us that philosophy must be consistent with an understanding of humans as natural beings. If we set aside metaphysics in the manner Price proposes, he thinks that Brandom has no reason to worry about identifying with subject naturalism: 'His account only looks nonnaturalistic (to him) because he tries to conceive of it as metaphysics. If he had stayed on the virtuous (anthropological) side of the fence to begin with, there would have been no appearance of anything nonnaturalistic, and no need to retreat' (Price, 2010a: 283; see also Rorty, 2007: 158).

On the two issues that appear to divide Price and Brandom, Price's position can be seen to be very similar to Rorty's: both are metaphysical quietists, and both are resolutely naturalistic (in the subject naturalist sense). However, Price thinks there is a difference between himself and Rorty too. This is that, once pragmatism has turned its back on metaphysics, there remains a role for the notion of representation (in a use-explanatory sense of the term).

To explain, consider such a seemingly obvious instance of representation as a thermometer varying according to the temperature of the outside world. In contrast to his understanding of Rorty's anti-representationalism, Price argues that there is a perfectly respectable way to render this in representationalist terms. In order to do so, he argues that we need to draw a distinction between two kinds of representation, which he calls '*external* representation' and '*internal* representation'. *External* representationalism is the view that there is a privileged class of representations which most accurately track the external world, and, as such, is dismissed by Price. This is however very different to, and not implied by, a second, *internal*, sense of representation. This second sense is inferential, according to which something counts as a representation by reference to its role in an inferential structure. Something functions as a representation only by reference to its role in norm-governed social practice, but, once a practice is in place, that something can be said to represent some thing in the world. According to internal representationalism, 'A token counts as a representation, in this sense, in virtue of its position, or role, in some sort of cognitive or inferential architecture – in virtue of its links, within a network, to other items of the same general kind' (Price, 2011: 20). So, for instance, the token 'Sydney' is the representation picked out by such relations as 'state capital of New South Wales', 'east of Perth', 'usually warmer than London', etc.

Price unpacks the differences between notions of representationalism by claiming that external representationalism bundles together two ideas about language which ought properly to be kept separate. The first he calls the 'content assumption', which holds that language is a medium which encodes bits of factual information, specifically the contents of beliefs and assertions. The second is the 'correspondence assumption', which holds that these packets of information represent some item in the external world. The content assumption is a central and necessary part of language, but Price argues that it must be separated from the correspondence assumption. If it is separated, we are left with a richer understanding of the various roles that language plays in our lives: 'According to an inferentialist, the internal logical machinery of language creates packets of information, or contents, but these may be associated with many different functional relationships, in the complex interaction between language users and their physical environment' (Price, 2008: 15–16). Rorty is said to miss the importance of the content assumption because of his anxieties about representationalism, but Price claims that acknowledging it poses no problems for Rorty's project if it is separated from the correspondence assumption. For Price, pragmatism is consistent with an account of some representational forms of discourse, as long as those representations are seen as use-explanations and as operating within a context of inferentialism. In so doing, they avoid the problems usually facing representationalism.

Truth as a norm of inquiry

What Price calls the idea of *in-game externality* implies a role for truth; that, within particular vocabularies, there are truths about the contents of different packets of information. He agrees with the classical pragmatists that we must approach the subject of truth by examining the role which it plays in our lives. But, like most contemporary pragmatists, he rejects the view that truth can be reduced to justification or warranted assertability (even Peirce's ideal assertibility at the end of inquiry). The mistake made by the classical pragmatists lies, Price claims, in not resting content with showing up the flaws in the correspondence and coherence theories but in going on to offer an alternative analysis of what truth might be. He writes that, 'given standard objections to metaphysical answers, it is understandable that Peirce's alternative should seem attractive. But the attraction is that of methadone compared to heroin. Far better, surely, from a pragmatist's point of view, to rid ourselves of the craving for analysis altogether' (Price, 2003: 184).

But even if we turn our backs on the attempt to offer a metaphysical analysis of truth, Price argues that this leaves us with the task of explaining the role truth plays for us as members of linguistic communities. In his paper 'Truth as Convenient Friction', he stakes out his position by further engagement with Rorty. Price's position takes off from Rorty's claim that concern with truth makes no difference to our practices. He argues that the truth *does* make a difference, and he undertakes to explain what this difference might be.

In his paper, Price claims that conversation among members of a linguistic practice contains three identifiable and identifiably different norms. These he labels 'sincerity', 'justification' and 'truth'. The norm of sincerity is a matter of asserting that which one believes to be the case. The norm of justification goes further: it is the norm of asserting only that which one is warranted in so doing in the light of the reasons and evidence one possesses. The third is the norm of truth. This norm holds that, when one makes assertions, one is asserting what one believes to be correct, and therefore takes those who think differently to be mistaken. This norm is said to be necessary for us to be able to make sense of ourselves as participants in conversation, something which Price thinks Rorty is unable to account for: 'What is missing – what the third norm provides – is the automatic and quite unconscious sense of engagement in common purpose that distinguishes assertoric dialogue from a mere roll call of individual opinion' (Price, 2003: 169).

Rorty's claim, it will be recalled, is that although there is a difference between justification and truth, it is not a difference that makes a difference to our practices. Shifting attention from justification to truth does not lead to a difference in behaviour – in both cases, we seek to justify ourselves to each other by offering reasons and evidence, and by responding to objections that others might have. Price, in contrast, claims to have identified a behavioural difference. He asks us to imagine a community of speakers who, though they criticize each other for insincerity or for lacking sufficient ground for making their assertions, do not regard differences of opinion as indicating error. Price labels this community 'Mo'ans', after their form of speech, which is 'merely-opinionated assertion'. The problem with the Mo'ans is that in not thinking that differences in belief amount to error, they miss something that is important for understanding our practices of communication: 'what matters is that disagreement itself be treated as grounds for disapproval, as grounds for thinking that one's interlocutor has fallen short of some normative standards' (Price, 2003: 179).

The point that Price is leading up to is that without the norm of truth, in addition to the norms of sincerity and of justification, we have no way of explaining disagreement, and have no way of accounting for our desire to improve our beliefs and commitments in the light of it: 'It [the norm of truth] positively encourages such improvement, by motivating speakers who disagree to try to resolve their disagreement' (Price, 2003: 180). Rorty would agree that the disposition to criticize those with whom one disagrees is an essential part of the need to secure justification, but Price's point is that that disposition requires the norm of truth: 'Without truth, the wheels of argument do not engage; disagreements slide past one another' (Price, 2003: 185).

Price's insistence that truth is a norm, separate from the norm of justification, leads him to claim that his is a *realist* form of truth. By this he does not, of course, mean to associate himself with the kind of metaphysics that usually accompanies realism. He simply means that it resolutely resists reducing truth to justification. In all this, his remains a pragmatic understanding of truth because it shows how the norm of truth 'plays an essential role in a linguistic practice of great importance to us, as we currently are' (Price, 2003: 190).

The essay 'Truth as Convenient Friction' led to an exchange between Price and Rorty which helped to clarify their differences. As might be anticipated, Rorty responds by insisting that the norm of truth produces no behaviour different from that associated with the attempt to secure justification. Commenting on Price's paper, he raises two objections. The first is to deny that it is possible to separate different aspects of our behaviour into two distinct norms. He thinks the Mo'ans, a community whose members do not think that difference and disagreement points to error, are not a possibility. Belief is only possible in the context of communication, something which means that one could not adhere to Price's second norm without necessarily adhering to the third as well: 'One cannot justify by one's own lights if one does not know what it is to justify by the lights of others' (Rorty, 2010c: 255). This he thinks is a lesson of the work of pragmatists such as Davidson and Brandom, who argue that knowledge is only possible through the process of exchanging ideas and arguments about how far one is justified in holding the beliefs that one does. Second, Rorty goes on to question whether Price is accurate to describe the various tasks that we pursue with each other as expressing a single norm, the norm of truth. He writes that: 'the disagreement between Price and myself boils down to whether the practice of intersubjective justification is evidence of obedience to a big wholesale norm ("the norm of truth") or just to a recognition of the many concrete benefits resulting from social cooperation' (Rorty, 2010c: 255). We undertake different tasks with one another, but there is no single norm under which they might all be brought together.

Price demurs. He agrees with Rorty that the Mo'an community is an impossibility, but thinks that impossibility instructive, precisely because it demonstrates the inescapability of the third norm. The norm of truth is the only way in which we can account for disagreement, and, in the light of that disagreement, make sense of errors and of the idea that the purpose of inquiry is to correct them and thereby improve our practices. The norm of truth forces us evaluatively to rank our justifications not only because they fit with the evidence available to us individually but in terms of their truth. In turn, he agrees with Rorty that there are lots of different local uses of language employed in the course of pursuing our various goals, but holds that each of these local uses deploys the third norm:

> If I'm right, asserting, calling, describing, and denying are all activities that already embody the third norm – not in the sense that they depend on an ability to make it explicit, to describe oneself as 'seeking the Truth,' but simply in the sense that to do any of these things is to engage in a social practice, one key feature of which turns on the default normative status of disagreements. (Price, 2010b: 259)

As we saw above, Price presents a 'two-level picture of assertoric language'. He agrees completely with Rorty that different vocabularies serve different functions, but argues that they are all nevertheless united in their commitment to the norm of truth, the norm which he sees as central to the game of giving and asking for reasons.

Conclusion

One of the themes illustrated in this book is that pragmatism is a living tradition. The most interesting contemporary pragmatists are, in my view, those who are largely indifferent to the question of their fidelity to the classical writers and instead draw selectively on their ideas in order to take them forward. This is seen, for instance, in the way in which Rorty moves between the classical pragmatists and analytic philosophers, Bernstein's examination of pragmatism in the context of European traditions of thought, and the work of Price, who takes pragmatist ideas to be found in versions of Humean expressivism, quasi-realism and inferentialism. That these and other pragmatists have engaged with alternative traditions is surely a good thing. The fruits of doing so are an enriched pragmatism, one which has helped ensure that it remains a philosophy worthy of our attention today.

We have seen that pragmatists are united in acknowledging the importance of what Putnam calls 'the supremacy of the agent point of view' and Brandom 'the primacy of the practical'. Rorty sees in the primacy of the practical opportunities for re-description and self-creation, thinking that philosophy is of value when it is in service to this end. Brandom and Price are concerned to offer a pragmatist account of knowledge and communication, arguing that the game of giving and asking for reasons is central to our lives. And, in different ways, Haack, Putnam and Habermas address our cognitive relations to the world and our responsibility to get things right in relation to that world. It has been argued that these are very different commitments, and that pragmatists can in consequence be distinguished by which they take to be 'the most fundamental' (Talisse and Aikin, 2011: 4). However, I suggest that these elements hang together, and that none is more fundamental than any other. Offering re-descriptions of ourselves and others requires the conceptual resources provided by our shared practices (as Rorty acknowledges). Conversely, one of the reasons that the game of giving and asking for reasons is worth playing is that it provides us with the freedom and capacity to make *novel* moves in that game (as Brandom makes explicit). And pragmatists of all kinds are clear about the importance of getting things – rabbits, colours, triangles – right, recognizing that the only way to do so is to participate in conversation with each other, and, in so doing, possibly altering the focus of that conversation by introducing new candidates for belief and knowledge (evolution, feminism, human rights, etc.). All of this falls out of the seriousness with which pragmatists take our living practices.

In the Introduction, it was noted that critics of pragmatism fault it for its refusal to look beyond the contingencies of lived experience. Russell disparagingly wrote that pragmatism 'appeals to the temper of mind which finds on the surface of this planet the whole of its imaginative material' (Russell, 1910: 110). Russell's allusion to the *surface* of the planet hints at superficiality, and carries the implication that the proper task for philosophy is to dig through that surface in order to attain something deeper (in every sense) and more substantial. But this book has indicated that, by paying attention to the surface of the planet in all its richness, pragmatists are attentive to something that Russell and others miss. This is the 'imaginative material' offered by our practices, material which pragmatists argue provides a way of accounting for knowledge and for progress in inquiry by providing (in Putnam's term) *a middle way* between contestable metaphysical claims and an unthinking relativism.

Russell and others connect the narrowly philosophical problems they find in pragmatism (its supposed conflation of truth and practical success, etc.) to a larger concern, which is that it refuses to accord sufficient respect to the world beyond the point of view of situated, fallible, human beings. Against the pragmatists, Russell sets those, such as himself, 'who do not find Man an adequate object of their worship'. For them, 'the pragmatist's world will seem narrow and petty, robbing life of all that gives it value, and making Man himself smaller by depriving the universe which he contemplates of all its splendour' (Russell, 1910: 111). By combining his anxieties about the intellectual weaknesses of pragmatism with its supposed moral failings, Russell raises a form of objection that has been expressed by more recent critics. Thomas Nagel, for instance, shares Russell's animosity towards historically inclined philosophies such as pragmatism, writing that: 'To the extent that such no-nonsense theories have an effect, they merely threaten to impoverish the intellectual landscape for a while by inhibiting the serious expression of certain questions. In the name of liberation, these movements have offered us intellectual repression' (Nagel, 1986: 11). It should hopefully be clear, however, that pragmatists think of their philosophy as combining intellectual and moral concerns in a beneficial way. What Nagel sees as repression, pragmatists do indeed see as liberation, and for good reason. Inquiry is inescapably local and time-bound but, in accepting this, pragmatists do not think of themselves as robbing life of value or as diminishing humanity's role and status, but rather as enhancing these things precisely by viewing human beings as answerable to each other. The insistence on attending to the views of one's fellow inquirers, and the duty to examine and respond to the objections and suggestions that they put forward, are thought by pragmatists to reflect the splendour of the universe and our place within it. For pragmatists, our responsibilities are owed to each other, something which, if accepted, leads to a shift both in our self-understandings and in our relationship with the world. As Dewey remarks, 'William James was well within the bounds of moderation when he said that looking forward instead of backward, looking to what the world and life might become instead of to what they have been, is an alteration in the "seat of authority"' (Dewey, *LW* 4: 227).

Of the differences between philosophers, Nagel is close to the truth when he writes that 'here, as elsewhere, we are stuck with the clash of standpoints' (Nagel, 1986: 11). But it is perhaps better to speak, with James, of a clash of temperaments. Pragmatists remind us of the ways in which our practices contain errors and injustices, and draw upon those practices in order to offer re-descriptions with a view to making our lives and our world richer and freer, but deciding whether they succeed in doing so is left to the reader.

Works Cited

Adoulafia, Mitchell, Myra Bookman and Catherine Kemp (eds.) (2002) *Habermas and Pragmatism*. London: Routledge.

Bernstein, Richard J. (1966) *John Dewey*. Atascadero, Calif.: Ridgeview Publishing Co.

(1971) *Praxis and Action: Contemporary Philosophies of Human Activity*. Philadelphia: University of Pennsylvania Press.

(1976) *The Restructuring of Social and Political Theory*. Oxford: Basil Blackwell.

(1983) *Beyond Objectivism and Relativism: Science, Hermeneutics, and Praxis*. Philadelphia: University of Pennsylvania Press.

(1986) *Philosophical Profiles: Essays in a Pragmatic Mode*. Cambridge: Polity Press.

(1987) 'One Step Forward, Two Steps Backward: Richard Rorty on Liberal Democracy and Philosophy'. *Political Theory* (15.4): 538–63.

(1990) 'Rorty's Liberal Utopia'. *Social Research* (57.1): 31–72.

(1991) *The New Constellation: Ethical-Political Horizons of Modernity/Postmodernity*. Cambridge: Polity Press.

(1995) 'American Pragmatism: The Conflict of Narratives'. In Herman J. Saatkamp Jr (ed.) *Rorty and Pragmatism: The Philosopher Responds to His Critics*. London: Vanderbilt University Press.

(1998) 'Community in the Pragmatic Tradition'. In Morris Dickstein (ed.) *The Revival of Pragmatism: New Essays on Social Thought, Law, and Culture*. Durham, NC: Duke University Press.

(2005) *The Abuse of Evil*. Cambridge: Polity Press.

(2006a) 'The Pragmatic Century: The Corruption of Politics and Religion since 9/11'. In Sheila Greeve Davaney and Warren G. Frisina (eds.) *The Pragmatic Century: Conversations with Richard J. Bernstein*. Albany: State University of New York.

(2006b) 'Creative Democracy – The Task Still Before Us'. In Shelia Greeve Davaney and Warren G. Frisina (eds.) *The Pragmatic Century: Conversations with Richard J. Bernstein*. Albany: State University of New York.

(2010) *The Pragmatic Turn*. Cambridge: Polity Press.

Bradley, F. H. (1914) *Essays on Truth and Reality*. Oxford: Clarendon Press.

Brandom, Robert B. (1979) 'Freedom and Constraint by Norms'. *American Philosophical Quarterly* (16.3): 187–96.

(1994) *Making It Explicit: Reasoning, Representing, and Discursive Commitment*. Cambridge, Mass.: Harvard University Press.

(1997) 'Study Guide'. In Wilfrid Sellars, *Empiricism and the Philosophy of Mind*, ed. Robert B. Brandom. Cambridge, Mass.: Harvard University Press.

(2000a) 'Vocabularies of Pragmatism'. In Robert B. Brandom (ed.) *Rorty and His Critics*. Oxford: Blackwell.

(2000b) *Articulating Reasons: An Introduction to Inferentialism*. Cambridge, Mass.: Harvard University Press.

(2000c) 'Facts, Norms, and Normative Facts: A Reply to Habermas'. *European Journal of Philosophy* (8.3): 356–74.

(2002a) *Tales of the Mighty Dead: Historical Essays in the Metaphysics of Intentionality*. Cambridge, Mass.: Harvard University Press.

(2002b) 'Pragmatics and Pragmatisms'. In James Conant and Urszula M. Zeglan (eds.) *Hilary Putnam: Pragmatism and Realism*. London: Routledge.

(2004) 'The Pragmatist Enlightenment (and its Problematic Semantics)'. *European Journal of Philosophy* (12.1): 1–16.

(2009) *Reason in Philosophy: Animating Ideas*. London: The Belknap Press of Harvard University Press.

Davidson, Donald (1984) *Inquiries Into Truth and Interpretation*. Oxford: Clarendon Press.

(1990a) 'A Coherence Theory of Truth and Knowledge'. In Alan Malachowski (ed.) *Reading Rorty: Critical Responses to Philosophy and the Mirror of Nature (and Beyond)*. Oxford: Basil Blackwell. Also in Davidson, 2001.

(1990b) 'Afterthoughts'. In Alan Malachowski (ed.) *Reading Rorty: Critical Responses to Philosophy and the Mirror of Nature (and Beyond)*. Oxford: Basil Blackwell. Also in Davidson, 2001.

(1990c) 'The Structure and Content of Truth'. *Journal of Philosophy* (87.6): 279–328.

(2001) *Subjective, Intersubjective, Objective*. Oxford: Clarendon Press.

(2004) *Problems of Rationality*. Oxford: Clarendon Press.

(2005) *Truth, Language, and History*. Oxford: Clarendon Press.

Dewey, John (1969–90) *The Collected Works of John Dewey 1882–1953 (Early Works, Middle Works* and *Late Works)*. Carbondale: Southern Illinois University Press.

Dickstein, Morris (1998) 'Introduction'. In Morris Dickstein (ed.) *The Revival of Pragmatism: New Essays on Social Thought, Law, and Culture*. London: Duke University Press.

Haack, Susan (1993) *Evidence and Inquiry: Towards Reconstruction in Epistemology*. Oxford: Blackwell.

(1998) *Manifesto of a Passionate Moderate: Unfashionable Essays*. London: University of Chicago Press.

(2009) *Evidence and Inquiry: A Pragmatist Reconstruction of Epistemology*. Amherst: Prometheus Books.

Habermas, Jürgen (1986 [1981]) *The Theory of Communicative Action*, volume I: *Reason and the Rationalization of Society*, trans. Thomas McCarthy. Cambridge: Polity Press.

(1987 [1985]) *The Philosophical Discourse of Modernity: Twelve Lectures*, trans. Frederick Lawrence. Cambridge: Polity Press.

(1992 [1962]) *The Structural Transformation of the Public Sphere: An Inquiry into a Category of Bourgeois Society*, trans. Thomas Burger and Frederick Lawrence. Cambridge: Polity Press.

(1996 [1992]) *Between Facts and Norms: Contributions to a Discourse Theory of Law and Democracy*, trans. William Rehg. Cambridge: Polity Press.

(2000) 'Richard Rorty's Pragmatic Turn'. In Robert B. Brandom (ed.) *Rorty and His Critics*. Oxford: Blackwell.

(2001) 'Why Europe Needs a Constitution'. *New Left Review* (11): 5–26.

(2002) 'Postscript: Some Concluding Remarks'. In Adoulafia et al., 2002.

(2003 [1999]) *Truth and Justification*, trans. Barbara Fultner. Cambridge: Polity Press.

James, William (1977) *The Writings of William James: A Comprehensive Edition*, ed. John J. McDermott. London: University of Chicago Press.

Lewis, Clarence Irving (1929) *Mind and the World-Order: Outline of a Theory of Knowledge*. London: Charles Scribner's Sons.

Macarthur, David, and Huw Price (2007) 'Pragmatism and Quasi-realism'. In Cheryl Misak (ed.) *New Pragmatists*. Oxford: Clarendon Press. Also in Price, 2011.

Menand, Louis (2001) *The Metaphysical Club: A Story of Ideas in America*. London: HarperCollins.

Misak, Cheryl (2000) *Truth, Politics, Morality: Pragmatism and Deliberation*. London: Routledge.

(2004a) *Truth and the End of Inquiry: A Peircean Account of Truth*. Expanded paperback edition, Oxford: Oxford University Press.

(2004b) 'Making Disagreement Matter: Pragmatism and Deliberative Democracy'. *Journal of Speculative Philosophy* (18.1): 8–22.

(2007a) 'Introduction'. In Cheryl Misak (ed.) *New Pragmatists*. Oxford: Clarendon Press.

(2007b) 'Pragmatism and Deflationism'. In Cheryl Misak (ed.) *New Pragmatists*. Oxford: Clarendon Press.

(2010) 'Rorty's Place in the Pragmatist Pantheon'. In Randall E. Auxier and Lewis Edwin Hahn (eds.) *The Philosophy of Richard Rorty*. Chicago: Open Court.

Nagel, Thomas (1986) *The View From Nowhere*. Oxford: Oxford University Press.

Peirce, Charles Sanders (1958) *Collected Papers of Charles Sanders Peirce*, volumes 8, ed. Arthur Burks. Cambridge, Mass.: Harvard University Press.

(1992) *The Essential Peirce: Selected Philosophical Writings volume 1 (1867–1893)*, ed. Nathan Houser and Christian Kloesel. Bloomington and Indianapolis: Indiana University Press.

(1998) *The Essential Peirce: Selected Philosophical Writings volume 2 (1893–1913)*, ed. Nathan Houser and Christian Kloesel. Bloomington and Indianapolis: Indiana University Press.

Perry, Ralph Barton (1935) *The Thought and Character of William James: As Revealed in Unpublished Correspondence and Notes, Together with his Published Writings*, volume II: *Philosophy and Psychology*. Boston: Little, Brown, and Company.

Price, Huw (2003) 'Truth as Convenient Friction', *Journal of Philosophy* (100.4): 167–90. Also in Price, 2011.

(2004) 'Naturalism Without Representationalism'. In Mario De Caro and David Macarthur (eds.) *Naturalism in Question*. Cambridge, Mass.: Harvard University Press. Also in Price, 2011.

(2008) 'Two Readings of Representationalism', René Descartes Lectures, lecture 2. Available at: http://philsci-archive.pitt.edu/archive/00004430/

(2010a) 'One Cheer for Representationalism?' In Randall E. Auxier and Lewis Edwin Hahn (eds.) *The Philosophy of Richard Rorty*. Chicago: Open Court. Also in Price, 2011.

(2010b) 'Reply to Rorty's Further Remarks'. In Mario De Caro and David Macarthur (eds.) *Naturalism and Normativity*. New York: Columbia University Press.

(2011) *Naturalism Without Mirrors*. Oxford: Oxford University Press.

Putnam, Hilary (1981) *Reason, Truth, and History*. Cambridge: Cambridge University Press.

(1987) *The Many Faces of Realism*. LaSalle, Ill.: Open Court.

(1990) *Realism With a Human Face*. Cambridge, Mass.: Harvard University Press.

(1992) *Renewing Philosophy*. Cambridge, Mass.: Harvard University Press.

(1994) *Words and Life*. Cambridge, Mass.: Harvard University Press.

(1995) *Pragmatism: An Open Question*. Oxford: Blackwell.

(1998) 'Pragmatism and Realism'. In Morris Dickstein (ed.) *The Revival of Pragmatism: New Essays on Social Thought, Law, and Culture*. Durham, NC: Duke University Press.

(1999) *The Threefold Cord: Mind, Body and World*. New York: Columbia University Press.

(2000) 'Richard Rorty on Reality and Justification'. In Robert B. Brandom (ed.) *Rorty and His Critics*. Oxford: Blackwell.

(2002a) *The Collapse of the Fact/Value Dichotomy and Other Essays*. Cambridge, Mass.: Harvard University Press.

(2002b) 'Comment on Robert Brandom's paper'. In James Conant and Urszula M. Zeglan (eds.) *Hilary Putnam: Pragmatism and Realism*. London: Routledge.

(2004) *Ethics Without Ontology*. Cambridge, Mass.: Harvard University Press.

Quine, Willard Van Orman (1960) *Word and Object*. Cambridge, Mass.: MIT Press.

(1969) *Ontological Relativity and Other Essays*. London: Columbia University Press.

(1980 [1953]) *From a Logical Point of View: 9 Logico-philosophical Essays*. Second edition. Cambridge, Mass.: Harvard University Press.

(1981) 'The Pragmatists' Place in Empiricism'. In Robert J. Mulvaney and Philip M. Zeltner (eds.) *Pragmatism: Its Sources and Prospects*. Columbia, SC: University of South Carolina Press.

Ramberg, Bjørn (2000) 'Post-ontological Philosophy of Mind: Rorty versus Davidson'. In Robert B. Brandom (ed.) *Rorty and His Critics*. Oxford: Blackwell.

Rescher, Nicholas (2000) *Realistic Pragmatism: An Introduction to Pragmatic Philosophy*. Albany, NY: State University of New York Press.

Rorty, Richard (1979) *Philosophy and the Mirror of Nature*. Princeton: University of Princeton Press.

(1982) *Consequences of Pragmatism*. Minneapolis: University of Minnesota Press.

(1989) *Contingency, Irony, and Solidarity*. Cambridge: Cambridge University Press.

(1991) *Objectivity, Relativism, and Truth: Philosophical Papers Volume I*. Cambridge: Cambridge University Press.

(1995) 'Response to Susan Haack'. In Herman J. Saatkamp Jr. (ed.) *Rorty and Pragmatism: The Philosopher Responds to His Critics*. London: Vanderbilt University Press.

(1997a) *Truth, Politics and 'Post-modernism': The Spinoza Lectures*. Amsterdam: Van Gorcum.

(1997b) 'Introduction'. In Wilfrid Sellars, *Empiricism and the Philosophy of Mind*, ed. Robert B. Brandom. Cambridge, Mass.: Harvard University Press.

(1998) *Truth and Progress: Philosophical Papers Volume III*. Cambridge: Cambridge University Press.

(1999) *Philosophy and Social Hope*. Harmondsworth: Penguin.

(2000) 'Reply to Ramberg'. In Robert B. Brandom (ed.) *Rorty and His Critics*. Oxford: Blackwell.

(2007) *Philosophy as Cultural Politics: Philosophical Papers Volume IV*. Cambridge: Cambridge University Press.

(2010a) 'Reply to Cheryl Misak'. In Randall E. Auxier and Lewis Edwin Hahn (eds.) *The Philosophy of Richard Rorty*. Chicago: Open Court.

(2010b) 'Reply to Huw Price'. In Randall E. Auxier and Lewis Edwin Hahn (eds.) *The Philosophy of Richard Rorty*. Chicago: Open Court.

(2010c) 'Further Remarks'. In Mario De Caro and David Macarthur (eds.) *Naturalism and Normativity*. New York: Columbia University Press.

Russell, Bertrand (1910) *Philosophical Essays*. London: Longmans, Green, and Co.

(1991) *History of Western Philosophy*. London: Routledge.

Scharp, Kevin and Robert B. Brandom (2007) 'Editors' Introduction'. In Kevin Scharp and Robert B. Brandom (eds.) *In The Space of Reasons: Selected Essays of Wilfrid Sellars*. Cambridge, Mass.: Harvard University Press.

Sellars, Wilfrid (1963) 'Philosophy and the Scientific Image of Man'. In Wilfrid Sellars, *Science, Perception and Reality*. New York: Routledge & Kegan Paul.

(1997) *Empiricism and the Philosophy of Mind*, ed. Robert B. Brandom. Cambridge, Mass.: Harvard University Press.

(2007) 'Some Reflections of Language Games'. In Kevin Scharp and Robert B. Brandom (eds.) *In The Space of Reasons: Selected Essays of Wilfrid Sellars*. Cambridge, Mass.: Harvard University Press.

Stout, Jeffrey (2004) *Democracy and Tradition*. Oxford: Princeton University Press.

(2007) 'On Our Interest in Getting Things Right'. In Cheryl Misak (ed.) *New Pragmatists*. Oxford: Clarendon Press.

Talisse, Robert B. (2007) *A Pragmatist Philosophy of Democracy*. London: Routledge.

Talisse, Robert B., and Scott F. Aikin (2008) *Pragmatism: A Guide for the Perplexed*. London: Continuum.

(2011) *The Pragmatism Reader: From Peirce Through the Present*. Princeton: Princeton University Press.

Westbrook, Robert B. (1999) *John Dewey and American Democracy*. London: Cornell University Press.

(2005) *Democratic Hope: Pragmatism and the Politics of Truth*. London: Cornell University Press.

Williams, Michael (2009) 'Introduction to the Thirtieth-Anniversary Edition'. In Richard Rorty, *Philosophy and the Mirror of Nature, Thirtieth-Anniversary Edition*. Princeton: Princeton University Press.

Index

Adorno, Theodore 123, 124,
        126
Aikin, Scott F. 200
American Civil Liberties Union
        59
American Civil War 3, 122
analytic philosophy 7–9
    and Bernstein 135, 136, 139,
        141
    and Brandom 176
    and Price 189, 192
    and Rorty 105
analytic–synthetic distinction
    in Kant 94, 95
    Quine on 64–6, 66–7, 81
    Rorty on 96
ancient Greece
    and the European
        Enlightenment 119–20
anti-representationalism
    Price on 185, 188, 192, 193
    Rorty on 96–9, 100–1, 103,
        179
a priori method of fixing belief
        22–3
Arendt, Hannah 144
Aristotle 2, 16, 57, 93
    on truth 151

authoritarianism
    anti-authoritarianism and the
        Enlightenment 103–4,
        119–20
    and reflective transcendence
        119
authority method of fixing belief
        22

Bain, Alexander 21
behaviouristic semantics, Quine
        on 69–70
belief
    and Brandom's normative
        pragmatics 177
    Davidson on truth as justified
        belief 89–90
    in Dewey 46, 49
    Haack on
        standards of evidence for
            147–50
        truth and 151–2
    and inferentialism 179–80
    James on
        morality and 38–9
        and the pragmatic maxim
            28–9, 30–3
        truth and 34–5, 163

Misak on truth and 162,
163–4, 165–6, 168–9
Peirce and fixing belief through
inquiry 20, 21–4
Quine on 65–6, 68
Rorty on justification of belief
102–3
Bentham, Jeremy 39
Berkeley (University of California)
James' lecture and introduction
of the term 'pragmatism'
1, 2, 36
Berlin, Isaiah 105, 142
Bernstein, Richard 2, 8, 12,
135–46, 199
The Abuse of Evil 144, 145
*Beyond Objectivism
and Relativism* 136, 139,
140
on Cartesian Anxiety 135–8,
145
on democracy 142–3
and Dewey 135, 140, 141,
142–3, 145
and Gadamer 139–40, 141
and Habermas 140–1, 142
John Dewey 135
and Misak 163–4, 169
on morality 144–6
*Philosophical Profiles:
Essays in a Pragmatic
Mode* 139
on pluralism 137–8
and political questions
13–14
The Pragmatic Turn 135, 138
Praxis and Action 135–6
*Radical Evil: A Philosophical
Interrogation* 144
*The Restructuring of Social and
Political Theory* 140
and Rorty 137, 138–9, 142,
144
'Bifurcation Thesis' and
expressivism 190
Blackburn, Simon 189
Bradley, F. H. 5

Brandom, Robert B. 10, 13, 48,
171–84, 199, 200
on expressive freedom and
normative constraint
182–4
on I-thou/I-we relations 181–2
Making It Explicit 176, 177
and normative pragmatics
175–9
on objectivity 179–82
and Price 185, 190–1, 192–4,
197
and rationalist pragmatism
171, 172–5
and Rorty 171, 172, 179, 180,
182, 183
and Sellars 72, 73, 117, 172
buried secrets, Peirce on 24, 151
Bush, George W. 145

cable metaphor *see* cord/rope
metaphor
Cambridge, Massachusetts
Metaphysical Club 2–3, 6
Carnap, Rudolf 8, 9
and Putnam 113–14, 117
and Quine 63, 66–7, 68
Cartesianism *see* Descartes, René
/ Cartesianism
Christianity
doctrine of transubstantiation
26, 27–8
Judeo-Christian moral
framework 130
and science 93
classical pragmatism 2–9, 199
and Bernstein 135, 139
and Brandom 171, 172–3,
174–5, 178, 183
and Davidson 89, 90
and the eclipse narrative viii, 7,
8–9
and Haack 148, 152–3, 155
and Habermas 125
and logical positivism 63
and the natural sciences 4–5,
6–7

classical pragmatism (cont.)
and the pragmatic maxim vii,
3–4
and Price 184–5, 195
and Putnam 108, 115, 119
and Quine 66
and Rorty 96, 99
and Sellars 72, 74–5
Clifford, W. K.
'The Ethics of Belief' 30–1,
32–3
coherence theory of truth 33, 34,
83, 89, 91, 195
Cold War 7
communicative rationality
in Habermas 125, 126–7, 134
communities of inquiry
Misak on 164
Peirce and fixing belief through
inquiry 20, 23
philosophers and scientific
inquiry 55
Putnam on 108, 120–1
Rorty on 100–1, 102
concept acquisition/formation
in Davidson's three varieties of
knowledge 85–6
in Sellars 74–7
consciousness
Habermas and the philosophy
of 124–5
constitutional patriotism in
Habermas 134
Continental philosophy
and Bernstein 135, 136, 141,
199
and Haack 148
and Rorty 105
Copernicus, Nicolaus 48
cord/rope metaphor
in Peirce 20–1, 150
in Quine 66
correspondence theory of truth
24, 34, 92
and Davidson 83–4, 89, 91
and Dewey 55
and James 33

and Misak 163, 169
and Putnam 108
and Price 195
and Rorty 101–2
critical theory 123, 135
cruelty, Rorty on 106, 107
cultural politics 103, 118
culture
scientific culture and
pragmatism 4–5

Darwin, Charles 4, 13, 115
On The Origin of Species 48–9
Rorty on representationalism
and 97–8
Davidson, Donald 9, 80–91
and Bernstein 140
and Brandom 172
'A Coherence Theory of Truth
and Knowledge' 86–7, 91
on conceptual relativism 81–2,
83–4
Haack's critique of 149
*Inquiries Into Truth and
Interpretation* 88
'The Myth of the Subjective'
84–5
'On the Very Idea of a
Conceptual Scheme' 81–2,
84
and Peirce 88, 90, 91
and pragmatism as relativism
88–9
and Price 197
on the principle of charity 86–7
and Quine 80–1, 82, 86
and Rorty 81, 92, 95–6, 98,
99, 102
and scepticism 84–5, 87–8, 91
on the scheme–content
distinction 81–4, 87
'The Structure and Content of
Truth' 89
on three varieties of knowledge
85–8
on triangulation 98, 100
on truth 86–7, 89–91

deconstruction 135
deliberative democracy
  and Dewey 143
  and Habermas 133–5
  and Misak 159, 166–8
democracy
  Bernstein on 142–3
  critics of 168, 169
  and Dewey 58–62, 105–6,
    106–7, 133, 142–3, 165
  and Habermas 14, 132–5,
    168
  and liberalism 13–14, 59–61,
    142
  Misak on 165–8
  and Peirce 14, 165, 166
  and pragmatic fallibilism 146
  Putnam on the Enlightenment
    and 120–1
  and Rorty 105–7, 166–7
  and scientific inquiry 55
deontic scorekeeping (Brandom)
  176–7
Descartes, René / Cartesianism 3,
  9, 13
  and Bernstein 135–8, 145, 165
  and Brandom 171
  and Davidson 83, 84–5, 87
  and Dewey 135
  and empiricism 36, 37, 52, 72
  and Peirce 3, 15–21, 24–5,
    32–3, 36, 76, 135
  and Quine's naturalism 67, 84
  and Rorty 93, 95, 96, 98, 135,
    138–9
  and self-knowledge 85
  and Sellars' Myth of Jones
    75–6
  and warranted assertibility
    53–4
Dewey, John 7, 9, 43, 44–62, 63,
  201
  and Bernstein 135, 140, 141,
    142–3, 145
  and Brandom 171, 172, 183,
    184
  and classical pragmatism 7

'Creative Democracy – The
  Task Before Us' 61
  and Darwin 48–9
  and Davidson 90
  on democracy 58–62, 105–6,
    106–7, 121, 133, 142–3,
    165
'Does Reality Possess Practical
  Character?' 5–6
  and the eclipse narrative 7, 12
  on experience 44, 50–3
Experience and Nature 50
'experimentalist' philosophy
  49–50, 55
  and Haack 154
  and Habermas 122, 130, 132
  and Hegelianism 44, 48, 60
  on human growth 58
  on liberalism 59–61
Logic: The Theory of Inquiry
  50, 53, 56
  on the meaning of pragmatism
  2
  on morality 45, 49–50, 56–8
  and the natural sciences 5, 10
  and Peirce 44, 49, 50, 53, 54, 61
  on philosophy as the quest for
    certainty 44–7
  and Price 187, 189, 190, 192
The Public and Its Problems
  61, 142
  and Putnam 109, 121
The Quest for Certainty 45,
  47, 50
  and Quine 67
  on reconstructing philosophy
    47–50
Reconstruction in Philosophy
  45, 47, 50
  and Rorty 92, 96, 99, 105–6,
    108, 109, 139, 142
  on truth 44, 55–6
  on warranted assertibility
    53–6, 90
'What Pragmatism Means by
  Practical' (review of James'
  Pragmatism) 7

Dialectic of Enlightenment
(Horkheimer and Adorno)
123
dialogical rationality 141–2
direct realism 111
discourse ethics 131, 132
doubt
Dewey on 54
Peirce on 19–20, 21–2
Duhem, Pierre 65

Eastern Europe
totalitarian states in 60
eclipse narrative (Talisse) viii, 7,
8–9, 12
empiricism
British empiricists 50, 51, 52,
93
Davidson's third dogma of
81–5
Dewey on 45–6, 50–3
and individualism 59
James on 28–9, 30, 35–7, 38,
51–2
Quine's two dogmas of 9, 63,
64–5, 66–7, 81
and Sellars' Myth of the Given
72–3
see also logical positivism
(logical empiricism)
the Enlightenment 59
Brandom and Enlightenment
epistemology 177
Dewey on 59
Habermas on 123, 124,
131
and negative liberty 184
Putnam on 118, 119–21
Rorty on 103–5
epistemological behaviorism 96
epistemology *see* knowledge
ethnocentrism, Rorty on 101,
138, 168
European Union 134–5
evil
Bernstein on 144–5, 146

experience
Dewey's re-description of 44,
50–3
James' re-description of 36–7
'experimentalist' philosophy in
Dewey 49–50, 55
explication project in Haack
148–50
expressivism, Humean 189–91,
192–3, 199

fact/value dichotomy
Putnam on 111–15, 116–17
fake reasoning
Haack on 153–4
fallibilism
and anti-scepticism 6, 19–21,
125
and Bernstein 137–8, 140,
145–6
and Haack 151
and Habermas 125
and Misak 162, 164
in Peirce 19–21, 170
and Quine 66
and Rorty 101
false consciousness
and Habermas 126
Feyerabend, Paul 99
forced options, James on belief
and 31–2
Foucault, Michel 174
foundationalism viii, 9, 16–17
and Bernstein 136, 138
and Davidson 83
and Dewey 53–4, 56
and Haack 141, 148–9, 150,
151, 155–6
and Quine 67, 68
and Peirce 3, 19, 20
and Rorty 93–6, 100, 104
and Sellars 72, 75, 77
foundherentism (Haack) 150,
151–2, 157
franchise reform 3
Frankfurt School 11, 122–3

freedom 200
  Brandom on expressive 182–4
  Dewey on 59–60
  Habermas on 123–4, 133
  negative liberty 105, 184
  Putnam on 118, 119–20
  and restraint 13
  Rorty on 103, 105–6
free will, Peirce on 160
Frege, Gottlob 94
Freud, Sigmund 144

Gadamer, Hans-Georg 139–40,
    141
Galileo 48–9
genuine options, James on belief
    and 31–2
Gibbard, Allan 189
global expressivism
  Price on pragmatism as
    188–92
Greece *see* ancient Greece
Green, T. H. 184

Haack, Susan 10, 12, 13,
    147–59, 199
  and classical pragmatists 148,
    152–3, 155
  and Davidson 149
  double-aspect theory
    (foundherentism) 150,
    151–2
  Evidence and Inquiry 147–50,
    155–7, 158–9
  explication project 148–50
  and foundationalism 148–9,
    155–6
  and Misak 159
  and 'New Cynics' 154–5, 158
  and 'Old Deferentialists' 154
  and Peirce 151, 152, 154
  and Quine 148
  ratification project 148, 151–2,
    157
  reconstruction of epistemology
    147–50

  and Rorty 149, 153, 155–9
  on warrant and acceptance
    158–9
Habermas, Jürgen 10, 122–35,
    199
  and Bernstein 140–1, 142
  Between Facts and Norms 130,
    132–3
  and Brandom 183
  and communicative rationality
    125, 126–7, 134
  on constitutional patriotism
    134
  and democracy 14, 132–5, 168
  and Dewey 122, 130, 132
  and discourse ethics 131, 132
  and the Frankfurt School
    122–3
  Habermas and Pragmatism
    125
  and the ideal speech situation
    129
  *Knowledge and Human
    Interests* 125
  on liberalism 133
  and Misak 129, 168–9
  on morality 129–32
  and Peirce 122
  and performative self-
    contradiction 127, 128
  *The Philosophical Discourse of
    Modernity* 130
  and the philosophy of the
    subject / of consciousness
    124–5
  on republicanism 133
  and Rorty 128, 129, 130
  *The Structural Transformation
    of the Public Sphere*
    123–4, 132
  *The Theory of Communicative
    Action* 127
  and transcendental pragmatism
    11, 125–7, 129, 140–1,
    168–9
  on truth 125, 127–9

Hegel, G. W. F. 4
  and Bernstein 144
  and Brandom 171, 175, 180,
    183, 184
  and Dewey 44, 48, 53, 60
Heidegger, Martin 92, 172
the Holocaust 122
Horkheimer, Max 122–3, 124,
  126
Hume, David 2, 36, 37
  and Brandom 183
  and Davidson 81
  Humean expressivism 189–91,
    192–3, 199
  and Price 184, 189–91,
    192–3
  and Sellars 72, 74, 75

idealism, Price on 191–2
ideal speech situation
  in Habermas 129
individual–society relations
    13–14, 59–60, 184
  and the European
    Enlightenment 120–1
inferentialism 179–80, 199
  and the correspondence
    assumption (Price) 195
  and global expressivism
    190–1
inferential nature of knowledge,
    Peirce on 19
inferential semantics
  Brandom on 176–8
instrumental norms
  Brandom and the
    classical pragmatists
    172–3
instrumental rationality
  Habermas on 123, 126–7
intellectualism
  Brandom on 178
  James on 33, 34
intentionality, Sellars on
    personhood and 80
internal realism 109–10
ironism 106

James, William 7, 9, 26–40, 63,
    201
  and Bernstein 137, 144
  and Brandom 171, 172, 178
  and Cartesianism 36
  and Davidson 90
  and empiricism 28–9, 30,
    35–7, 38, 51–2
  Essays in Radical Empiricism 27
  and Habermas 128
  The Meaning of Truth 27
  on the moral life 37–9
  'The Moral Philosopher and
    the Moral Life' 38–9
  and new pragmatism 12–13
  'On a Certain Blindness in
    Human Beings' 38
  and the origins of pragmatism
    1, 2
  and Peirce 15, 26, 34, 40, 43
  'Philosophical Conceptions and
    Practical Results' 26
  on pluralism 37–9, 105
  and the pragmatic maxim vii,
    6, 25, 27–30, 42, 158
  *Pragmatism: A New Name For
    Some Old Ways of
    Thinking* 2, 5, 7, 27, 28,
    33, 37, 40
  and Price 186–7, 187
  Principles of Psychology 26
  and Putnam 110–11, 115, 117,
    119
  and Quine 35, 69
  and radical empiricism 35–7
  and Rorty 35, 96, 108, 159
  theory of truth 33–5, 35–6
  'What Pragmatism Means' 27,
    100
  'The Will to Believe' 27, 30–3
Judeo-Christian moral framework
    130
justification
  Haack's theory of epistemic
    149–50, 151, 155–9
  justification norm in Price
    196–7

and truth
  Davidson on 89–90
  Habermas on 128–9
  Rorty on 102–3, 128–9
  see also foundationalism

Kant, Immanuel 36
  and Bernstein 136, 144
  and Brandom 171, 172, 175,
    176, 180, 183, 192
  and Davidson 81
  and Dewey 48
  and empiricism 51
  and Habermas 125, 130–1
  and Rorty 93–4, 95, 107
  and Sellars 72
Kepler, Johannes 48
knowledge viii, 1
  and classical pragmatism 8–9
  Davidson on 83, 85–8
  Dewey on 50–3, 54, 121
  Haack's reconstruction of
    epistemology 147–50
  Habermas on 125
  James on 36–7
  Kant on 93–4
  Peirce on Cartesianism and 3,
    16–19, 20–1, 76
  Quine on
    naturalized epistemology
      67–9
    as a web of belief 65–6
  Sellars on
    manifest and scientific images
      78–80
    Myth of the Given 72,
      73–5
    Myth of Jones 76–7
  spectator theory of 52–3
Kuhn, Thomas 81–2
  The Structure of Scientific
    Revolutions 99

language
  Brandom on 174, 183–4
  and conceptual schemes 82
  and Habermas on morality 131

Price on 185–8, 189, 191, 192,
    194–5
  and representationalism 179
  Rorty on 97–9
  and Sellars' psychological
    nominalism 73–5
laws, Habermas on the
  nature and legitimacy of
    132–3
Lewis, C. I. 8–9
  and Davidson 82–3
  and Haack 149
  and Quine 66–7, 68
liberalism
  Bernstein on 142
  and democracy 13–14, 59–61,
    133
  Dewey on 59–61
  and the Enlightenment 120
  Habermas on 133
  Misak on 166–7
  negative liberty 105, 184
  and pluralism 37–8, 130
  Rorty on 105–7, 129, 142
Lippmann, Walter 62, 143
  Public Opinion 61
local expressivism 190
Locke, John 2, 59
  and Rorty 93, 94, 95
  and Sellars 74, 75
logical inference 177–8
logical positivism (logical
    empiricism) 8, 9
  and hypotheses 160
  and the pragmatic maxim 27
  and Quine 63–4, 65, 66, 116

Macarthur, David 185
manifest image of personhood
    78–9, 80
Marx, Karl 124, 184
material inference, Brandom on
    177–8
materialism, Dewey on 58
meaning of pragmatism 1–2
means–ends continuum (Dewey)
    53

medieval Scholasticism
   and Cartesianism 15–17
meliorism, James on 39
Menand, Louis 7, 122
*The Metaphysical Club: A
   Story of Ideas in America*
   2–3
Metaphysical Club 2–3, 6
metaphysical quietism
   in Price 185, 188–9, 193
metaphysical realism
   and Bernstein 136
   and Putnam 108–11, 114–15,
      117–18
metaphysics 7
   Dewey on 46
   and new pragmatism 11, 12
   and the pragmatic maxim 26,
      29–30
Mill, John Stuart 39, 105, 107,
   142
the mind
   and Cartesianism 16–17
Misak, Cheryl viii, 10, 11,
   159–70
   and Bernstein 163–4, 169
   on democracy 14
   and Haack 159
   and Habermas 129, 168–9
   and 'moderate pragmatism'
      168–70
   and Peirce's account of truth
      99, 159–65, 170
   and Rorty 164, 169–70
   Truth, Politics, Morality 163,
      165–8
   Truth and the End of Inquiry
      159–60, 163, 164, 165,
      166, 168
   on truth in politics and
      morality 164–8
modernity
   and Habermas 123, 130
morality
   and analytic philosophy 8
   Bernstein on 144–6
   and Dewey 45, 49–50, 56–8

and expressivism 189
and the fact/value dichotomy
   113
Habermas on 129–32
and Humean expressivism 189
James on pluralism and the
   moral life 37–9
and metaphysical quietism 185
Misak on 160, 164–8
Peirce on 41
and pluralism 188
Murdoch, Iris
   The Sovereignty of Good 113
Mussolini, Benito 117
Myth of the Given 72–5, 77, 83,
   173, 177
Myth of Jones 75–7

Nagel, Thomas 201
naturalism
   in Dewey 58
   in James 29
   in Price 186–7, 193
   in Quine 66–9, 71, 148
   in Rorty 97–8
naturalized epistemology
   in Quine 67–9, 84
natural sciences
   and analytic philosophy 8
   and classical pragmatism 4–5,
      6–7
   cognitive science 148
   Dewey on 46–7, 48–9
      and democracy 61–2
      the 'method of science' 54–5
      and morality 56–7
   and the Enlightenment 104,
      119
   and epistemology 148
   Haack on 154–5
   James on 28, 29
   and logical positivism 63–4,
      112
   Misak on truth and 161–2
   and new pragmatists 10
   Peirce on 6–7, 10, 23–4, 26,
      40–1, 55

Price on 186–7, 188
Putnam on 114–15, 115–18
Quine on 9
and religion 10, 46
Rorty on 10, 92–3, 97–8, 99,
    104
Nazi Germany 7, 113, 117, 122
new pragmatism 9–14
New Pragmatists (ed. Misak)
    vii–viii, 11
Nietzsche, Friedrich 106, 174
nihilism 136–7
nominalism
    and Peirce 42
    psychological nominalism in
        Sellars 72, 73–5
normative constraint
    and expressive freedom 182–4
novelists, Rorty on 105, 107

objectivity
    Brandom on the structural
        conditions of 179–82
    and new pragmatism 11, 12
    Putnam on 117–18
    Rorty on 99–101
object naturalism 187, 193
ontological relativity in Quine
    70–1, 107–8

participatory democracy 105–6
Peirce, Charles Sanders vii,
    15–26, 40–3, 63
    and Bernstein 135, 137, 145
    and Brandom 171, 172, 183
    on Cartesianism 3, 7, 15–21,
        24–5, 32–3, 36, 76, 135
    and classical pragmatism 3–4,
        7
    and Davidson 88, 90, 91
    and democracy 14, 165, 166
    and Dewey 44, 49, 50, 53, 54,
        61
    'The Fixation of Belief' 21–3,
        25, 42
    and Haack 151, 152, 154
    and Habermas 122

'How to Make Our Ideas
    Clear' 1–2, 23–4, 24–6, 40
    and James' theory of truth 34,
        35, 36
    and logical positivists 64
    Misak on truth and 99,
        159–65, 170
    and new pragmatism 9, 12, 13
    and nominalism 42
    and the origins of pragmatism
        1–2, 2–3, 40
    and the pragmatic maxim vii,
        3–4, 24–6, 27, 30, 43,
        158, 160
    and Price 186
    and Putnam 112
    'Questions Concerning Certain
        Faculties Claimed for Man'
        17–19
    and Quine 67, 69, 71
    restatement of pragmatism
        40–3
    and Rorty 96, 99, 101, 108
    and scholastic realism 42
    and scientific inquiry 6–7, 10,
        23–4, 26, 40–1, 55
    and Sellars 72
    'Some Consequences of Four
        Incapacities' 19–21
    on truth 24, 56, 90, 102, 151,
        170
    'What Pragmatism Is' 41–2
performative self-contradiction
    in Habermas 127, 128, 168
Perry, Ralph Barton vii
personhood, Sellars' framework
    of 78–80
philosophical anthropology 193
Plato 93, 120
    and Dewey 46, 52
pluralism
    Bernstein on 137–8
    Habermas on 130
    James on 37–9, 105
    Misak on 167
    Price on 187–8, 191
    Rorty on 105

political life
  and analytical philosophy 8
  Bernstein on politics, religion
    and morality 145–6
  Brandom on 184
  Misak on truth in 164–8
  and new pragmatism 13–14
  role of pragmatism in 1, 6–7
  and Rorty 105–7, 139
  see also democracy
positivism
  and the fact/value dichotomy
    112
  see also logical positivism
    (logical empiricism)
pragmatic fallibilism 145–6
the pragmatic maxim vii, 3–4, 6
  in James vii, 6, 25, 27–30, 42,
    158
  in Peirce vii, 3–4, 24–6, 27, 30,
    43, 158, 160
Price, Huw 10, 184–98, 199
  on assertoric language 191,
    198
  and Brandom 185, 190–1,
    192–4, 197
  on external representation
    194–5
  on horizontal pluralism
    187–8
  on internal representation 194
  on linguistic priority without
    representationalism 185–8
  on metaphysical quietism 185,
    188–9, 193
  and Misak 164
  on naturalism 186–7, 193–4
  on pluralism 187–8, 191
  and pragmatism as global
    expressivism 188–92
  on representationalism 186,
    187, 189, 192, 194–5
  and Rorty 185, 189, 190, 191,
    192, 194, 195–8
  on truth 185, 186, 195–8
  'Truth as Convenient Friction'
    195–7

and use-explanatory quietism
    189, 193
  on vertical pluralism 188, 191
Protestant Reformation 29, 119
psychological nominalism
  in Sellars 72, 73–5, 77, 78
public sphere
  in Habermas 123–4, 134
Putnam, Hilary 6, 10, 61,
    107–21, 186, 199
  and Brandom 172, 174–5
  *The Collapse of the Fact/Value
    Dichotomy* 112
  on the Enlightenment 118,
    119–21
  on the fact/value dichotomy
    111–15, 116–17
  on the 'God's-eye view' 108,
    110, 114, 115
  and Habermas 132
  on metaphysical realism
    108–11, 114–15
  and new pragmatism 10, 12,
    13
  and political questions 13–14
  'Pragmatism and Realism' 110
  'A Reconsideration of Deweyan
    Democracy' 121
  on reflective transcendence
    119, 121
  on scientism and relativism
    115–18
  *The Threefold Cord: Mind,
    Body, and World* 109, 111

quasi-realism 189–90, 199
Quine, W. V. O. 63–71
  and behaviouristic semantics
    69–70
  and Bernstein 137
  and Brandom 172
  and Carnap 63, 66–7, 68
  and Davidson 80–1, 82, 86
  and Haack 148
  on James' theory of truth 35
  and logical positivism 63–4,
    65, 66, 116

and naturalism 66–9, 71, 84, 148
on ontological relativity 70–1
and Peirce 67, 69, 71
and pluralism 187–8
'The Pragmatists' Place in Empiricism' 69
and Putnam 112, 115–16
the Quine–Duhem thesis 65
and Rorty 92, 95–6, 97, 100
on truth 64–5, 66–7, 71, 81, 90
'Two Dogmas of Empiricism' 9, 63, 64–5, 66–7, 81
Word and Object 69–70

radical empiricism
James on pragmatism and 35–7
radical scepticism
and Cartesianism 16
Davidson on 87–8
Ramberg, Bjørn 98
ratification project in Haack 148, 151–2, 157
rationalism
James on 28–9, 30, 36, 38
and practical activity 41
rationalist pragmatism
in Brandom 171, 172–5
Rawls, John 166–7
realism
direct 111
internal 109–10
quasi-realism 189–90, 199
see also metaphysical realism
reductionism, Quine's concept of 65, 81
Reichenbach, Hans 8, 63, 113, 117
relativism vii, 12, 200
and Bernstein 136–7, 139
and Haack 148
and Habermas 123, 126
and Putnam 115–18
and Rorty 101

religion 6
Bernstein on morality and 144–5
Christian doctrine of transubstantiation 26, 27–8
Dewey on 45, 46–7, 187
James on 28–9, 30, 31, 32, 34, 51
and morality 130, 132
and natural science 10
and the rise of liberalism 37–8
Rorty on the Enlightenment and 104
representationalism
Brandom on 175, 177, 178–9, 179–80
James on empiricism and 37
and pluralism 188
Price on 186, 187, 189, 192, 194–5
Putnam on 110–11
see also anti-representationalism
republicanism, Habermas on 133
Rescher, Nicholas 12–13
rights
individual rights and liberalism 60–1
Rorty on 106–7
Romanticism 104–5, 174
Rorty, Mary Varney 138
Rorty, Richard 10–11, 12, 13, 92–107, 199
on anti-representationalism 96–9, 100–1, 103
and Bernstein 137, 138–9, 142, 144
and the 'Bifurcation Thesis' 190
and Brandom 171, 172, 179, 180, 182, 183
and Cartesianism 93, 95, 96, 98, 135, 138–9
Consequences of Pragmatism 102

Rorty, Richard (cont.)
  *Contingency, Irony and
    Solidarity* 105
  and cultural politics 103, 118
  and Davidson 81
  and democracy 105–7, 166–7
  and Dewey 92, 96, 99, 105–6,
    108, 109, 139, 142
  'Dewey's Metaphysics' 99
  and epistemological
    behaviorism 96
  on ethnocentrism 101, 138,
    168
  and Haack 153, 155–9
  and Habermas 128, 129, 130
  on ironism and liberalism
    105–7
  and James 35, 96, 108, 159
  and Kant 93–4, 95
  and Misak 164, 169–70
  on objectivity 99–101
  *Philosophy and the Mirror of
    Nature* viii, 7, 8, 92, 93,
    95, 96, 100, 102, 105, 138
  and Price 185, 189, 190, 191,
    192, 194, 195–8
  and Putnam 108, 111, 116–18
  on relativism 101
  and romantic polytheism 105
  and Sellars 72, 92, 95–6, 99,
    100, 157
  on truth 90, 101–3, 128, 129,
    169–70
Russell, Bertrand 5, 35, 55–6, 94,
    163, 200–1

Santayana, George 52
scepticism
  Davidson on 84–5, 87–8, 91
  and empiricism 36, 37, 51
  fallibilistic anti-scepticism 6,
    19–21, 125
  Misak on 164, 169–70
  Peirce on 16, 19–21, 20, 25
  Price on 186
  Putnam on ethics and 118
  Rorty on 93

Scharp, Kevin 72
scheme–content distinction
  Davidson on 81–4, 87
  in Kant 94
  and Rorty 96
Schmitt, Carl 168, 169
scholastic realism
  in Peirce 42
Scholastics
  and Cartesianism 15–17
science *see* natural sciences
scientific image of personhood
  (Sellars) 78–9, 80
scientism
  Haack on 147–48
  Habermas on 123
  Price on 187
  Putnam on 115–18
self-consciousness
  Peirce on Cartesianism and
    17–18
Sellars, Wilfrid 71–80, 85
  and Bernstein 137, 145
  and Brandom 72, 73, 117,
    172, 173
  and Davidson 88
  'Empiricism and the Philosophy
    of Mind' 9, 12, 72–4, 77–8
  Myth of the Given 72–5, 77,
    83, 177
  Myth of Jones 75–7
  'Philosophy and the Scientific
    Image of Man' 78–80
  and Price 192
  and psychological nominalism
    72, 73–5, 77, 78
  and Rorty 72, 92, 95–6, 99,
    100, 157
  'Some Reflections on Language
    Games' 74–5
semantic pragmatism in Brandom
    175–6
semantics 6
  behaviouristic 69–70
  Price on linguistic priority
    186
Shklar, Judith 106

social contract theory 10, 59–60
  and the Enlightenment 120
Socrates 2
Spencer, Herbert 49
Stout, Jeffrey
  on objectivity 181
  'On Our Interest in Getting
    Things Right' 11
subject naturalism 187, 188,
    193–4
subject–object dualism
  and Dewey on experience 50,
    51–2
  and Habermas on the
    philosophy of
    consciousness 124–5
  and Putnam 111

Talisse, Robert B. viii, 7, 200
tenacity method of fixing belief
    22
tender-minded philosophers,
    James on 28, 29, 33
totalitarianism 60
tough-minded philosophers,
    James on 28, 29, 33, 39
transcendental idealism 93
transcendental pragmatism
  in Habermas 11, 125–7, 129,
    140–1, 168–9
transubstantiation, Christian
    doctrine of 26, 27–8
truth 1, 200
  coherence theory of 33, 34, 83,
    89, 91, 195
  Davidson on 86–7, 89–91
  and democracy 14
  Dewey and warranted
    assertibility 55–6
  Haack and the project of
    ratifying 151–2
  Habermas on 125, 127–9
  James' theory of 33–5, 35–6,
    102

Misak on
  Peirce's account of truth 99,
    159–65, 170
  and Rorty 169–70
  truth in politics and morality
    164–8
  and new pragmatism 12
  Peirce on 24, 56, 90, 102, 127,
    151
  Price on 185, 186, 195–8
  Putnam on 108
  Quine on 64–5, 66–7, 71, 81,
    90
  Rorty on 90, 101–3, 128, 129,
    169–70
  see also analytic–synthetic
    distinction; correspondence
    theory of truth

United States
  American Civil War 3, 122
  and democracy 60, 62
  politicians and the language of
    evil 144, 145
universal moral norms, Habermas
    on 130–1, 132
use-explanatory quietism (Price)
    189, 193
utilitarianism, James on 39

verificationism
  and the pragmatic maxim
    27–8
Vienna Circle 63

warrant and acceptance 158–9
warranted assertibility 53–6, 90
Williams, Bernard 114, 115,
    118
Williams, Michael 187
Wittgenstein, L. 52, 92, 131
  and Brandom 172, 174, 176,
    179
  and Price 184, 189